SLAYING DRAGONS

SLAYING DRAGONS

The Truth Behind the Man Who Defended Paula Jones

John W. Whitehead

Publishers Since 1798

THOMAS NELSON PUBLISHERS®
Nashville

Published in Nashville, Tennessee, by Thomas Nelson, Inc.

Unless otherwise noted, Scripture quotations are from THE NEW KING JAMES VERSION. Copyright © 1979, 1980, 1982, Thomas Nelson, Inc., Publishers.

Scripture quotations noted RSV are from the REVISED STANDARD VERSION of the Bible. Copyright © 1946, 1952, 1971, 1973 by the Division of Christian Education of the National Council of the Churches of Christ in the U.S.A. Used by Permission.

Library of Congress Cataloging-in-Publication Data

Whitehead, John W., 1946–
    Slaying dragons : the truth behind the man who defended Paula Jones / John W. Whitehead.
        p. cm.
    Includes index.
    ISBN 0-7852-6937-1 (hc)
        1. Whitehead, John W., 1946– . 2. Christian lawyers—United States Biography. 3. Jones, Paula, 1966– —Trials, litigation, etc. 4. Clinton, Bill, 1946– —Trials, litigation, etc.
    I. Title
KF373.W457A3 1999
340'.092—dc21
[B]
                                                                                    99-39347
                                                                                    CIP

Printed in the United States of America
1 2 3 4 5 6 BVG 04 03 02 01 00 99

This book is lovingly dedicated to my parents,
and to my wife, Carol, who has stood with me all these years.

CONTENTS

ACKNOWLEDGMENTS

I hope I have not left anyone out of this book who would want to be in it. Some I left out on purpose, for reasons only they would understand. Others not mentioned in the text who have been a great help to me over the years and whom I would like to recognize include: Mike and Patrice Masters, Fred Willson, Nancy Deane, Debbie Gwinn, James Sammons, Mark Stuart, Al Larson, and Peggy Kelly. There are, of course, many others who in small ways have helped me fight the good fight. To all of you, I offer my most heartfelt thanks.

It was unseasonably warm for a winter day—December 6, 1997, a day I will never forget.

We were having a Christmas party at our home that evening, and my wife, Carol, had asked me to go to the store to get a few last-minute things. So, about ten o'clock that morning, I got in our Chevy Blazer with Joshua, the youngest of our five children, and started down our gravel driveway.

We live in the countryside—near the Blue Ridge Mountains in a heavily wooded area of central Virginia. No one finds our house by accident, so door-to-door salespeople, strangers, and passersby are rare. We notice anything out of the ordinary.

As Josh and I drove toward the road, I suddenly slammed on the brakes. In the field across from our driveway, slightly hidden behind some trees, an ominous-looking black van with no markings was parked. It was a sleek-looking vehicle, and I could see two men in white shirts sitting in the front. I looked straight at them; they looked straight at my son and me.

"What in the world?" I said.

"Dad, who are those people?" Joshua asked.

Instinctively, I knew that something was wrong. I didn't want to frighten my son but thought I should be truthful.

"I think the government is watching us, Josh," I said.

The only reason I could think of that the United States government would care enough to spy on me was that I was involved in a lawsuit against Bill Clinton, the president of the United States. My family watches the television show The X-Files, *and although those stories are fiction—we hope—suddenly Josh and I felt like we were part of some unbelievable story ourselves.*

Not knowing exactly what to do, we went on our way, finished our errands, and returned home. The black van was gone.

When I arrived at work the following Monday, I got the telephone number of a private investigator who had helped "debug" our offices earlier.

When *The Rutherford Institute entered Paula Jones's case against the president, we had been advised to hire someone who could conduct a security check of our offices. I again contacted our investigator, who had worked for the National Security Agency, and asked him about the black van. He wouldn't talk about it over the telephone. "When you're a security risk, anything you say over the telephone is probably being picked up by surveillance devices," he said.*

"It's either the FBI or NSA that is watching you, John," he said later in my office. "Since you saw them, they wanted you to realize you are being watched. It's a warning. You're being treated as a national security risk. My advice is to take it seriously."

I remember thinking, Me, an enemy of the state? *And anyway, what would I do to "take it seriously"? I really couldn't believe that I was a national security risk just because I was in the middle of a lawsuit against the president. I was only a lawyer representing my client.*

The investigator then told me a lot more about how the government can actually watch an individual. "Did you know, John, that our government can record your conversations from several miles away? They now have a device that can actually pick up the vibrations from your voice off your windowpanes."

As I listened to the private investigator talk, I began to think about the movies I had seen and the novels I'd read about how the future would one day be controlled by an all-seeing state. But those days that seemed to be in the far-distant future were now here—and I was part of them. Few law-abiding citizens believe they could ever be the target of surveillance or be seen as an enemy of the state. These thoughts were sobering, especially since I had dedicated my life to the fight for freedom.

This was hard to take—and I certainly had no idea what lay ahead. When I took on the Jones case, I had no idea that this lawsuit would lead to a virtual civil war that pitted the core values of truth and integrity, morality and monogamy against national interests in privacy and perhaps the very rule of law.

I had no idea that the Jones case would compel the National Organization for Women and its leaders to expose their own hypocrisy and discredit more than thirty years of work for women's rights.

I had no idea that Paula Jones's sexual harassment lawsuit would lead ultimately to the impeachment of the president of the United States.

I had no idea that so many evangelicals would attack and eventually disown me.

I had no idea.

PART ONE

INTO THE STORM

Throughout history, women have generally not been accorded the respect and status of men, even in societies that did not actively harm or persecute females. This is true in today's American society.

—John W. Whitehead
Women's Rights and the Law

The heading on the file says it all.

I'm speaking the truth and need help.

—*Paula Jones*

The *Washington Post* headline on Tuesday, September 9, 1997, caught my eye:

PAULA JONES LAWYERS ASK TO QUIT CASE

The article, written by Peter Baker, reported that the White House was "rejoicing" over the fact that Jones had lost her lawyers.

"The development threw the lawsuit into disarray and was welcomed in the president's camp as a sign of weakness in a case that has dogged Clinton and threatened to tarnish his legacy," Baker wrote. "With the departure of her top defenders, some Clinton advisors reasoned, Jones may be severely handicapped."

Several things about this article seized my interest. Paula Jones had no attorneys and was without the help she needed to pursue her case. After a long struggle by a woman who felt she had been wronged and horribly mistreated by Bill Clinton, the case looked dead. Paula Jones had taken on the most powerful man in the world and was running into a formidable and impenetrable legal fortress, buttressed by expensive lawyers and certain media pundits determined to save a liberal-leaning president.

Two years before that, I had written a short book for Moody Press entitled *Women's Rights and the Law*, in which I discussed the Christian view of women and the biblical model for male-female relations. I gave a brief history of the modern women's movement, reviewed contemporary topics related to the role of women, and discussed the current law regarding women's rights and responsibilities.

"A true understanding of the message of Jesus Christ regarding the treatment of women inevitably leads to the rejection of any social and legal patriarchy," I argue. While I reject "gender deconstruction"—which treats gender as a state of mind rather than a physical characteristic—I also insist that Christ challenged some of the patriarchal views of women held in His day.

One of the theses of *Women's Rights* is this: "In the kingdom of God, there will be no domination and subjugation. And Jesus Christ prayed that God's will would be done on earth, as in heaven. The corruption of the liberating tradition of Jesus Christ must give way to a clear focus on social justice and the proper use of power and hierarchy."

The Paula Jones story seemed like a clear assault on Christ's view of how men and women should relate to each other in the workplace. I thought it would be a great opportunity for Christians to say, "We really do care about sexual harassment in the workplace." In my opinion, we were long overdue for the first foray of Christians into a significant sexual harassment case.

I placed the newspaper clipping in my briefcase and began my hour-long drive to The Rutherford Institute (TRI) office. When I got there, I gave the story to Ron Rissler, my legal coordinator.

"Ron, take a look at this," I said. "See if you can contact this woman who is listed as Paula Jones's spokeswoman: Susan Carpenter-McMillan."

It took Ron several days to track Susan down, but he finally spoke with her on September 12. I had authorized him to offer help with Paula's case.

Carpenter-McMillan said, "I know John Whitehead. I appreciate the work of The Rutherford Institute. Let me talk to Paula."

Nearly a week went by. I had essentially forgotten about the issue—so many of these cases do not pan out that I keep short tabs on initial contacts.

On September 18, however, Ron received a call that would rock our world. He came into my office and said, "Steve and Paula Jones have decided to accept our help."

After he left, I closed the door to my office and sat in silence for several minutes, listening to the air rushing through the cooling vents, thinking, *What have I gotten myself into this time?*

No Turning Back

Since TRI's cases are defended by a nationwide network of affiliate attorneys who basically donate their time, I immediately thought of asking Donovan Campbell, a member of TRI's board of directors, to take the case against the president of the United States. I needed a group of attorneys who would be aggressive and professional and who wouldn't be intimidated by taking on the world's most powerful man. Don is known for his tenacity and aggressiveness, and he had the necessary infrastructure—a firm with support staff and equipment—that would be essential for a case in which the president's attorneys filed motions on literally a daily basis.

On September 19, I called Don and got right to the point. "I've offered to help Paula Jones with her case, and I need a lead attorney. Can you do it?"

Don was understandably hesitant. "Gee, I don't know, John. I'm swamped right now, and a case like that could bury us."

He thought for a moment, then added, "I'm also concerned about being involved in such a politically charged case. But let me talk to my partners and call you back. Just keep in mind that my answer could be in the negative."

I was asking a lot from Don. Having worked with TRI before, Don knew he would get reimbursed for his expenses. But there was the possibility of no lawyer fees—and this would be a massive undertaking, time-wise. Could his firm survive financially if they had to devote months or even years of their time to a single, nonpaying case?

The next day, I snatched the phone off the headset when I was told that Don was on the other line.

"I talked to my partners," he said. "We discussed it and prayed about it. We'll work with TRI on the case. What's the next step?"

"First, we need to know that Paula's story is credible. I'd like you to fly out to meet with her."

Don and two of his law partners flew out on a weekend, met with Paula, and returned on Sunday, September 28. He called me that evening and said, "John, I believe her story. I think we should move forward."

There would be no turning back if we decided to go forward now.

"All right," I said, "but let me talk to Paula, too."

"The Governor Would Like to Meet with You"

I talked with Paula on the telephone that week.

"Are you a Christian?" I asked her.

"My Lord, why would you ask me a question like that, John?" she replied.

"Because it's important to me. Also, I've read the story and seen the photographs of you that were in *Penthouse*. That raised some questions in my mind."

"I was raised in a Christian home. I was never perfect, but I've always been a Christian," she responded.

"I'm not saying anyone has to be perfect, Paula. But I know I'm going to be asked if you're a Christian. I want to know for myself, too. As you know, I'm a Christian, and so are the other attorneys who'll be handling your case. Faith is important to us all."

I paused, then added, "Tell me your story, Paula. What did Bill Clinton do to you that has caused you to sue him for sexual harassment?"

Paula's tale was as simple as it was disturbing. I listened carefully to her tone and probed for any inconsistencies in her testimony. She impressed me as a straight shooter who felt she had been wronged and who wasn't going to suffer in silence any longer.

This is what she told me.

It all started in 1991 when Paula, an Arkansas state employee, was working at the registration desk of the Governor's Quality Management Conference at the Excelsior Hotel in Little Rock. After talking with Paula and her coworker earlier in the day, state trooper Danny Ferguson came up later that afternoon, handed Paula a piece of paper with a room number written on it, and said, "The governor would like to meet with you."

Excited by the prospect of being introduced to the governor of Arkansas and thinking that it might lead to a better job with the state, Paula went with the trooper to Governor Clinton's suite. Clinton answered the door and invited Paula in. Ferguson, who Paula noticed was wearing a gun, waited out in the hallway.

Unknown to Paula, but later revealed in depositions, Clinton had told Ferguson that Paula gave him a "come hither" look earlier in the day, which Clinton took to be a sign that she would be open to sexual advances.

According to Paula, for ten minutes, Clinton made small talk with her. He then started stroking her arm, rubbing her hair, and then even began to run his hand up toward her crotch.

"I like your body," he said, but Paula responded with a forceful, "I'm not that kind of girl."

Clinton persisted. Paula turned away, but when she turned back around, she saw that Clinton had dropped his pants and was exposing himself.

"Kiss it," he said.

Paula told me that she was "repulsed." According to Paula, Clinton fondled himself in front of her as he urged her to perform a sexual service.

"I have to leave," she told Clinton.

By Paula's account, as soon as she said this, Clinton blocked the door. His tone changed dramatically. "I know your boss," he said. "He's a friend of mine. If you need help with anything, let me know."

Though the words spoke of advancement, Paula was able to read the veiled warning. In case she missed it, Clinton became even more explicit. "You're a smart girl. Let's keep this between ourselves."

Paula rushed by him to get out the door, passing the state trooper. She was shaking and terrified, which I can understand. Paula is a small woman. Clinton is at least six-two. If the governor had wanted to rape her, Paula didn't think there was anything she could have done to prevent it.

Seeing that her friend was visibly shaken when she returned, Paula's coworker asked, "What's wrong, Paula?" Paula gave a general account of what had happened and then left the conference to visit one of her close friends, who also noticed that Paula seemed upset. They discussed the incident as well.

Although Paula's friend urged her to report what had happened, Paula decided not to because she was afraid of losing her job and endangering her relationship with her fiancé (and later husband), Stephen Jones. Paula also shared what had happened with her immediate family and, to a lesser degree, with Steve.

When I asked her why she had decided to remain quiet, Paula told me, "I just wanted to put the entire incident behind me and get on with my life."

From my research over the years, I've found that this is a very common statement for women who have been sexually assaulted, so it wasn't hard for me to believe it in Paula's case.

The January 1994 issue of *American Spectator* magazine had disclosed the incident, quoting an Arkansas state trooper who alleged that a girl named Paula was a willing participant in a brief affair with the governor at the Excelsior Hotel.

"I began to worry what my husband, family, and friends would think about this and me," Paula explained. "I tried to get the magazine to retract its story. They just put me off. I knew then that I had to step forward and try to right this horrible wrong."

By this time, Bill Clinton had been elected president of the United States. On September 6, 1994, Paula filed suit against the president, alleging that while governor of Arkansas, Bill Clinton had sexually harassed her. Like many cases, it changed attorneys' hands and was mired down in wranglings until I decided to enter the fray in September 1997.

All Rights Hang Together

When the news broke that The Rutherford Institute was involved in the Jones case, the usual volley of attacks and criticism started rolling in from evangelicals. Charges were made that TRI had diverted from its purpose and vision and that we had become "political."

If these critics had paused to consider my book *Women's Rights and the Law* or paid attention to TRI's foundational principles, they might have better understood our interest and intent. TRI was founded on the principle that no person—not even the president of the United States—is above the law.

The Jones case was not about politics. It was about a woman's fundamental human and constitutional right to be free from sexual harassment in the workplace. We must remember that all rights hang together. If one freedom can be violated, they all can be, including religious freedom.

When asked on various television shows what TRI brought to the Jones case, my immediate answer was "aggressiveness." When we take on a case, we throw everything we have into it.

This aggressiveness may help to explain how we eventually found a young woman named Monica Lewinsky.

Monica and "X"

Early in October of 1997—just days after we took the case—Ron Rissler received a call from an anonymous woman (whom I will call X). X's voice broke often, leading Ron to believe she was very nervous, maybe even a little frightened.

"There's a woman who worked at the White House," X said. "She had a sexual relationship with President Clinton."

The reason we believed this woman would be relevant to our case was because she might help us establish a pattern of how Clinton treated female employees.

"What's her name?" Ron asked.

"Monica."

"What's her last name?"

"I don't know."

Ron tried to get X to give her own name, but she refused. She wouldn't even tell him where she worked or her sources for her allegations. She then asked an interesting question.

"Have you obtained a list of White House employees?"

"I'm not sure," Ron answered, "but I'll contact the attorneys who are handling the case and ask if they have done so."

"I'll call again if I come across any other relevant information," X said.

"Can you give me your phone number?" Ron asked. "In case I need to contact you?"

"No."

X hung up, but just before Thanksgiving, she called again.

"I have a last name for Monica," she told Ron. "It's Lewinsky."

Ron was now sitting on the edge of his seat. This was definitely something we could use.

"I believe she's in her early twenties," X said, "and has long, dark hair."

After a pause, X added, "She was moved from the White House

to the State Department because of the Paula Jones case, and then moved back into the White House at a later date."

Ron furiously scribbled all this down.

X fed us even more information. "Lewinsky viewed the screening of *Air Force One* in the White House theater with President Clinton. That incident raised the eyebrows of the White House staff. In fact, it's my understanding that some on the staff were infuriated at Clinton's arrogance for allowing her to return to the White House."

As Ron related to me the details of the call, I asked him, "Who do you think X is?"

"I don't know," he said, "but she has to have pretty good access or contacts to know what happens at the White House theater and how the staff feels about it." He paused. "In both calls, she sounded very articulate, but the more she talked, the more nervous she seemed to get."

"Well, we've got a full name," I said. "Finding 'Monica' shouldn't be too difficult."

We hired private investigators to locate Ms. Lewinsky. Rumors had her living in New York, but much to our surprise, the private investigators found she was staying at—of all places—the Watergate complex in Washington, D.C.

Although we would never have the opportunity to depose her, on December 5, we placed Monica Lewinsky on our witness list, thus alerting the White House that we had found her—and inadvertently setting in motion the president's alleged obstruction of justice, for which he would be impeached by the House of Representatives.

When the Lewinsky allegations became public knowledge, Washington, D.C., came to a near standstill. Even George Stephanopoulos, the president's former adviser, was uttering the "I" word—*impeachment*.

In late January, X called for the last time.

"Although I believed that what I had shared with you was true," she said, "it wasn't until I saw it on TV that I said, 'Oh my God, it is true!'"

Then X became forceful with Ron. "You must obtain the White House telephone logs," she insisted. "My sources tell me that the president made several calls to Lewinsky in the middle of the night, mostly in the A.M."

"Where were the calls placed from?" Ron asked.

"The Oval Office."

Ron's heart nearly stopped beating.

X went on. "You should also subpoena Hillary Clinton's secretary and the president's receptionist, as well as the Secret Service personnel."

We never heard from X again.

I don't believe X was Linda Tripp or Lucianne Goldberg (Tripp's literary agent). Ron and I have listened carefully to both Tripp and Goldberg on television and believe that it was neither of them. My best guess is that X is someone who works or worked in the federal government and who overheard conversations at social gatherings. Some of what she heard was merely gossip, but some of it was fact. X, like "Deep Throat" in the Nixon Watergate scandal, will remain anonymous unless and until she chooses someday to make her identity known.

Willey and Other Wiles

It was also through private detectives that we were able to locate and then depose Kathleen Willey. She later claimed that the president fondled her when she visited him to inquire about employment at the White House. These allegations created a momentary stir among some of the feminist groups, with one leader even saying, "If true, this isn't sexual harassment; this is sexual assault."

But, like a slight breeze on a sunny day, this consternation soon passed, and once again the president was excused by the women's groups.

One of the reasons I believe Willey's allegations to be true is that she was so reluctant to come forward. No one could accuse her of deliberately setting out to destroy the president. When we finally found Willey, she was literally hiding out in southern Virginia, and it was very, very difficult to serve her with a subpoena. When Willey went outside her house—fully aware from an article that appeared in *Newsweek* that she was wanted—she frequently wore disguises and dark sunglasses. When our investigators walked up to her car, she refused to roll down her window, thus preventing herself from being served with a subpoena.

If I could have controlled events, none of these revelations would ever have come out in the press. Justice would have been better served if the public hadn't found out about Monica Lewinsky and Kathleen Willey until after the legal process was completed. But, of course, the media were heavily involved in breaking many of these stories. However, instead of talking about the real issues—sexual harassment and the abuse of power—many reporters routinely focused on the political implications, thoroughly muddying the waters.

The aggressiveness that I promised the Joneses and Susan Carpenter-McMillan was clearly justified. Although all sides had known about Lewinsky for months, both Ken Starr's and Clinton's legal teams failed to pursue her. In my mind, once you take on a case, you go at it with everything you've got. If your client is accusing the defendant of being a sexual assaulter, you go after him, even if he is the president of the United States. You find out everything you can about the defendant, and you leave no stone unturned in your efforts to build your case.

Breakfast with Paula

It was in between the first and second telephone calls from X that I first met Paula Jones in person, on November 12, 1997, in Little Rock, Arkansas. It was a stressful day, as Paula was scheduled for a deposition by the president's lawyers. We knew the president's team would be as brutal and as tough as we had been aggressive toward the president by taking this case.

Don Campbell and I met for breakfast before Steve and Paula showed up.

"Steve called me last night," Don said. "You're not going to believe this, but he doesn't want you to be present during the deposition."

"Why not?"

"He read in an interview that you said you weren't personally opposed to Bill Clinton."

"But that's not what I said! I stated that I liked Clinton when I knew him while we were at the University of Arkansas School of Law."

"I tried to tell him that," Don explained, "but by now it's become sort of personal, as you might imagine. Steve, for quite obvious reasons, doesn't like Bill Clinton, and he's wary of any lawyer who doesn't share his views."

"How did you leave it?"

"I explained that this is a cocounsel case, you have a right to be there, and you're the guy I want to help me win this case. He's willing to live with it."

I made a mental note to be careful about how I analyzed the comments of others.

After breakfast, Don and I met Steve and Paula in the hotel lobby. Steve had a pompadour hairdo, vest, and cowboy boots. His demeanor toward me was visibly cold, though Paula was cordial and warm. As we drove across town, I tried to put Steve at ease.

"I think you and Paula are both courageous for taking this on," I said sincerely. "I appreciate your willingness to stand for principle. Not too many people will do that these days."

Steve's attitude seemed to warm some after that.

The deposition took place at the offices of a Little Rock law firm. We sat down in a well-lit room, where I got my first good look at Paula. The big, curly hair had been replaced with a shorter, straighter look.

The heavy makeup was toned down to incorporate softer, more subtle colors. What surprised me most was how tiny and delicate she looked.

Life, however, had dealt Paula a difficult hand as far as physical appearance goes. Paula's most prominent feature—at that time—was her nose. Sitting a couple of seats from her, I could not make myself *not* look. I felt sorry for her, knowing her nose would be the one feature emphasized and exaggerated by political cartoonists. I knew that Paula would have to be one tough woman to continue this battle.

Any doubts I had about this aspect of her character were completely erased during the deposition. Paula exceeded all my expectations. Although I am restricted by the attorney-client privilege in how much I can share, a couple of vignettes will demonstrate what I mean.

Even an experienced and hardened lawyer like Bob Bennett, the lead attorney for the president, couldn't intimidate Paula. He asked her pointed and personal questions, and she fired the answers right back at him.

After a while, Bennett realized that Paula wasn't likely to crack. "Paula," he said at one point, "as one of your court expenses, you've listed boarding for your dog. Just what kind of dog do you have?"

Without flinching, Paula answered, "A pit bull."

I saw Bennett's face drop. He let out a long, deep breath, and I could imagine him saying to himself, *I can believe that's the kind of dog you would have.*

Paula also handled herself extremely well during what could have been a very embarrassing grilling when she was asked to describe the president's penis.

"Could you draw a picture of it?" Bennett asked.

"Certainly," Paula said.

A comical scene followed. Every lawyer in that room—including the women—leaned forward to see the picture of the member that Paula had verbally described as somewhat short and thin, with a decided crook to the left. This is undoubtedly the only artistic depiction of a president's member that has become a matter of official record. As absurd as it sounds, that picture had to be preserved and is part of the public record.

Bill Bristow, the attorney for Arkansas State Trooper Danny Ferguson, a codefendant in the case, really put Paula on the hot seat when he started asking questions about her own sexual history. At one point, Paula looked in his eyes, leaned forward, and said, "You really like talking about this, don't you?"

She had done everything a lawyer could hope for. After the deposition, Paula left by the back door. I decided to leave by the front and walked right by a host of media, none of whom had any idea who I was. It was the last time I would enjoy such anonymity. In the long and arduous months that followed, I thought back to my roots and all the events that had brought me to this momentous place in history.

PART TWO

SHADOWS OF THE PAST

You're traveling through another dimension—a dimension not only of sight and sound, but of mind; a journey into a wondrous land whose boundaries are that of the imagination. Next stop: The Twilight Zone!

—Rod Serling

My dad and mom with me in 1946

CHAPTER 2

As I stand here and look out on the thousands of Negro faces and the thousands of white faces, intermingled like the waters of a river, I see only one face—the face of the future.

—*Martin Luther King Jr.*

My father doesn't remember the incident. I was only three or four at the time—no older than that. My father is a tall, thin man, as was the black man approaching us from fifteen or twenty feet away.

As my dad held my hand, we continued walking toward the man. I was on the outside, near the street. When the black man came within a couple of yards of us, I started to move closer to my dad to let him pass. Before reaching us, though, the black man stepped off the curb into the street and lowered his head, allowing us to pass before he moved.

"Why did he do that, Daddy?"

"That's the way it is in the South, son. The colored folks honor the whites."

This was Pulaski, Tennessee, in 1952. Pulaski had a town square, as it still does. And at the courthouse, the rest rooms were marked "Colored" and "White," one among many things that black people and white people did not share. This was segregation, and by the late fifties, it was inspiring protests in the South.

Pulaski is my hometown, the place where I was born. I was forcibly delivered, pulled from my mother's womb by forceps that left indentations and black-and-blue marks on my tiny head, just before midnight on July 13, 1946.

Because of the superstitious stigma attached to the number 13, my mother's doctor gave her the choice of having me born on that day or waiting a couple of minutes and cutting the umbilical cord on the fourteenth. She waited, and I began life straddling two separate days. I had given my mother, twenty-three-year-old Alatha Wiser Whitehead, thirty-six hours of intense labor pains. She had no idea, though, that this was just the beginning, a mere foreshadowing of the difficult child I was to become.

My mother is a tough woman, but she had to be. She grew up in a poor family with four brothers. One, Raleigh, was shot down over the Pacific during World War II. Another was nearly burned to death on an aircraft carrier when a Japanese kamikaze plane crashed on the deck.

However, I would be her toughest challenge. And it all started with my birth. Exhausted, my mother vowed on the delivery table never again to give birth. True to her word, within a few years, because of medical problems possibly related to my birth, she was forced to undergo a hysterectomy. The surgery ensured that I would never have the brother I always wanted, making me a lonely, only child.

I sometimes rebelled against this by inventing a brother. My lack of a sibling and the loneliness I felt as a child I came to see as dragons, personal dragons I slayed one by one by avoiding the truth or by diversions into mischievousness. Later in life, I would confront dragons of a different sort—ones that really existed and placed me in battles that I didn't always win.

I was christened John Wayne Whitehead because my father admired the famed movie actor. In like manner, my hometown of

Pulaski had been named after someone famous: Count Casimir Pulaski, a Polish-American patriot who was an aide to George Washington and a Revolutionary War hero.

Pulaski is a small town about an hour's drive south of Nashville. With less than six thousand people in 1946, it hasn't grown much since then and remains virtually unchanged except for some fast-food restaurants and a Wal-Mart Super Center.

But Pulaski has a historical significance nonetheless. It is the birthplace of the Ku Klux Klan, which was founded in 1865 by a group of young former Confederate officers as a social club of sorts. The name Ku Klux Klan is a corruption of the Greek word *kuklos*, which means "circle." The original purpose of the group was to relieve boredom and revive some of the excitement of the Civil War. I've read that the founding group invented elaborate rituals and other activities to amuse themselves.

The Klan members soon discovered, however, that the sight of night riders in white frightened blacks. As the organization grew in the South, the KKK turned its attention from recreation to controlling the behavior of the former slaves and disrupting their political meetings.

A new version of the group, which was dedicated to white supremacy, emerged in 1915 in Georgia. The so-called invisible empire attracted a membership of nearly 100,000 throughout the country within six years and employed terrorist tactics against blacks, Jews, and Roman Catholics, especially in the South.

Painfully aware of the KKK legacy, Pulaski city authorities have done everything they can to discourage any memory of the Klan's origins in Pulaski. In fact, the plaque attached to the front of the building on Madison Street, where the Klan was founded, was turned to face the wall in 1989, a sad reminder of a dark past and an unresolved future. Like all history, however, it isn't possible to erase it. The best we can hope for, as individuals or as any part of society, is to redeem that which we repudiate.

Shadow of the Bomb

I was brought into the world on the cusp of the momentous change born of the atomic bomb, a change in the basic design of life, death—and living. The new reality of mass destruction changed the consciousness of mankind, even if you couldn't really notice it right away in Pulaski.

On August 6, 1945, the *Enola Gay*, an American B-29 bomber named after the mother of the pilot, Colonel Paul W. Tibbets Jr., dropped an atomic bomb on Hiroshima, Japan. Four square miles of the city were flattened. In an instant, some eighty thousand people were killed, and about the same number died later of the new man-made death, radiation sickness. President Harry S. Truman announced the bombing by saying, "Sixteen hours ago, an American airplane dropped one bomb on Hiroshima . . . If they do not now accept our terms, they may expect a rain of ruin from the sky, the likes of which has never been seen on this earth."

On August 9, America dropped a second atomic bomb on Japan, killing at least forty thousand and leveling almost half of the target city of Nagasaki. Those who were not lucky enough to instantly die suffered in agony and hopelessness. As a ten-year-old eyewitness to the Nagasaki bombing later wrote, "After a few minutes, I saw something coming up the road along the river that looked like a parade of roast chickens. Some of them kept asking for 'Water! Water!' . . . I would rather blind myself than ever have to see such a sight again!"

While Hitler's atrocities were so horrible that it took the general populace, especially noncombatants, a long time to comprehend them fully, it didn't take long for the world to begin worrying about what nuclear weapons meant. The scientists who delivered the new death, however, already knew. As atomic bomb developer and refugee Dr. J. Robert Oppenheimer watched the blinding light and scalding wind give birth to a gray mushroom cloud rising slowly into the early morning sky of Alamogordo, New Mexico, on July 16, 1945, he recalled the words from the *Song of God*, a sacred Hindu text: "I am become Death, the shatterer of worlds, waiting that hour that ripens to their doom."

Americans, fearful of the possibilities of destruction, began to justify taking control of people, places, things—an attitude that would ultimately result in the Cold War and wars in places such as Vietnam, Bosnia, and Iraq.

Like thousands of other young men, my father joined the army in July 1943, less than a month after he and my mother were married, and was sent to the battlefields of England and Europe. After completing his military duty, he returned home to Pulaski in October 1945. His homecoming was marked in history by the end of shoe rationing and my conception.

John M. Whitehead didn't have a middle name. Instead, his parents gave him an initial, for reasons still unknown. He grew up dismally poor outside Pulaski, Tennessee.

Dad's parents moved a lot, trying to get work to feed their daughter and two sons. This meant, among other things, that the children's education was sketchy, at best. They were able to spend only portions of the year in school before pulling up stakes and starting over wherever work was available.

One of the earliest stories I know about my dad's childhood still makes me sad for him. As a young boy, he was sent to the Red Cross to get some chicken soup for his mother, who was near death. The Red Cross sent him away empty-handed, and his mother died. He never forgave them.

Dad never talked much about those days, and he still won't. But he once told me that when he was in the fifth grade, he spent part of the year with a teacher who worked with and encouraged him, recognizing that he was intelligent and had a lot of potential. But, as usual, the family had to pull up stakes again and take the kids out of school.

The next year, he wound up in the same grade, with the same

teacher. When he walked into the room, the teacher looked at him quizzically and said, "John M."? She was simply surprised to see him back and was not trying to embarrass him or be cruel. But he never forgot the shame and humiliation. That was the last year of his schooling.

My dad is a smart man who did well for someone with only a fifth-grade education. He has lived his life one challenge at a time. For many like my father, feeding and sheltering a family was heroic work. And he, with my mother's help, did it the best way he knew how.

My parents lived their young married lives under the pressure of the Cold War and its prospects for immediate and total destruction. And, in the process, they simply tried to survive and figure out what in the world to do with me.

Falling Through Space

Several stories during my first three years I don't remember, but my parents told them to me all my life. One time as I sat playing in the backyard of our house, my mother stepped out on the porch to check on me. To her horror, she saw a three-foot chicken snake lying across my lap with a series of large lumps descending from its head to its tail—the chicken eggs it had recently swallowed. The snake, drowsy as it digested its last meal, was oblivious to my loving strokes as I proclaimed to my mother, "Look, Mommie, see the big worm!"

I don't really know how to explain some of the things I did while growing up. I was always hyperactive, something I might have inherited from the genes of some distant relative. Being an only child, I was alone a lot when I was small and needed something to occupy my active mind. So I ended up doing some things that, looking back now, seem a bit strange.

My dad bought a basset hound as a companion for me. I liked to carry the dog up the stairs of our back porch and drop it to the ground, a few feet below. The dog would yip as he hit the ground. I would then repeat this bit of cruelty throughout the day. Finally, by the time I was finished with him, the poor dog was so dopey that he would just sit and look at me.

My first real childhood memory is from 1949. I remember falling through space, helpless, screaming as blood shot through the air. I was about three years old when I tumbled from the back porch of an old house we rented—the same porch I dropped my dog from. Although it was a mere three or four feet to the ground and the corrugated steel that lay waiting to rip my tiny arm open, it seemed that I fell for an eternity.

My next memory is being held down by my dad, mom, and two others as an old country doctor, without the mercy of effective anesthetics, crudely sewed the gaping wound together. I remember screaming and sobbing with each new stitch. The four-inch scar still imprinted on my left arm is a gruesome reminder to this day.

But like most youngsters, I mended quickly, I am told. Before long, I was jumping off that back porch again. And around the corner lay a new world, some nine hundred miles to the north.

A Mischievous Kid

By the time we moved north, one thing had become abundantly clear: I was turning into a mean—or at least very mischievous—kid. Whether I was born that way or was just a victim of circumstances makes no difference. I do like to think that I've changed over time, though, and maybe even mellowed a bit.

I don't think I'm mean to the core—I just appear hard from the outside. From my earliest days, I've always had a soft spot for the downtrodden, the underdog. I still do. I collect dogs that have been abandoned, and most people who come to me with their troubles go away with my help, concern, and sympathy. But I can't deny that the soft inside is often covered with a hard outer layer. Perhaps I've just been protecting that soft core all my life, as I'm sure a lot of people do.

In 1950, my parents moved to Peoria, a central Illinois factory town known as "Little Chicago." "It was because of the higher wages they were paying up north," my dad would tell me. In October of that year, my dad went to work at Caterpillar Tractor Company.

My uncle Kenneth, my mom's brother who had told my parents of the work opportunities in Peoria, came to visit us and brought a bottle of whiskey to share with my dad. I asked for a drink, and then another and another. I still remember leaning over the toilet vomiting when I was five years old, while my uncle and dad laughed.

My mom and dad subscribed to the work ethic that you got a job, showed up every day, and did it well, hoping either for a raise or more overtime. Corporate politics were unknown to people like my parents. Thus, my father worked at Caterpillar until his retirement and left with a pension and health benefits. This was the life philosophy my parents hoped to instill in me, but I would eventually head in a different direction.

Although my family had a steady income, it wasn't much, even for those days. I remember one Christmas I wanted a cowboy gun and a holster from Santa Claus. I got the pistol, but I guess Santa couldn't afford a holster. So my dad made one for me out of one of my mother's old leather purses. It didn't look like the ones on television, but it worked pretty well. When my friends asked, "What is that?" I felt a little bit ashamed. But I remember feeling good that my dad cared enough to do what he could to make a little boy's Christmas dream come true.

Money was always tight, and we lived in a series of low-rent apartments for years. As a result, I was cooped up and full of energy. Since I wasn't in school yet, my mother became the target of my energy. Mom tells the story of walking by the kitchen table one day when, motivated by some unknown impulse, I leaped out and bit her on the back of her leg and held on, drawing blood. She had to beat me off with a broom. Thankfully, such events were rare—or at least the family recollection of them seems to have faded.

This painful event prompted my mother to look for ways to

channel my energy somewhere other than her body. She decided to gather old bricks and give me a hammer to break them up. I would sit there and smash the bricks on a newspaper on the kitchen floor for hours while she cooked dinner.

Uncle Paul, my dad's younger brother, came to live with us in 1951 and got a job at Cat, like my dad. But he worked the brutal third shift, the one from 11:00 P.M. until 7:00 A.M. That meant he had to sleep during the day.

By this time, my mother had also taken a part-time job to help make ends meet. As a result, I was left at home unattended for several hours each day, while my uncle slept. Television was fairly primitive at that time and, to a five-year-old, even boring at times. So there was plenty of time for mischief. And I was up to the challenge.

On various occasions, just to liven things up, I would sneak into the darkened room where Uncle Paul was sleeping and slap him across the face with my dad's leather belt. One time, he got so angry he chased me outside into our front yard with only his underwear on. I stood on the sidewalk and laughed at him. Other times, when it looked as if my uncle might catch me, I would yell, "Paul, I'm on your side. I really am." He'd then throw his hands in the air and say, "Aw, heck, I give up." Times like these taught me how to verbally manipulate situations and be quick on my feet.

My parents knew they had to do something with me—Uncle Paul probably helped them reach this decision. So they put me in day care. I hated it. It only lasted a few months, but I managed to make it an eventful time.

There was an iron grate over a ground-level window near to where the kids had recess. We were carefully instructed not to throw any objects into the grate, especially rocks. I took that as an invitation.

So the first chance I got, when I thought no one was looking, I tossed a handful of rocks into the grate. The next day, as we all sat down to eat the mysterious food big people serve to little ones, I found only a handful of rocks on my little plate. Everyone else had meat and peas or whatever it really was. Two of the day-care wardens announced to the room that I would have to eat the rocks on my plate. All the children were looking at me, and I was frightened out of my mind.

I remember sitting there and screaming, staring at those rocks until way into the afternoon. Although I never threw any more rocks in that grate, I found other ways to cause trouble.

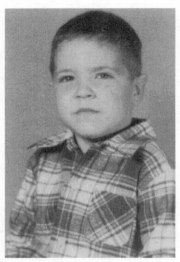

At age six I was already a handful.

My own little "aliens"—
Elisabeth, Josh, Me, Jon, and Joel (Halloween 1986)

CHAPTER 3

Gort! Klaatu barada nikto.

—Patricia Neal
The Day the Earth Stood Still

On July 2, 1947, a bright, disk-shaped object was seen flying over Roswell, New Mexico, heading northwest. The following day, widely scattered wreckage was discovered about seventy-five miles northwest of Roswell by a local rancher.

Officers from the nearby air force base investigated the wreckage. When they returned to Roswell, an official press statement was released confirming that wreckage of a flying disk had been recovered. Later, the U.S. Air Force retracted the statement, saying a weather balloon had crashed. Despite the "correction," the possibility that aliens from outer space were watching earthlings and perhaps invading our planet was an idea that is still gaining momentum.

Other unidentified flying objects were reported routinely after that. Indeed, some fifteen million Americans claimed to have seen UFOs in a twenty-five-year period following the Roswell incident. More than half of all Americans say they believe in UFOs, and many believe they are manned by creatures from other planets, despite the seemingly inexhaustible supply of alternative explanations provided by the government.

I, too, have doubts about what has been seen in the sky. I look up at the stars at night, sometimes through my telescope, and wonder what the truth is. I believe there are legitimate questions concerning extraterrestrial life that have yet to be answered. It is something we cannot hide from.

My views on this are pretty well known, especially to my staff at The Rutherford Institute. One year, for my birthday, they staged a mock alien abduction at the office, complete with masked alien captors, a black van, everything that went with it. To humor them, I went along with it, although I saw through it immediately. My alien experience is, after all, long-standing and extensive.

It began in 1952 when my mother went to work for Ben Schwartz at his grocery store on Main Street in downtown Peoria. Actually, this wasn't an alien experience, per se. But it was a major development in my life, since there were several movie theaters within walking distance of Schwartz's. My mother knew that if I hung around her job, she would not be able to get her work done. In fact, I was so unpredictable and uncontrollable that she probably even feared I would get her fired. So she would give me some nickels and dimes, and off to the Palace, Madison, or Rialto Theater I would go and enter the dreamworld of movies.

To this day, I believe this is one of the best things my parents ever did for me. It changed my life and opened worlds that I would never have known otherwise. At that time, the science fiction craze was just beginning to hit Hollywood, where film directors were churning out cheap "B" flicks primarily aimed at the kiddie market. I was particularly susceptible, being only six at the time.

Not that I was scared or fearful. To the contrary, by this time I had already seen *The Day the Earth Stood Still*. The main alien figure, who comes to earth to save us from our destructive weapons, is killed. At the end of the movie, he rises and ascends toward the heavens.

Later, when I began to study film, I realized that the theme of the movie mirrors the birth, death, and resurrection of Jesus Christ in a kind of allegory that Hollywood tends to avoid or, at the least, downplay. However, the film didn't move me as a child. It simply wasn't ominous enough.

More to my liking at the time was *The Man from Planet X*, which depicted people as being as cold and heartless as the aliens from outer space. And I even had trouble sleeping after seeing *The Thing*. This is a genuinely good film about an alien creature that survives on the blood of humans. I recently watched it again and was impressed by how well it was made. *The Thing* is as good as any modern film of its genre.

For me, a little boy lost in the amniotic darkness of the movie theater, these films fused fantasy and reality. Instinctively, I developed an imagination so I wouldn't be caught off guard by the real world, which to me, of course, included aliens. I would routinely scan the skies for a saucer sighting. Where were they? Behind the clouds? In the dark alleys between the theaters and my home? I even hid and eavesdropped on my father and mother so I could find out if they had been captured by aliens and if they were planning to abduct me and turn me into an automaton.

While this was happening to me, it was also happening to the thousands upon thousands of kids who were also watching films like these. The theaters in Peoria were populated with what sounded like hundreds of screaming, unruly children. A constant stream of popcorn boxes and ice flew toward the movie screen. The kids in the balcony poured their drinks on the kids unlucky enough to be sitting in the seats below. It was a wild time, but it was these films that were forming our minds—we who would be the sixties rebels and eventual leaders of the nineties.

Virtually no adults were there. They were neither wanted, at least by the youthful moviegoers, nor necessary in those days. The America of 1952 was much different than today. Parents could let their children walk to the movies alone. Mothers didn't have to worry about their children being molested in a dark theater or in the rest room. The milk carton children weren't the ever-present tragedy they represent these days. The language and generally the themes of the films respected Judeo-Christian values. Indeed, this was probably the last era in our history where there was some semblance of innocence in popular culture.

But for me, when I was in a movie theater, the changing world outside did not exist. Generally, I would sit in my seat and watch the double feature over and over again until I had to leave—which was usually in the early evening. Then I would amble down to Schwartz's Grocery, and my mother would take me home where I would continue to feed on the cathode-ray tube.

The movie theater is where I virtually lived during the early years of my life when I wasn't at school. I ate there. Boy, did I eat: hot dogs, popcorn, Cokes, Milk Duds, pickles. One of my favorite treats was a hot dog with mustard, topped with popcorn lined up in a row across the top. (I've tried but haven't yet convinced my children that this is gourmet food.) I would take an entire box of Milk Duds and cram them into my mouth, making a huge caramel ball that I would suck on. What a life for a kid who lived in his head!

By the end of 1953, while I was lost in the world of aliens and flying saucers, Walt Disney entered my life. I was fascinated by the animated film *Peter Pan* and must have seen it a hundred times before it left Peoria. I dreamed of being one of the "lost boys"—free of the real world of parents, day care, and school. In actuality, I was a lost boy, lost in movies and my imagination.

Scared Stiff

Halloween was one of my favorite times of the year. Christmas is a magical time, but my parents didn't really celebrate it much after I was four or five. So, as a young boy, I put my energies into themes of a darker kind.

By 1953, my family had moved to an old house at the top of a hill on Knoxville Avenue in Peoria. The house seemed spooky to me, with an upstairs and a cold, damp, dirty basement. I had become a jumpy, nervous seven-year-old, having been frightened out of my wits in the movie theaters, even though I loved it. Occasionally my parents, out of some sense of fun, would take advantage of my weakened state. I remember one of those times.

I was returning from seeing my usual fare of fright films, something along the line of *Them*—a film about giant flying insects, mutated by human nuclear activities, which threatened to take over the planet.

The side door to our house had a glass window at the upper part, which made it possible to see into the kitchen area. As I was about to enter the kitchen, a weird, white ghostly figure rose up, squealed, and floated away. I nearly jumped out of my skin and ran back into the yard. Thinking that maybe I was having another of my recurring fantasies, I tried to go back in—but the ghost reappeared. I screamed and ran for my life, only to hear my mother calling to me. She was shedding an old sheet, and laughing, while I stood there weeping.

By this time, films that could attract my attention had expanded to include anything that was showing in the theater. Although I was just a little kid, I saw all the great films of the fifties on the big screen, from *The African Queen* to *High Noon* to *Marty* to *On the Waterfront*.

I was now old enough to walk by myself down Knoxville Avenue to the wonderful world of movies. A twenty-minute walk and a few quarters could buy escape from a world that was looking more hostile each day.

But my parents were having trouble understanding their strange child who lived in his head more and more. This sometimes resulted in my receiving severe spankings, often out of my parents' complete frustration over how to deal with me.

I remember one time when I had just seen a double feature of fright and had to walk home alone. It was twilight, and the sun was beginning to hide behind the rooftops. As I was lumbering up the long, winding alley that ran behind my house, I thought I heard footsteps following me. I stopped. The footsteps stopped. I looked to see if anyone was there. I saw no one. I started walking again, and the footsteps quickened. I began to run and didn't stop running until I reached my house, even though it must have been a mile or more. I crashed through the front door of the house, screaming and crying.

My parents, sitting around the television set, were startled—so much so that my dad leaped up, turned and pulled his belt from his pants, and whipped me. I was put to bed immediately, where I sobbed myself to sleep—still believing that something from another world had been tracking me.

No doubt I was a frustrating child. And this was probably most intense at Halloween. I was so transfixed by the possibility of getting treats that I visited homes the night before, the night of, and the night after Halloween. The neighbors would literally curse me by the third visit.

As I grew older, if people didn't treat me, I would trick them. My favorite method of revenge was writing obscene words backward on their windows. I did this so they could read what I had written when they opened their drapes the next morning. I even used paraffin wax instead of soap because the wax was so much harder to wash off. This was done intentionally to punish those who had rejected me. My mother-in-law claims that I waxed her windows one year even after she had given me candy. I don't know how she knew it was me, but she insists it was.

When our own kids were small, we would take them trick or treating but explained the dark nature surrounding the day to them. A couple of times, I put on a scary mask and growled at them through the closed window. They simply looked at me and said, "We know it's you, Dad." I've kept different masks I've gotten over the years, including a Bill Clinton mask someone gave me the first Halloween he was in office.

School Troubles

I hated school. I can't remember one good day spent in elementary or high school. To me, school was hell spilled over into time.

I was a daydreamer and could not sit still in class. Books were a bore, and teachers were wardens in a prison from which there was no escape, except at the movie theater. Years later, *Gentlemen's Quarterly* magazine quoted one of my staff members and longtime friends, Alexis Crow, as saying that I had the worst case of attention deficit hyperactivity disorder she had ever seen. If my parents had been aware of Ritalin when I was a child, there is little doubt that I would have been my town's leading consumer of it.

In 1952, I started my education at Greeley School. Since my parents did not celebrate Christmas in the traditional sense, they would give me my presents either a few days before Christmas or on Christmas Eve. On one Christmas morning when I was about nine, I got up early and decided to play Santa Claus. I went into the kitchen, got a few grocery bags, and filled them partially with cans and boxes of food. After putting on my coat, I gathered my bags of goodies and quietly sneaked out the back door, trying not to wake my sleeping parents.

I went from door to door and left a bag on each front porch, feeling proud of myself for sharing our bounty with others on Christmas morning. When my mother got up and realized what I had done, she got quite upset because we were poor and didn't have extra food to spare. But this had been done from whatever kindness I had in my little heart.

By the third grade, I was attending White School, where the head warden, believe it or not, was named Principal White! An aging, balding man, he never gave any indication that he liked me. My fascination with movies, I soon found out, didn't sit well with him either.

When I saw *The Day the World Ended*, it blew me away and is still a film that makes me feel uneasy. The story focused on a group of people who had survived the nuclear holocaust. Radiation clouds swept the earth and caused a race of grotesque devil-like creatures to roam the earth. These devil people searched out the remaining humans in order to kill them. Then, with a stroke of divine blessing, it rained for the first time in years. Fortunately for the remaining humans, the falling rain melted the devil creatures, making them sizzle away. From there, the humans could begin building anew in a world ripped apart and contaminated by nuclear fallout.

I was ten years old at the time, and my teacher told the students to write a story. "Use your imagination," she said. I ripped off the plot from *The Day the World Ended* and wrote my story about the devil creatures. The next day, Principal White called me to his office. To my surprise, my mother was seated in front of his desk because he had called her at work about my story. It seems that after reading what I had written, my teacher believed I was a "very troubled child." Principal White felt the story showed a mental imbalance in me and instructed me not to write about such terrible things. My mother was shocked that I would write such horror and was irritated that she had to leave work to tend to her "problem" child, as she referred to me. Mom took me out in the hallway and gave me a spanking I didn't soon forget. So much for encouraging creative writing.

My third-grade teacher, Mrs. Pauli, believed I had a speech impediment because I stuttered a bit and had trouble saying certain words. As a result, I spent many afternoons with speech therapists dressed in clean white coats. It was like I was actually in a film, being probed by aliens disguised as therapists. They kept asking me, "Are your parents from a foreign country?"

I will never forget third grade. Mrs. Pauli was an older woman with yellow-gray hair, large rabbitlike teeth, and breath that smelled like it came from Methuselah's grave. One day she told the class that for every library book we read, she would post a star on a board in front of the class for all to see. I got busy and chalked up a long row of stars. Mrs. Pauli even commended me in front of the other students for all the books I had read.

But then my personal D-day arrived. Mrs. Pauli asked the students to give reports on the books we had read. I hadn't read a single book and stammered and stalled in front of the class. When it became obvious that I had lied and attempted a scam, the teacher told me to sit down. That evening, Mrs. Pauli called my father and told him what a liar his son was, whereupon my father took care of the situation in his usual manner. These types of incidents, as well as the spankings, continued on into high school.

By the mid-fifties, the boom of the wartime economy was beginning to wane. My dad was laid off from Caterpillar, which eventually forced us out of our home on Knoxville Avenue. I changed schools yet again, this time winding up in Peoria Heights at an elementary school where I knew no one and no one knew me.

My grades were not improving. Instead of homework, my reading material consisted of a steady diet of comic books. For ten cents, I could fly with Superman, crawl up walls with Spiderman, or swim underwater with Aquaman. Of course, teachers didn't like comic books, but without them, I don't think I would have learned to read.

By the winter of 1957, a cold wind blew across the factory rooftops of Peoria. As I lay cuddled up in my bed with visions of monsters dancing in my head, little did I know that a big change was coming in my life.

My second year of high school (1961-62),
I was still getting into a lot of trouble.

Our pre-fab house and my first motorcycle

CHAPTER 4

You ain't nothin' but a hound dog.

—Elvis Presley

Sometime in 1955, I was jolted by a song I heard on the radio, "Maybelline" by Chuck Berry. America had its first black rock 'n' roll hero, and when I saw him on television duckwalking across the stage, playing his guitar, there was no turning back. Rock 'n' roll was becoming part of my soul and soon joined movies as my true love.

Then came Elvis. Although Chuck Berry had moved me, Elvis became part of me. John Lennon was right when he said years later, "Before Elvis there was nothing." Elvis combined all the images of rebellion—James Dean and Marlon Brando, among others—into one solitary figure.

I totally identified with Elvis Presley. About ten years old at the time, I dressed up in tight pants and drew mascara sideburns. Grabbing my toy guitar (with no strings), I stood in my front yard serenading little girls who would stare listlessly at me. Two favorite songs, "Hound Dog" and "All Shook Up," sometimes seemed to stir my young audience, though. One little girl, I remember, said I even looked a bit like the King except I was shorter and not as good-looking.

"They're Not Like Us"

I grew up during the golden age of television. I would watch it from the time I got home from school until I was forced into bed. I never did homework, content to merely pass and go on to the next grade. I was a TV addict, watching virtually everything from *Alfred Hitchcock Presents* to Dick Clark's *American Bandstand* to the *Mickey Mouse Club* to *Lawrence Welk* to *Leave It to Beaver*.

In 1958 we moved again, this time to Bartonville, a suburb of Peoria. I was used to going to school with people of every color, but Bartonville was all white, "Vanilla City." I would finish my last year of elementary school and high school in Bartonville.

We initially moved into a rented house. But a "prefab" subdivision was being built near the high school, and for $13,000, financed by a thirty-year mortgage, my parents bought their first home. With three tiny bedrooms, a small living room-dining room, a kitchen, one bathroom, and a basement (which soon became my haven), it wasn't much to brag about, but it was one of the biggest houses in the cul-de-sac. No matter how small it was, though, we were proud because it was ours. And it would be my home until I left for college in 1965. Several years ago, I went back to see the old house and, peeping in through the windows, was amazed to see how small the rooms actually were.

Before moving in, we drove out to see the house being put up. *Fast* was not the word to describe how quickly it was built. Once the basement was poured, the house was put together in several weeks—the miracle of prefabricated construction.

The smell of a new house is hard to describe. It's a good smell, the smell of a new beginning—a type of hope for the future. But when we moved, the new house brought with it the same old problems with the same people. It was still the four of us: a problem child, my parents, and Uncle Paul, who served as a surrogate big brother to me.

We had new neighbors. Down the street lived a family named Marx. One day, while playing with some of the neighborhood kids, an older girl stood nearby, straddling her bicycle. She began talking about the Marxes. "They're Jews, you know," she said. We all looked up. "Did you know that Jewish men bleed like women? They have menstrual periods, except they bleed from the privates."

I was only twelve at the time and didn't really know what she was talking about. But whatever it was, it didn't sound good. She had more: "They're not like us. They don't celebrate Christmas. They're odd. So stay away from them." I didn't give much thought to what she said and often played with the Marx kids. But I never forgot this incident.

I am amazed at the prejudice of people. Many hate and in turn teach their children to hate. Hate builds upon hate, and it infests everything it gets near, even Christians. In fact, every time The Rutherford Institute takes a case on behalf of Jewish people, I receive anti-Semitic mail from people professing to be Christians. This is astonishing, since Christ Himself was a Jew. I now understand why many Jewish people fear Christians.

Things That Go Bump

Even with my parents' excitement over a new house, I was still getting more than a fair share of spankings. The strain of getting ahead, paying for a new house, and dealing with my erratic behavior caused an ever-present tension in my home.

But there was escape. Although I was farther from the movie theaters, I learned to hop a bus to see *The Brain Eaters* and *The Fly*. *I Was a Teenage Frankenstein* added gore to the package. *Monster on the Campus* gave me a lesson on reverse Darwinism, and *Teenage Caveman* portrayed life after a nuclear war. Paranoia was still a theme for popular culture to exploit.

It was about this time that I entered my insomnia period. There was a small tree outside the window of my tiny room. At night, the moon would throw the tree's shadow on the wall in my room and the hallway just outside it. Watching the shadow twitch and shake with its tentacle-like branches greatly unnerved me. Also, the sounds of the night—the things that go bump—were picked up by my highly sensitive ears.

Around midnight, still unable to sleep, I would call for my father until he came to my room. As I anxiously shared my fears, he would try to reassure me, although he had to be up before dawn for work. But when I called out at 2:00 A.M. a few too many times, he would just spank me and tell me to go to sleep, which somehow helped me pass out. This went on for several months.

Something strange happened one night during the sleepless era, something I often think about even now. As I lay awake one night, I turned over on my side so as not to see the wiggly shadows. I felt a hand lightly touch me on the shoulder and turned, but no one was there. A warm, comforting feeling came over me, and a small voice in my head said, "Christ is with you." I dropped off into dreamland.

I was not brought up in a religious home. We went to church maybe on Christmas or Easter, and that was it. My parents were not atheists but simply the type of individualists who believed that God was on your side if you worked hard enough. They were suspicious of anyone asking for a handout or a donation, including a church or its pastor. I personally never thought that much about religion until I converted to Christianity many years later. Thus, the childhood incident described above with Christ was highly unusual.

My father at times took me on hunting trips, where I would be the only child among a group of whiskey-drinking, tobacco-chewing men. I remember one time begging my dad until he let me take some "chaw." The sweet taste of the tobacco was pleasant at first. I was warned not to swallow it, but I did and got so sick and dizzy that I couldn't stand up.

It was on one of these hunting trips that I shot a small rabbit that was bobbing and weaving in front of me. I walked up to grab what I thought was a dead rabbit from the ground and put it in my hunting pouch. But the rabbit was still alive, and as I walked up, it looked at me with bulging eyes and started to scream. I freaked out and unloaded a shotgun on it, leaving it in a bloody mess. That was the last time I went hunting.

Pinned to the Mat

The summer of 1960, a few months before I entered the ninth grade, proved to be pivotal in my life because of an acquaintance I made. I spent a lot of time riding my bike and playing with the kids in my neighborhood. A new family had moved onto my street, just around the corner from my house. One day, when a bunch of us were playing "kick the can" in the street, I saw a cute little pudgy girl watching us. I decided to go say "Hi," not realizing this would lead to a lifetime commitment.

Carolyn Nichols was eleven years old and the second of five children. Although she was born in Mississippi, her family moved to Peoria when she was a baby in search of a better living, just as mine did. She was shy but showed an interest in me, and we would meet and talk in her garage over the summer. I remember kissing her on the cheek once, and she recoiled, saying, "Don't sweat all over me!" Her mother wouldn't let her stay outside after dark, and I would sneak around to her bedroom window where we would continue our conversations.

When the summer ended, though, I decided that since I was going into high school and she was just a sixth grader, our little fling had to end. Although we passed each other occasionally (we lived on the same street, and she entered high school when I was a senior), we didn't speak to one another for the next five years. I didn't find out until years later that after I broke up with her, she cried herself to sleep every night for an entire year.

I entered Limestone High School in September of 1960. An all-white school, Limestone was comprised of middle- to upper middle-class students who congregated in social cliques. You had to dress a certain way, play sports, and be in school plays and the like to be accepted—to be popular.

There was another way to become popular, and that was to be outrageous. I soon learned how to perfect the art of outrageous.

The sixties can really be divided into three general epochs: the Kennedy years, the age of the Beatles, and the Vietnam era. I participated in all three.

John F. Kennedy made a trip to Peoria in the summer of 1960 as part of his political campaign for the presidency. On his way to the Peoria Airport, JFK had to pass through Bartonville, and my dad and I lined Garfield Hill along with about fifty other people. The turnout was disappointing, and the crowd was quiet and solemn as JFK passed by. Kennedy was sitting on the back of a convertible when my dad raised his fist and yelled, "You're the man, JFK!" Kennedy looked him right in the eye and said, "Thank you. Thank you very much." No one else said a word.

It was a curious campaign. I remember my dad arguing with neighbors about Kennedy's Catholicism. A Baptist minister vehemently argued that if Kennedy became president, the pope would run America. "We have to fight the Catholics," he demanded.

The Kennedy-Nixon television debates inaugurated the beginning of the television era and its influence on presidential politics. Kennedy was the perfect television candidate, with his good looks, tanned skin, white teeth, and athletic physique. And he was a skilled debater. I remember watching in amazement as Kennedy smiled and even laughed at Nixon. But Nixon, on the other hand, simply looked sweaty. The television camera was unkind to him, and the debates damaged Nixon's appeal.

Inaugurated on January 20, 1961, Kennedy declared: "The torch has passed to a new generation of Americans." Calling for idealistic sacrifices, he demanded of Americans, "Ask not what your country can do for you; ask what you can do for your country." Hope for the future was the Kennedy theme and his eventual legacy. We who were young then—people like Bill Clinton, Bob Dylan, Gloria Steinem—could draw our inspiration for civic and social involvement from Kennedy's vision of America. In a rare and fleeting moment in American history, the young felt connected to their leaders. Even the dirt of politics couldn't soil us because we were working for a better world. And JFK was leading the way.

Hope is exactly what I needed as I began my first year of high school. I didn't come from a family with money. When other students learned that I lived in a "prefab" subdivision, they made fun of my house. I wasn't a great athlete, either—a good basketball player, maybe—but I was small for my age then. I didn't start growing until I was a senior in high school and went from five feet, six inches to six feet, two inches in the next couple of years. At the time, though, I was a runt from a factory laborer's home in a school of mostly snobs. But I had something many of the other students didn't have—a strange imagination, the nerve to be outrageous, and a mean streak.

I wanted to play basketball, but since I was skinny and short, I decided to join the wrestling team. The physical conditioning for wrestling is like no other sport. In fact, the football players joined the wrestling team simply to get in shape for the upcoming season.

I weighed 113 pounds and, at that weight class, was routinely getting pinned. So I decided to diet to get to the 109-pound class. I had no fat on me but went on a strict diet of Jell-O, lettuce, and skim milk, with an occasional raw egg. I got down to 109.

I made the team but as a second stringer. My first match was against Galesburg, a school that had a state champion class program. The day before the meet, our first stringer got sick, and I was forced to wrestle in his place. My opponent had been the state champion the year before, and this was my first time on the mat.

My dad and uncle came to see me wrestle, the first high school event they had attended. They finally had something to be proud of in me. But the Galesburg wrestler pinned me in under thirty seconds, like I wasn't even there. Humiliated, I crawled off the mat. Dad told me at home that night that he had felt my humiliation, too.

By this time, I had moved into my second year of high school, and the country continued in turmoil. There was a social war going on that was played out on the television screen each night.

Election Time

In my sophomore year, I decided to run for school office, thinking it might help me get a girlfriend. I wasn't popular, so I knew I would never be class president or anything close to it. But there might be an outside chance that I could be elected representative to the student council. After all, there were a lot of representatives, and "with the right campaign strategy," I told myself, "I might eke out a victory."

My closest friend, Kenny Barth, and I sat down to plan my campaign strategy. Sure, we could put out flyers and shake hands and all that. But the popular kids would be doing that, too. And I wouldn't win on looks, for sure. I hadn't been a pretty child, and I was no Errol Flynn look-alike in high school. So we needed something extra—payoffs and a bit of muscle on the right people.

Thus, with whatever money I could scrape up, I bought candy and gum and handed it out. We preyed on smaller, weaker students, telling them that if they voted for me, they wouldn't get beaten up (by us). Kenny and I worked hard on the day of the election, using the same menacing tactics. And miracle of all miracles, I actually got elected by a slim margin. For the first time in my life, I had actually accomplished something outside of my head. My dad and mom were surprised and even acted a bit proud of their only child.

The next day, I was seated with the other council members. I listened as my name was called as a newly elected member. Now I had hope. I was going to be the JFK of Limestone High School. I was going to seek new frontiers, and I wasn't going to ask what I could do for myself, but what I could do for good ol' Limestone High. I felt good.

Good feelings have a way of lasting only a short time, though. Mine lasted only a day. As I was sitting down with the council members for the next day's meeting, the teacher in charge, our student adviser, asked me to step out in the hallway. I knew this routine, and it never meant something good was about to happen.

"John, you do not have a C average. This means that you can't sit on the council," the adviser told me. There was a slight echo from his words as I slunk down the hallway with a riveting echo in my head. I had been cool for exactly one day.

I was led to an empty room where I was to sit and study, hopefully to bring my grades up so I could rejoin the council. But putting me in an empty room with no one watching me was like putting a monkey in the zoo. All I did was play.

It was now clear to me that there was no way people like me were ever going to be part of the system.

Kenny Barth and I also had a falling out. He and I were playing basketball when a kid came in to play with us. But he had no ball shoes and played only in his socks. Barth started making fun of the kid and even stepped on his toes.

I felt sorry for the boy because he was too poor to afford a pair of cheap athletic shoes. So I went up to Barth and punched him in the face. He stormed out—but called me at home later. Still mad, I cursed him out. It took a while for us to be friends again. And at the same time, my problems at school increased.

I began to get in trouble more and more. I would get bathroom passes but not return to class. I would dart down the hallways, using them as a racetrack, knocking other students to the ground and occasionally running into a teacher. For such activities, I received detention slips. I used to get them in five-hour blocks—the max. This meant staying an hour after school for an entire week.

By this time, I had run up debts borrowing money from other students. It was clear that my life needed to change, and I needed a job.

My friend Ken Barth got me a job as a dishwasher at a country club north of Peoria. I would go to work right after school and usually got home around midnight, leaving no time for homework. The next morning I would have to get up early for school, and I ended up dozing through many classes. I did this for most of my junior year of high school.

I was going nowhere as the world around me seemed to be cascading out of control. By October 1962, the world was on the brink of nuclear war. For two terrifying weeks, the United States and the Soviet Union came face-to-face in what has come to be known as the Cuban Missile Crisis. It began on October 14 when an American spy plane detected a ballistic missile on Cuban soil. Nikita Khrushchev, the Soviet premier, claimed that the weapons he had sent to Cuba were defensive and nonnuclear. However, the Soviets had never deployed nuclear arms in the Western Hemisphere.

President Kennedy responded by ordering a blockade of Cuba. On October 22, in a nationally televised address, JFK warned, "I have directed the armed forces to prepare for any eventuality." His message was clear. We were braced for war.

Finally, the stalemate lifted. Khrushchev agreed to remove the missiles, and everyone breathed a deep sigh of relief.

The discussion at school was intense, especially in history class. One of the few teachers I ever liked to any degree taught American history. His name was Mike Owens, and he was a young former college basketball player who had a rapport with the students. For once, school was actually interesting. While people were building fallout shelters and hiding in fear of an atomic holocaust, I was finally getting something out of school. I still hadn't read a book or gotten a grade higher than a C, but I actually tuned in to this part of history. It just goes to show that a good teacher and the right topic—even a possible nuclear holocaust—can help someone learn.

The sight of the thalidomide children, on the other hand, was shocking. Once advertised as the "sleeping pill of the century," thalidomide was the villain of one of the darkest chapters in pharmaceutical history. By 1962, when it was removed from the market, the drug had caused up to twelve thousand infant malformations (mostly in West Germany). Nearly half of the deformed babies died shortly after birth. The drug was thought to have no side effects. Yet, following its introduction in Europe in 1957, thousands of babies whose mothers had taken the drug were born with flipperlike appendages instead of arms and legs. Eyes, ears, and internal organs were often damaged as well. Modern science had produced a nightmare.

The thalidomide children still haunt me. It has always given me pause when science in any way begins tampering with people or the world around us. That is one reason I have been vocal against genetic manipulation and why The Rutherford Institute has fought it.

"They Killed Him!"

I still had not read a book from cover to cover. When it came time to do book reports, I would buy a Classic comic book. These were great tools for lazy or bored kids like me because they covered all the classics. So when I had to write a report on the French Revolution, I bought the Classic comic book on the subject. I was even caught in French class reading a Classic comic book by my teacher, Michael Rule. One of the few good teachers I ever had, Mr. Rule looked over my shoulder and said, "At least you're reading something, Whitehead."

Not many people, however, encouraged me. "The boy looks like he has no future. We've got to do something with him," I heard my dad say. Then the sound of my mother's voice, "But what can we do? He's almost a man."

I was sitting in my small room with my door slightly ajar. I got up and put my ear to the crack, but the rest of what they were saying was muffled.

I began to hear the dismal theorem from others. My high school guidance counselor was a man named Frank Bailey. A redhead who wore a bow tie, he had surveyed my school educational and discipline records. Mr. Bailey also analyzed what he believed to be my mental acumen and summoned me to his office for "guidance" counseling. After reviewing my negative progress in high school, Mr. Bailey offered me what he believed to be his best advice. "John," he said in his baritone voice, "I really see no future for you in higher education. In my opinion, it would be a waste of time and money for you to attend college. My best advice is to learn a trade or follow in your father's footsteps. Get a job at Caterpillar."

I had watched my dad wake before daybreak and march off to his job at Caterpillar Tractor Company, day in and day out. He would come home tired and often frustrated. Although I had no idea what I wanted to do, I did know that working at Cat was not the answer for me.

Several days later, my parents announced to me that they had talked with a Navy recruiter who wanted to meet with me. He was coming over the next night.

The man in the uniform was what he said he was, a recruiter. A better title would have been "salesman," for he spun a yarn of advancement and career opportunities that to the trained ear would sound ridiculous. But to my parents, who were hoping for some direction in a directionless boy, the Navy sounded great. I even believed him and signed on the dotted line.

Before I knew it, I was in the Navy Reserves, drilling once a week. Then that Christmas, over my school winter break, I was sent to the Great Lakes Naval Training Center in Chicago. If there is a hell on earth, that's where it was for me at that time in my life. Waking at 4:00 A.M. with a drill instructor screaming in your face, and then standing at attention in subzero weather, is enough to break you. And it did break some of the kids—we were just seventeen and eighteen years old. A number of them deserted but were caught and brought back.

I stuck it out for my two weeks, with my shaved head, frozen fingers and feet, and the putrid existence of boot camp. However, my mental wheels began to turn. How was I going to get out of this mess?

I had already been dazed and confused a month earlier by something that both numbed me and shook the foundations of the country. The killing of John F. Kennedy in November of 1963, one of the most profound acts of the twentieth century, set the pattern for an assassination mosaic that dominated the sixties and altered irrevocably the flow of history.

But not until I saw Abraham Zapruder's home movie of the assassination did I truly understand the horror of what had happened in Dallas. The first bullet hit its target with deadly aim. Horror-struck, Zapruder screamed, "They killed him! They killed him!" And for a few appalling, petrifying seconds, time seemed to stop in Dallas's Dealey Plaza. Kennedy seized his neck and slumped forward. Then the second bullet hit, ripping his flesh and jerking his head back as if it had been struck by a cannon. Half of his head splattered on the trunk of the black Lincoln convertible he rode in. A red halo of blood seemed to encircle what remained of his head. Jackie Kennedy, cool under fire, climbed back on the trunk, retrieved her husband's bloody scalp, and laid it on her lap. Kennedy was dead.

The grisly nature of the killing of John Kennedy was kept from the American public for decades. If we had been allowed to see the Zapruder film shortly after the killing in 1963, the impact of JFK's assassination would probably have been entirely different. It was not simply a shooting; it was a slaughter.

Watching the funeral on television, I cried for Kennedy's small, saluting son and myself. The pain inside was great, and there was a sense that more than a man had died in Dallas on that sunny day in November 1963. The American Dream left on the funeral plane with the slain president.

The nation was in mourning. Everyone needed a lift, even the children. We needed to smile again and have a sense of innocence, something that was robbed from us with the death of JFK.

That's when I heard "I Want to Hold Your Hand" on the radio by a group I had never heard of—the Beatles. It sounded so bright, fresh, and new, and it soon topped the American music charts.

By the time the Beatles landed in New York in February of 1964, they were a hit. And after their appearance on the *Ed Sullivan Show*—the highest rating for any television show at the time—they were a sensation. Beatlemania was born.

The dramatically different responses to the television appearances of Elvis Presley in 1956 and the Beatles in 1964 demonstrated vividly how much American society had changed in a mere eight years. Elvis's blatant sexuality provoked a rash of outraged sermons. Politicians and newspaper editors rallied against him. Adults found him ridiculous or dangerous, while the kids screamed and swooned. There was virtually no crossover.

In 1964, however, respectable adults and even intellectuals were listening to the Beatles. At first, the older generation even seemed to like John, Paul, George, and Ringo, although that would change later. But initially, the "boys from Liverpool" did indeed seem enviably like boys, rather than men, with their English schoolboy haircuts. Exuberant, fun-loving, and generous, they seemed to suggest a world that was a fun place to be.

The Outer Limits

When I received my SAT scores, I knew I was in trouble. They were low. And with my bad grades—I was near the bottom of my class—any hopes of going to college seemed far-fetched.

Somehow I had wasted my four years of high school and had virtually nothing to show for them. I had been known in school as part clown, part bad boy. After all, Ken Barth and I had sung "White

Lightning" and "Does Your Chewing Gum Lose Its Flavor on the Bedpost Overnight?" at the Limestone football pep rally in the fall and brought the house down. My future wife, Carol, was a freshman that year and watched my performance. I walked right by her, she tells me, without even noticing her. This hurt her because she still had a crush on me from the summer of 1960.

One thing was clear to me by now: Being funny would not get me too far. Then I got some encouragement. My father didn't like the science fiction television show *The Outer Limits,* so when I wanted to watch it, I went to my friend's house. Rick Lawless was a tall, freckle-faced kid who was a good student. He associated with me because we both loved science fiction.

Rick had been accepted at a number of colleges and eventually opted for the University of Missouri. He asked me one day where I was going to college. I said that because of my grades, I didn't think I was going anywhere. Then Rick said something that struck me. "You know, John, you're a lot smarter than you think. You should apply to some schools and, if possible, go to a university. You have more to offer than you think."

Words of encouragement—especially about my intelligence— were something rare for me. That night I went home and decided to apply to some schools. I didn't tell my parents because they were expecting me to pull a stint in the Navy and then come back to work at Caterpillar.

I intercepted the mail every day to see what the responses to my applications were. I was rejected by every school I applied to. No one wanted a bad student like me. I felt like I was stuck in a hole and couldn't get out.

For me, high school ended not with a bang, but a whimper. My parents came to my graduation ceremony, grateful that their problem child had made it over the academic hurdle, had received his high school diploma, and now could get a real job.

I was still in the Navy Reserves and attending weekly meetings. I needed a job, and my dad helped me get one at Cat, sweeping floors from 11:00 P.M. to 7:00 A.M. I never could sleep during the daytime and walked around like a zombie. I applied and eventually was put on a first-shift job cleaning motor parts. At least I could sleep now.

Then came an event that would forever change my life. My mother was dead-set against my going to college, even if perchance I might get into one. She had found out about my secret plans after getting her hands on several letters from universities where I had applied.

But in early October, Uncle Red, my mother's brother, was involved in a near-fatal automobile accident. She went to Pulaski for several months to help care for him.

One day, while reading the sports page, which was (and still is) my favorite part of the newspaper, I saw an article about the University of Arkansas and its Razorback football team, which was undefeated. On the spur of the moment, I wrote a letter asking for an application. Within two weeks, I had the application and quickly filled it out and sent it back. By November, I had been accepted and, with the money I had saved from working, bought a one-way airplane ticket to Fayetteville, Arkansas.

Ever the dreamer, I even wrote the freshman basketball coach and asked if I could try out for the team. I had been practicing every day but had never played any organized basketball. However, I thought I could walk on and play for the Arkansas Razorbacks. To my amazement, Duddy Waller, the coach, wrote back and said I could try out. But making the team would prove to be much more difficult than I had thought.

When my mother returned, she was upset with my dad and blamed him for letting me make what she considered at the time to be an incredibly stupid move on my part. Even years later, when I was practicing law, she would ask me when I was going to get a real job.

I finished my last day of work at Caterpillar in early January of 1965. And with a small suitcase of clothes, I boarded a plane at the Peoria airport, bound for a place I had never seen but one that would change my life forever.

At the University of Arkansas, still wild and crazy
(Winter 1966)

Carol and me on our wedding day
(August 26, 1967)

CHAPTER 5

If we are able to give the American male a few extra laughs and a little diversion from the anxieties of the Atomic Age, we'll feel we've justified our existence.

—*Hugh Hefner*

Life unfolds all around us, and most of the time we have no idea what is going on. In other words, God's invisible hand works in history. He works in us individually, without our knowing what he is doing most of the time.

Events that are seemingly unrelated to us can have a direct bearing on our lives. Things were happening in 1965 in parts of the world I had never seen, parts of the world that I thought had nothing to do with me. But what was happening in Southeast Asia would soon become a central part of my life. In 1965, the United States entered the Vietnam War in earnest.

President Lyndon Johnson was very conscious of the peace movement that was growing in response to it. Despite overwhelming congressional support for the war, there was little popular support. Johnson understood that, so he initially relied on airpower. But the South Vietnamese forces needed ground support, and eventually, by the year's end, 180,000 American soldiers were stationed in Vietnam.

However, American soldiers were not prepared for the war they were to fight in Vietnam. Combat there meant slogging through jungles and rice paddies in search of an enemy that was elusive, even almost invisible. Snipers and booby traps were everywhere. Friend and foe were hard to tell apart. The chief motivation for many who served there was simply to survive and get home.

The Peoria Kid

For me, landing in Fayetteville, Arkansas, from Peoria, Illinois, was as foreign as landing in Vietnam. I wasn't ready for the culture differential. I arrived on a cold January day dressed in blue jeans, a plaid shirt, white socks, sneakers, and a multicolored coat that zipped all the way up to my chin. To top it off, I had a crew cut, a haircut that made a comeback in the nineties but was not popular at the time on college campuses.

To the collegiates in the airport that day, I must have looked like a strange bird. Sport coats, slacks, penny loafers, and mod haircuts were the fashion on campus. The girls were generally beautiful and neatly dressed with hair that was big and stiff. I had never seen anything like it.

I wondered why students would turn their heads to look at me. Then I realized that I was dressed like the "Peoria kid." It took me several months to revise my "style" so that I would not stick out so much.

When I registered for classes, I learned that my entrance exams indicated I was deficient in certain areas, especially English. Thus, I was required to take remedial courses in English (which included a speed-reading course) and math. While I was not happy about the additional classes, when I received my first A in remedial English, I felt a sense of accomplishment I had not felt before.

During this first semester in college, I read my first book from cover to cover, Ian Fleming's *Goldfinger*. I was surprised how good it was and how it differed from the film (which I had seen, it seemed, a hundred times).

Living in the dormitories was a new experience for me, as it is for most young people. But since I had no brothers or sisters, I had virtually lived alone all my life. Not only did I have a roommate now, I also had a lot of fellow students living on the same floor.

The influences from the other students would change my life in many ways. Besides new fashions, music, and friends, sex was introduced in a big way. *Playboy* magazine was the new bible for most of the male students. There were some guys on my floor who kept every copy of *Playboy* neatly stacked in numerical sequence. A main topic of discussion in the evenings was the new Playmate of the Month and how cool Hugh Hefner was. Sex, sex, and more sex became our focus.

What this meant was partying and a lot of alcohol. Before I arrived in Fayetteville, I never drank much. By the end of the second semester, though, I was downing a couple of six-packs of beer a day, sometimes more. Getting drunk on the weekends was a ritual I looked forward to, along with dates that usually included sex.

I walked on to the freshman basketball team. Practices usually lasted three hours a day, and when I returned to the dorm, I was so exhausted that it was difficult to study. I got to play some in the games, but it became clear within a month or so that I really didn't have a future in basketball. Even if I had been a better player, the university was obliged to play its scholarship players. I saw I was wasting my time, and at the end of the first semester, I decided I wouldn't return to the team.

The Generation Gap

Movies once again became a mainstay in my life. So did music. Nearly everyone had a radio or a record player with the latest tunes playing. When I heard "(I Can't Get No) Satisfaction" by the Rolling Stones, I knew there were others out there who felt the same way I did.

One year after joining the "British invasion" of the United States by the Beatles, the Rolling Stones achieved superstar status with "Satisfaction." The song attacks the hypocrisy of the establishment world. At the same time, it screamed out the young man's plea for fun and sex, as Mick Jagger boasts of "trying to make some girl." This overt reference to sex, a far cry from the Beatles' "I Want to Hold Your Hand," helped change the vocabulary of popular music.

One reason many of us were brought full-fledged into the sixties was because of the music and the fact that the hit-makers were young, like us. They had our interests and our urges, and they expressed them. It was easy to follow someone your age who was successful and talked your language.

By 1965, there was a sense of freshness in the air, a feeling that something new was happening. A youth revolution was beginning, and its causes were the Vietnam War, the racial injustice in American society, and the fundamental hypocrisy of the materialistic older generation. For many of us, John Kennedy had embodied our noble cause. And as the social conflict heated up, many of us were radicalized.

Eventually, the changes we went through would mean challenging our parents. They were, in effect, seen as the enemy. They were the status quo, and they didn't and wouldn't understand us.

For me, this would mean increasing alienation from my parents. By late 1965, my parents and I weren't speaking very often. That this happened to many of my generation is one of the sad legacies of the sixties.

The cause of this so-called generation gap came from several sources. For one thing, our entire culture was undergoing rapid changes. No one had time to adapt. Forces were pushing the uprising in a new direction, away from traditional values and institutions. However, many in the older generation simply refused to deal with any change. Conflict and broken relationships were the result.

Although this was a sad time, it was almost unavoidable, given all the things that were being thrown at us. By year's end, my dad and I had actually exchanged blows. After an especially heated argument during Christmas break, I punched him in the face with my fist and he returned the blow, while my mother stood screaming. From that point on, there was a rift between my father and me, one that took nearly thirty years to repair.

I was still obligated to the Navy but had received a deferment for college. After those freezing weeks on the Great Lakes, however, I wanted to avoid the Navy at all costs and began looking into the Army ROTC program at the University of Arkansas. The Reserve Officers Training Corps would allow me to attend school and receive college credit for military service. Once completed, I would enter the Army as an officer either in the Reserves or active duty. I discovered that with some paperwork, I could transfer from the Navy to the Army, and this became my goal.

"Don't Get Serious"

During the summer of 1965, after my first semester of college, I worked at Caterpillar again, driving back and forth on my motorcycle, earning money to pay my tuition. And it was my motorcycle, the one I had bought during my junior year of high school, that brought me back into contact with my future wife.

Carol and I had not spoken in the five years since our initial meeting. It was now the summer of 1965, I had just completed my first semester of college, and Carol was sixteen years old. One evening, as it was just starting to get dark, I rode by her house on my motorcycle and saw her standing in her front yard. Thinking she might be someone I could have some fun with that summer, I stopped and asked her to go for a ride. She climbed on the back of my cycle for the first of many rides.

At that time, I was what is now referred to as a male chauvinist— I saw women basically as things to be used. Although I didn't know it then, Carol tells me she had never stopped loving me and desperately wanted to be part of my life.

For those five years, she had watched me drive by her house as if she were invisible. She had seen me in the hallways of Limestone High School and at dances and tried to get just a look from me. Her heart sank after watching Ken Barth and me perform at the pep rally, when I walked by her as if she didn't exist. So when I stopped that summer night on my motorcycle and asked if she wanted to go for a ride, she eagerly hopped on.

When we started dating, I warned her, "Don't get serious because I'm never getting married." Carol had taken an after-school job at a grocery store as soon as she turned sixteen and paid for many of our dates that summer. We spent a lot of time together, and when the summer ended and I was preparing to return to college, I gave her an aquamarine birthstone ring and said that meant we were "going steady." Although I told her that meant she couldn't date, I, of course, had no intention of curbing the pleasure-fulfilling activities I had begun the previous semester.

That summer, folk singer-songwriter Bob Dylan released "Like a Rolling Stone." The first time I heard his twanging, uneven voice, I couldn't believe what I was hearing. What is certain is the effect Dylan's lonely wail had on me and many who felt alienated at the time. We were all "like a rolling stone, with no direction home." From that time on, Bob Dylan's lyrics became part of my consciousness.

"We're More Popular Than Jesus"

Back at school that fall, I began to think seriously about the possibility of joining a fraternity because a friend of mine, Bob Roller, had pledged one. I attended the various dinners and social functions that potential pledges are required to go to. Finally, I was offered a place in the Sigma Pi fraternity. Since I already knew several of the guys in the fraternity, I decided to pledge.

In January 1966, I became an official pledge at the fraternity. Although I was still going steady with Carol, I continued to date and drink heavily.

Being a pledge was a crazy experience for me. The members continuously harassed the pledges. There was one member who would wake us up whenever he came in drunk. Whether it was 11:00 P.M. or 2:00 A.M., he would make us get out of bed and stand at attention while he screamed obscenities at us. One night a group of us decided to get even with him. We were going to teach him a lesson and make him think twice before ever waking us up again.

It was a cold night, and it was snowing. In came this fellow, yelling and screaming, telling us to get out of bed. We were ready for him. Six of us descended upon him and threw him to the ground. We tied his hands behind his back and put tape over his mouth. We then shoved him into a car and headed for the Arkansas backwoods.

About ten miles outside of town, we found a gate that led to some farmer's pasture. We pulled our antagonist out of the car and stripped him down to his underwear and T-shirt. We then tied him to the fence, with him sitting on the ground, and ripped the tape from his mouth. I can still see his angry, screaming face as we drove away in the falling snow. We never found out how he got loose and found his way back. But he never mentioned the incident or woke us up again.

My grades were suffering. I had close to a B average going into the fraternity. Now I was facing an F in at least one course. So I decided, as I did with the basketball team, that if I was to have any chance of succeeding, I would have to study. I quit the fraternity and kissed my carefree life as a frat boy good-bye forever. And with some serious studying, I passed all my courses. But my grades that semester hurt my overall average.

That summer I had my final stint with the Navy. I was required to go on a two-week training exercise aboard a destroyer. It departed from the Great Lakes and traveled down the Atlantic Coast to Boston and back.

While I was in Boston, the Beatles came to town. The big hit of the summer was their song "Yellow Submarine." But the headlines focused on a statement John Lennon had made about religion: "Christianity will go. It will vanish and shrink. I needn't argue about that. I'm right, and I will be proved right. We're more popular than Jesus Christ right now. I don't know which will go first, rock 'n' roll or Christianity. Jesus was all right, but His disciples were thick and ordinary. It's them twisting it that ruins it for me."

Critics used Lennon's statement to label the Beatles as evil. Traditional Americans, especially in the South, hoped to ban the group. In South Carolina, the Ku Klux Klan put a Beatles record on a wooden cross and set it on fire. In Birmingham, Alabama, radio station WAQY broadcast announcements every hour urging listeners to turn in their Beatles records and souvenirs for a great community bonfire. And the Grand Wizard of the Ku Klux Klan exhorted: "Get out there, you teenagers, and cut off your Beatle-style long hair. Join those at the bonfires and throw your locks into the fire! Burn, burn, burn everything that is Beatle!"

Sensing the damage it had done to the Beatles' image of innocence and the possibility of seeing their careers grind to a halt, Lennon publicly retracted his statement. "I'm sorry I opened my mouth," he said.

The significance of Lennon's statement cannot be underestimated, however. Lennon challenged some basic premises of American culture and helped undermine Judeo-Christian beliefs.

The intellectuals had already decided that traditional views had to go. *Time* magazine reflected this on April 10, 1966, with its red-on-black cover that asked, "Is God Dead?" The lead article's ending sentence read: "Perhaps today, the Christian can do no better than echo the prayer of the worried father who pleaded with Christ to heal his spirit-possessed son: 'I believe, help my unbelief.'" The same *Time* cover would appear several years later in the film *Rosemary's Baby*, a story about the birth of Satan's son.

Summer of Love

During the summer of 1966, Carol and I picked up where we had left off the summer before. We had professed our love to one another in our letters and telephone calls and during my infrequent trips home during the school year. And although I had not stopped dating while at school, I knew I wanted Carol to remain a part of my life. We got engaged that summer, and, because I told her I had to save the money I was earning for college, she paid the $90 for the wedding ring set we picked out, a set she still wears today.

My mom and dad had always liked Carol and admitted there was little affection in our family until she came along. She always hugged them hello and good-bye and every Sunday night would go over to their house, where she and my mother would share the letters I'd written them and talk.

By the time I returned to school in the fall, my radicalization had begun, largely as a result of lyrics being sung by the Beatles and Bob Dylan. My parents didn't understand what was happening. The schism between us continued to widen. The Beatles were on the verge of carrying a generation away, and I was gladly going.

June 1, 1967, was the beginning of the "Summer of Love" with the release of the Beatles' *Sgt. Pepper's Lonely Hearts Club Band*, now considered the most influential rock album of all time. Disparate social factions—prizewinning novelists, rock stars, hippie acid trippers, middle-class homeowners, and rebel professors—repeatedly came together to protest the Vietnam War and attempt to bring about a new age in which people would "make love, not war."

Sgt. Pepper was also an anthem to drugs. The Beatles had put words and music to the anthem of rebellion that swept over the disgruntled youth of the American middle class. And what most people seemed to miss was that the Beatles appeared to offer a spiritual alternative to a materialistic culture that had lost sight of its own values and principles— something that mainline evangelical Christianity was not doing. Looking back on those times, it's clear that it was spirituality we were searching for, a sense of meaning in a world that seemed out of control.

I couldn't revel in the Summer of Love yet because I had trans-ferred from the Navy to Army ROTC and had to spend two weeks at

Fort Sill, Oklahoma, for basic training. My days were spent training and my nights drinking and carousing in the nearby town of Lawton, which was a series of strip joints and houses of ill repute.

Although Carol and I had scheduled our marriage for late August, neither one of us was sure we were ready for it. During our two years together, I had not treated her well and had even been physically abusive, something that would continue through many years of our marriage. I had bragged to her about some of my sexual conquests and even told her the name of a student with whom I had carried on a long-standing relationship. I now realize I did this out of insecurity and a lack of self-worth, but at the time it was devastating for Carol, an eighteen-year-old just out of high school.

Perhaps in retaliation, she became involved with someone where she worked. After being confronted by my mother, she fled to Mississippi, where her mother was visiting relatives. When I returned from Fort Sill and heard my mother's side of the story, I knew I had to find out if there was a future for us and left for Mississippi immediately. I drove the more than seven hundred miles without stopping to rest. I grew so tired while driving that I even imagined pink elephants jumping out at me. I finally arrived in Magee. As I drove up, Carol saw me and ran to greet me. We hugged, we kissed, we talked, we made up. The wedding was on.

Some of my friends had come from Arkansas to be in the wedding, and I had my bachelor's party the night before the wedding. Held in the basement of my parents' home, I drank beer and whiskey until early in the morning while *Sgt. Pepper's Lonely Hearts Club Band* blared in the background. That night, I got so sick that I vomited on the bed. While my mother was cleaning it up, she said I kept sitting up, while in a drunken stupor, saying, "I don't want to get married. I don't want to get married."

The next day, I married the only woman I would have ever married. Unfortunately, by the time the candlelight service began, I was so hung over I could barely keep my eyes open. During our wedding vows, I struggled not to vomit and even had to cover my mouth at one point. Needless to say, our honeymoon night was not one to remember with fondness.

We got married at the Pentecostal church Carol had been raised in and where she became a Christian at the age of fourteen. We did not have time for a honeymoon because I had to get back to school. So we took a couple of extra days to drive the five hundred miles from Peoria to Fayetteville so we could enjoy one another and our new marriage.

Carol liked the apartment I had rented for us a few months earlier. It sat right across the street from the Greek Theater, a university-owned open-air facility used for pep rallies and other outdoor events.

No one can really tell a person what will be required in a marriage. Because of my hot temper and tendency toward violence, Carol and I had more than our share of bad times. I had an unusually large share of personal problems, dragons that needed to be slain. Although my parents were able to help some with my education and the student loan paid my tuition, Carol had to abandon any thoughts of going to college and get a full-time secretarial job to support us.

Although she was only eighteen, I quickly initiated Carol into one of my favorite rituals, drinking beer at George's Majestic Lounge. Along with a friend or two, we would usually meet around 5:00 P.M. when Carol got off work and drink beer and eat boiled eggs and potato chips until late in the evening.

While I drank and otherwise saturated my selfish urges, the images of the starving children in Biafra began to reach American news. While Dr. Irwin Maxwell Stillman's book, *The Doctor's Quick Weight Loss Diet*, taught Americans how to lose seven to fifteen pounds per week and American annual beef consumption reached 105.6 pounds per capita, babies and the weak in Biafra starved before America's eyes. Before it was over three years later, two million Biafrans would be dead.

Poverty, world hunger, the refugees from war—these all began to affect me. These and my inborn love for the underdog slowly pushed me to major in social work. I wanted to help people much as those in the Peace Corps were doing. Established in March of 1961 by President John F. Kennedy, the Peace Corps enabled young volunteers to work for two years in underdeveloped countries around the world. By 1968, there were some thirty-five thousand Peace Corps volunteers in sixty countries around the world. And I finally found myself responding to JFK's pleas to the young to be responsible for the world in which we live.

I declared my major. The University of Arkansas had a good social work program, and there were numerous course offerings and innovative programs. Important for me at the time, there was an understanding attitude toward the students. My goal was to help the poor and disadvantaged but to undermine the system that I was beginning to hate. The war machine that I believed killed Kennedy and that was now chewing up Vietnam had to be dismantled. My views showed up in my schoolwork. Papers I wrote for class spoke these views, often appearing radical enough for professors to comment on them.

Killing King

As 1968 dawned, the vision of peace and love, as articulated by the Beatles and the hippies, was splintering. The Beatles as a group were beginning to crack. Many who believed that peace and understanding were going to change things, as I did, began to question such assumptions.

I was one year away from graduating from college. Three years before, my high school counselor had told me I couldn't make a go of it in higher education. And now I was part of the rebellion that was gripping America.

The Vietcong Communists began what is now known as the "Tet Offensive" on January 30, 1968. The North Vietnamese forces attacked more than thirty South Vietnamese cities, including Saigon, in an effort to overthrow the generals who were supported by the United States. The power of the North Vietnamese impressed the world. Americans, in particular, were stunned. American government officials had reported that most of Vietnam was secure and an end to the war was in sight. Now, however, after years of war, things looked even worse.

In March, in a South Vietnamese village called My Lai, American soldiers "wasted" five hundred unarmed men, women, and children, but the news of it would be suppressed for almost two years.

Simply trying to understand what was going on at the time was impossible. Here I was scheduled to enter the Army after college, but I was against the war. I was still in the first year of my marriage, trying to learn how to be a decent husband. My parents were barely speaking to me. They believed, like a lot of parents during this era, that their child had lost his mind. Studying for classes was difficult. I began to drink more.

I was in a bar one evening after classes in April. It was crowded. The day was warm, and the cold beer felt good going down. All of a sudden, a student jumped up on a table and yelled, "Martin Luther King has just been shot and killed." The students cheered and burst out in applause.

I was stunned. King dead? The students cheering? What was happening to the world?

I went back to my apartment. My first thought, as I watched the news of King's assassination, was that "they" had killed him because he was challenging the system. King fought their racism. He was against the Vietnam War. He was a peace warrior who had gotten out of hand. So they killed him. He became part of what would become an assassination motif of the sixties. This may sound paranoid, but that's what I believed at the time—and I still have my suspicions.

The message I was receiving from these events seemed clear: If you resisted the people in power, you could get hurt. Change, loss of power, that's what they feared. This type of thinking radicalized many young people, including me, and produced the necessary mentality for social activism.

In October 1968, a personal tragedy occurred when my dad collapsed at work. He was rushed to the hospital, and it was discovered that he had suffered a heart attack. He was forty-five years old and had smoked Camel cigarettes most of his life. I received a telephone call from my mother, who was crying. The word was that he might die.

I headed for Peoria on the next flight out of Fayetteville. My relationship with my parents was extremely tense, and it had been months since we had talked. It was unfortunate that it took a heart attack to bring us together.

Uncle Paul met me at the airport and drove straight to the hospital, where my mom was waiting. Mom and I hugged for a long time.

A doctor led me into the room where Dad lay. Tubes were running everywhere, in and out of him. He looked so pale and vulnerable. I had never seen him that way. His eyes were closed, and he was breathing lightly.

I leaned over the bed and said, "It's going to be okay, Dad. You're going to pull through."

Then Dad slowly opened his eyes and smiled. He reached up and grabbed my arms with both of his hands and said, "Thank you for coming, son. I love you."

"I love you, too, Dad," I replied. He dropped off into a drugged sleep again.

"I love you" coming from my dad was a big surprise. He had grown up in an environment where "real people" didn't say such things. And this trend continued in our family, too, until Carol came along and brought genuine affection into our lives.

I walked out of the room. Mom and Uncle Paul were standing there, as if on a deathwatch. I telephoned Carol, who had to stay behind and work, and told her that my dad had told me he loved me, for the first time in his life. I had never seen him show that type of emotion before and hoped this was a new beginning.

Several days later, the doctors told us that Dad was going to heal. He was tough, having been hardened by life. And by early November, Dad was out of the hospital and back home, with a restricted diet and "no more Camels."

I called to check up on him often. Then Christmas break came, and Carol and I drove north to Peoria. When we arrived, Dad was more distant, as if nothing had intervened in our lives. His "moment of weakness" had passed, and I was my usual difficult, obstinate self. Thus, things returned to normal, which meant disagreements and discord.

Helter Skelter

Knowing my more radical inclination, several of my social work professors encouraged me to apply for a scholarship to the new experimental School of Social Work that the University of Arkansas had opened in Little Rock. With the support of my teachers, I received a scholarship with an eye toward a master's degree in social work and the opportunity to make a difference.

The night I learned about the scholarship, I remember sitting and drinking beer and listening to the Rolling Stones singing "Sympathy for the Devil." I didn't recognize that, as I looked the demon in the face, maybe I was looking at myself. Maybe, just maybe, I needed to help myself before I could help others. But I didn't know how to do that.

By year's end, *Rosemary's Baby* gave us Satan's son. Leaving the theater after seeing *Night of the Living Dead* with its message of godless nihilism, I felt a foreboding for both Carol and myself. Society seemed to be headed for a dead end. Any hope in a benevolent, caring God now seemed remote.

I graduated in January of 1969. Carol and I attended the ceremony; my parents stayed home in Bartonville.

After graduation, we packed all of our earthly belongings, which at that time fit neatly in the backseat of our old Chevy Malibu, and headed from Fayetteville to Little Rock. This adventure, like many others in my life, did not turn out as I had hoped.

These were dark days. We moved into a small duplex, and Carol got a job as a medical secretary for an orthopedic surgeon. She earned enough for us to get by, and I went back to school.

It only took a few weeks before I was routinely arguing with and offending my professors. As a student intern, I worked at the Veteran's Hospital in Little Rock. My immediate superior was a woman who compulsively chewed her fingernails until it drew blood. Working with her and the other social workers, it became clear that most of them did what they did because it was a job, a way to earn a paycheck. To me, it was a calling and a cause. I soon became disillusioned with the entire social welfare bureaucracy.

My relationships with my professors worsened. I saw no light at the end of the tunnel I was in. So I quit.

Disillusioned and filled with an anguished rage, I again packed our car and we headed north to Peoria in the summer of 1969. Since I was no longer in school, I would have to enter the Army as part of my obligation from ROTC.

I notified the Army and received papers to report for duty in August. I was designated an infantry officer with orders to report for active duty in Vietnam. But first, I had to report for basic training at Fort Benning, Georgia, which was the training ground for Vietnam.

My parents and I still had an uneasy relationship, so Carol and I rented a small apartment in Peoria and both got jobs.

On July 21, American astronaut Neil Armstrong stepped down from the *Apollo 11* landing craft, the Eagle, and onto the surface of the moon. Although much of the world watched, many Americans believed that the moonwalk was staged in a studio to divert attention from the Vietnam War. Millions more demanded that the money and technology be applied to more socially productive purposes.

As I sat watching the moonwalk unfold on our small black-and-white television in our hot, sweltering little apartment, I saw nothing but bleakness, for my country and for myself. I remember feeling so low that I had trouble looking up.

Here I sat, depressed, with little hope, and on my way to a raging war in Vietnam. The sixties movement I had embraced was coming to a screeching halt. There were signs everywhere, but none so telling as the discovery of the grisly murders of twenty-six-year-old Sharon Tate and friends at her house in Los Angeles on August 10. Messages such as "Helter Skelter" and "Death to Pigs" were found on the walls. The leader of the cult, Charles Manson, who saw the Beatles as prophets and used their lyrics to prophesy the end of the world, and his followers were eventually convicted as the murderers.

In October, Richard Nixon said, "I will say confidently that looking ahead just three years, the war will be over. It will be over on a lasting basis that will promote lasting peace in the Pacific." Nothing seemed to make sense anymore.

Here I am in ROTC training at
Fort Sill, Oklahoma (Summer 1967).

Christmas 1972 with Carol and Jayson, during my second year of
law school (and my long-hair period)

CHAPTER 6

Both doth suffer a sea change
Into something rich and strange.
—William Shakespeare
The Tempest

In mid-August 1969, some 400,000 young people flocked to the Woodstock Music and Art Fair for a three-day festival on a farm in upstate New York. The Woodstock event was a reflection of my generation—naive, defiant, optimistic, and finally indulgent. Many of the biggest names in the rock business as well as rebels like Abbie Hoffman, student activists, professors, druggies, hippies, yippies, and others showed up to celebrate one last time. But there were signs that Woodstock was about something more than simply love and peace. Even before the festival, a deal had been negotiated by the festival organizers for a film about the event. The yuppie entrepreneurism of the seventies and early eighties really began at Woodstock.

I was not at Woodstock to celebrate with my fellow alienated ones. Instead, I was trudging through the Georgia woods on day and night maneuvers in preparation for my stint in Vietnam. While they danced to the music of The Who at Woodstock, I danced to the sound of gunfire and the reality of war and death.

However, I made up my mind early on that I would not go gently into the dark night. I would struggle and, when possible, undermine whatever the military was trying to accomplish.

In basic training at Fort Benning, when the instructor would yell "kill" as we thrust our bayonets into the bags in front of us, I would counter with "peace" or "love." They were not going to turn me into a killing machine.

Fate would intervene and change the plans the Army had for me, however. Possibly as a result of growing about six inches my first year of college, I experienced episodes of severe back pain, an affliction that still plagues me and periodically puts me through weeks of intense pain. Often, while at attention, it became so painful that I had trouble standing.

Although I had been examined several years earlier and given a clean bill of health from the Army, I was suffering quite a bit when Carol worked for the orthopedic surgeon in Little Rock. After x-raying my back, he discovered that one of the disks was out of alignment, which caused my back to go out for unexplained reasons. When I reported to the Army infirmary, I was x-rayed and told that because of what was now viewed as a congenital back problem, I would not be able to serve in the infantry. No patrols in jungles where "Charlie" waited to blow my legs off. I would, they told me, be restricted to stateside duty.

My commanding officer called me in to inform me that I would never leave the United States in an Army uniform. "Too bad," he said, "you scored high in all of your combat skills, and you're an expert marksman with the rifle. We could have used you in 'Nam."

Despite his words, I volunteered for overseas duty in Korea, Australia, anywhere. I had never been out of the country and thought this would be my opportunity to see the world. Every request was turned down.

Instead, I was stationed at Fort Hood, the shipping-out grounds

for Vietnam and the home of the proud Second Armored Division
that once had General George Patton at its helm. Situated in the city
of Killeen, this Texas town is the hottest place I've ever been. In the
summer, it is invaded by millions of crickets that make a deafening
sound at night and crunch when you drive over them on the streets.

Dropping Acid

By this time, the United States death toll in Vietnam was hovering near forty thousand, surpassing the total American battle deaths of
the Korean War. And although he was beginning to withdraw troops,
President Nixon had stepped up the bombing. Amid this, our goals in
Southeast Asia were hazy, and our troops—with little emotional support from home—were losing morale. Drug use and desertion rates
soared. The killing of American officers by our own soldiers grew so
common that the word *fragging* was coined to describe it. Peace sym-
bols began appearing on GI camouflage covers. It was time for me to
fight my own private war, even if I was only going to be an infantry
supply officer. Although I entered the Army as a second lieutenant, it
didn't start off very smoothly.

I was introduced to my platoon by my new second-in-command,
Staff Sergeant Fahey, at reveille. I was supposed to walk in front of my
platoon, call them to attention, and then salute the American flag. I
completed the first two parts correctly but forgot to turn away from
my men toward the flag. As I stood there saluting with a band playing in the background, my men snickered. I couldn't figure out what
was so funny until Sergeant Fahey walked up and whispered in my ear,
"Sir, you're saluting your men instead of the American flag."

I knew I was in the Army for the short haul and wasn't making a
career of it. So I wasn't going to be an authoritative overlord to my
men. In fact, I got along with most of them and, although it was
against Army protocol, would have them over to eat and drink at my
house.

I was introduced to drugs in the Army, starting with marijuana. Several months into my hitch, one of my men asked me, "Lieutenant Whitehead, have you ever dropped acid?" In October 1969, as I lived nestled in a rented house outside Fort Hood, Texas, I took my first LSD trip. The tablet was tiny; in fact, I could hold it on the tip of my finger. But I had been instructed to take only "half a tab because it is powerful." So at about nine o'clock on a Saturday morning, not having duty that day and ignoring Carol's pleas not to, I split the tablet in half with a razor blade and washed it down with a gulp of beer.

A couple of hours later, nothing seemed to be happening, so I swallowed the other half of the tablet. By noon, I knew my trip had begun. I was sitting on the couch watching a basketball game. As a player shot the ball, it turned into a stream of balls flying across the screen. A car drove by outside, and the reflection off the bumper hit some words on the cover of a book lying on my end table, sending them across the ceiling in a rainbow of colors.

For the next twelve hours, I lay motionless, listening to music on the old couch that came with the house, moving only to use the rest room. Carol took care of me much the same way a nurse would have cared for an invalid.

Every record that Carol, who refused to even smoke marijuana with me, placed on the turntable—Led Zeppelin singing "Whole Lotta Love," The Band wailing out "The Night They Drove Old Dixie Down," the Beatles, Rolling Stones, Simon and Garfunkel—floated in and through my skull like nothing I had ever heard before. The colors flashed, a cockroach crawling across the floor looked like a rhinoceros, my teeth tingled as if they were trying to move out of my mouth. I knew then why Paul McCartney admitted that he dropped acid more than a hundred times—and people like Timothy Leary hailed LSD as the drug for the new age. It would open doors, we were told.

After that first trip, I dropped LSD on a number of occasions. However, I decided to quit for two reasons. After one trip, insisting that the effects had worn off, I was driving our car when I started to go under what looked to me like an underpass. Carol grabbed the steering wheel and yelled at me to stop. It wasn't an underpass; it was a heavy steel sign that was only about four feet off the ground. We would have hit it head-on.

Then one day Carol and I were driving south toward Austin for the weekend. I hadn't dropped acid for several weeks, but coming over the treetops about a hundred feet in the air were three motorcycles. I was starting to have flashbacks. From then on, I decided I would stick with the lighter stuff like marijuana and alcohol.

Undermining the System

There's something about the Army that is anti-hair. I wanted a mustache, but the commanding officer didn't like facial hair and called me in and ordered me to shave. I refused. Thereafter, every time there was extra duty, I somehow ended up pulling it.

I knew the Army wouldn't receive it well, but I decided to put a peace symbol decal on the window of my car, anyway. As I left the post, the military police would pull me over. A higher ranking officer, usually a captain or major, would emerge from the MP guard hut and order me to scrape the decal off. I had to do it in their presence, and they provided the razor blade. As soon as I got home, I would put another one on, though, and the scene would repeat itself.

After these skirmishes and a few other incidents like them, I found myself in the doghouse with my superiors. Then one day I was notified by battalion headquarters that I would be starting off 1970 with a new platoon, Headquarters and A Platoon. When I saw this group of soldiers—a ragtag bunch, consisting mainly of African Americans who had encountered some problems in the service—I knew this was the payback for showing any form of individuality.

I knew there was no way that these men, some of them Vietnam veterans and others black men who despised white officers, were going to show me any real respect. Moreover, I didn't really think that a greenhorn like me had the right to be telling somebody who had fought in the jungles of Vietnam what to do.

Thus, my first day I called my new platoon together. "Gentlemen, many of you are vets. Some of you just plain don't like me because of who I am. So, I'll make a pact with you. You don't have to salute me or call me 'sir' except when my superiors are around. I will bend over backward to make your stay under my command a sane experience. In return, do your job. That's all the respect I want." From that day on, I had one of the best-rated platoons on the post.

I never really understood Army life except to know that it didn't make sense a lot of the time. One particular incident illustrates the point.

My company was set to have its annual inspection. The platoon next to ours was run by a lieutenant who wanted to make the Army his life. He kept his area immaculately clean, and his men always treated him as they were supposed to treat an officer.

Of course, my men and I were treading water until we received our exit papers. But I had found out that putting on a show worked. Thus, I had my men make signs that read "By Order of Lt. Whitehead" and put them everywhere. Our area was clean, and when the small, swagger stick-carrying general drove up in his jeep to inspect us, we snapped to attention. We passed with flying colors. The general told me, "I know you're in command. Your name is everywhere."

The officer across the way, however, was relieved of his command after the general had pointed his swagger stick to a board that displayed the vehicles under the lieutenant's command and it had taken too long to find the vehicle to suit the general. The lieutenant's career was ruined.

The Army had told me that, because of my back condition, I couldn't carry a rifle and, after all, I was in the infantry. So I coached and played sports—basketball, softball, water polo, volleyball. I had good athletes in my platoon. We won a battalion championship in softball and could have done better in basketball except for the drugs. Some of my men would show up for games high on pot, and it hurt their play.

Racial tensions were high in the Army. My jeep driver was a hulking black man from New York's Harlem district. Nicknamed "the Babe," he played on my softball team and could knock the ball a mile, hence the nickname. He told me one night as we drove around on general duty that if he ran into me in Harlem, he might kill me. I believed him.

America's involvement in the war continued to widen, despite affirmations from Nixon to the contrary. In April, United States and South Vietnamese forces poured into Cambodia, although Nixon insisted that this was only a "limited incursion."

In the United States, the peace movement was in full swing. Jane Fonda led a peace march through the streets of Killeen up to Fort Hood but was stopped at the gate. Students went on strike across the nation, and on college campuses they burned draft cards and ROTC facilities.

The ROTC building at Ohio's Kent State University was still smoldering on May 4 when National Guard troops opened fire on demonstrators and onlookers, killing four unarmed students. Ten days later, in a similar incident, police shot and killed two student protesters at Jackson State University in Mississippi. The ensuing explosion of rage shut down seventy-five American colleges for the rest of the academic year.

The killings at Kent State would force me into a confrontation about a year later. I was on my way out of the Army in the spring of 1971 when I was placed in a transition platoon where I had a desk job. It was headed by a captain who took himself a bit too seriously and liked to put slogans on a blackboard as you walked in the door. Mostly the slogans were innocuous nonsense. But one day as I stepped inside on my way to my desk, I noticed his slogan of the day and stopped in my tracks. "Four for us, zero for them," it read.

When I asked the captain what it meant, he said, "The Kent State shootings, of course." I told him I was offended by his callousness. Four innocent people had died. It was not a joking matter and certainly not a subject to be used for sloganeering. I asked him to remove it. The captain refused. I asked again and warned him that I would go over his head. He again refused. After I complained to our commanding officer that afternoon, the captain erased the slogan.

My last six months in the Army were spent working on a top secret project dealing with sensors that could be deployed from the air. They mainly consisted of camouflaged bushes, animal feces, rocks, and other natural debris and could be deployed in areas for intelligence gathering. For example, if an enemy soldier brushed against a plastic bush in the dark, our forces knew he was there. It was a 9:00 to 5:00 desk job. The best thing about the job was that it gave me time to read.

I was batting a thousand. I had told Carol I never wanted to get married, and within a couple of years we were standing at the altar. Then I told her I never wanted children but fell hook, line, and sinker when our first child, Jayson Reau, arrived on October 11, 1970. Carol had suffered a miscarriage about a year earlier but delivered a healthy seven-pound, twelve-ounce baby after eight hours of labor. Jayson was named after one of my favorite authors, Henry David Thoreau.

Although I thought I had not wanted children, as soon as I held Jayson I became the classic doting father. In fact, fearing that he would go blind if any flashbulbs went off in his eyes, I wouldn't even take any pictures of him in the hospital.

"I'll Take Japan and Leave"

Fort Hood and surrounding Killeen could be boring, especially when you're young and restless as I was. So Carol and I would take frequent trips to see my friend from college, Bob Roller, who was attending law school at the University of Texas in Austin. It was Bob who encouraged me to attend law school. "Hey, if you want to change the system, the law is a more effective way." Eventually I decided he was right and applied to the University of Arkansas School of Law.

When I learned that I had been accepted to law school, I notified the Army and received a two-month early out. My time in the Army, to put it mildly, had been chaotic. So I was greatly surprised when a few months before my obligation was scheduled to end I was called into a colonel's office and offered a promotion to captain if I stayed in. I sat there stunned as the colonel told me, "You're the kind of man we're looking for." I thought, *You want someone who despises you?* I thanked the kind gentleman for the offer but declined what appeared to be sheer insanity. Leaving his office, I knew I had made the right decision.

In July of 1971, I loaded up my small family and headed back to Fayetteville in search of a way to continue the fight. We arrived in Fayetteville in early August and rented a small apartment. As I registered for classes, I noticed a small underground newspaper, *The Grapevine,* stacked on the floor of the law school. I flipped through it and liked its cynical nature and the fact that it attacked everything from the university itself to the president of the United States.

While in the Army, I had dabbled in poetry and short stories and decided to submit a poem to the editors of *The Grapevine.* To my amazement, they published it.

I started law classes with a sense of optimism. My hair was longer, and my mustache was beginning to thicken. I had all the markings of the counterculture. My love of motorcycles was still strong, and I bought a used Yamaha for transportation to and from school. Although Jayson was only a year old, I would fasten his helmet on his little head and put him in front of me on the motorcycle seat, and we would zoom down the road with his long blond hair blowing in the wind. At other times Carol climbed on the back, and the three of us took off as I zigged and zagged in between traffic. It was a lot of fun, but I shudder to think what would've happened to us if there had been an accident.

The law school years were some of the toughest ones Carol and I have faced. Our only income in the beginning was the GI Bill. If we went out to eat, Carol and I would share a meal at a cheap drive-in. Since Carol was still nursing Jayson and didn't want to leave him with a sitter, we got a paper route. Jayson liked to watch as we tossed the rolled-up *Northwest Arkansas Times* from our car as we sped down the highway. However, this didn't cover our expenses, so I got a job selling shoes on the weekends.

On top of all this, I had my studies. The first year of law school was grueling. The subjects were new, and the work was piled on unmercifully. Within two months, students were dropping out.

I was and still am an idealist. If possible, I would've taken a few courses like constitutional law and poverty law and gone right into the courts to fight for the oppressed. But the system doesn't work like that. Instead, I was faced with courses in property, contracts, torts, and other subjects I had no interest in. I quickly grew frustrated.

I made it through the first semester with average grades. By this time, my hair was long and my usual attire was blue jeans, a sweatshirt, and my old Army jacket. My political views were far to the left. I hated Richard Nixon and distrusted anyone who spoke positively about the United States. I was drinking heavily and smoking marijuana on a regular basis, which caused a lot of friction in my marriage. When I wasn't in class, I was behind a closed door in our apartment, studying. Carol and I weren't talking much, and when we did, I usually ended up yelling at her—or worse. She had stood by me and supported me in whatever I had decided to do, but it seemed we were headed for a breakup.

I was beginning to feel that I was always swimming upstream, and even when I got near the top, somehow I would always wind up at the bottom again. I look back on my early school years as a continual struggle; I fought with my teachers in college; the Army was one battle after another with some superior officer; and now I was in law school, taking what I saw at the time as mindless courses that had no relevance to my life.

We were supposed to be living in a democratic country. Millions were involved in the peace movement, and polls showed the American people did not support the war. But it raged on anyway. We were helpless before the war machine.

It was all too much. Carol and I were always broke. My parents and I were not talking. Although they had not seen me for some time, they sensed the worst—I looked like a freak. I grew angrier and angrier. I couldn't even drive a car without screaming at the driver in front of me. Total disillusionment finally set in.

By late March of 1972, halfway into my second semester, I decided to quit law school. I wasn't quite twenty-six, but I felt as though I had lived a century already.

There are crossroads in everyone's life where a decision is made that affects everything that follows. I had made my decision to abandon law school while sitting under a tree on campus, feeling sorry for myself. Most depression, I've come to see, is selfishness—thinking about yourself and forgetting about the people around you. After my decision, I drove back to our apartment and calmly informed Carol that I was finished with law school. "I'm quitting," I told her. "I can't go any further. I'm going to get a job." In the four and a half years we had been married, Carol had followed me and accepted whatever I wanted to do, so her reaction was totally unexpected. She looked me right in the eye and said, "What are you talking about, quitting law school? You've put Jayson and me through pure hell these past few months. First of all, you were going to finish college and then get a job. Then you were going to get your master's degree and go to work.

"Then you couldn't wait to get out of the Army, even though they offered to make you a captain. Then, after talking to Roller, you just had to go to law school because he was going to law school. Well, that's it!

"I've gone along with everything you ever asked, because I loved you more than anything in the world. But you never loved me and just treated me like a thing. I'm not going through anything else with you. Either you get your head screwed on right and finish law school, or we're through. I'll take Jayson and leave. I won't put my child through this. It's not worth it."

Carol was serious, and I knew it.

The next day I was back in class.

Carol had always been willing to help me in any way I needed her to. In college, she had typed my papers and worked to help put me through; she did the same during graduate school. Attendance in law classes was not mandatory, but if you wanted to know some of the key information that would be on the tests, you had to attend and take notes. The classes were usually big, and I always sat far back in the classroom, hoping not to be noticed or called on. Eventually I persuaded Carol to start going to some of my classes like Property and Contracts. She knew shorthand and would come home and type her class notes for me so I had the professor's comments verbatim. I had a good memory and would virtually memorize the notes for exams. This got me through my first year of law school.

After that, Carol often went to class for me in my last two years, making life easier and more tolerable for me. She always said her worst fear was that one of the professors would call on "me" when she was taking my place.

That summer we stayed in Fayetteville, delivering papers as I continued to sell shoes on weekends. My relationship with my parents was still tense, although Carol got along well with them, and my mom and dad wanted to see their grandson. So they, along with Uncle Paul, packed their suitcases and made the five-hundred-mile trip to Fayetteville. To say the least, my parents were shocked at my appearance. To them, long hair on a man represented everything they detested, and I now had hair below my ears. It was the counterculture, drugs, and the Beatles rolled into one. Also, Carol and I lived like hippies. We slept on a mattress on the floor and used old cable-wire wooden spools as tables—more because of a lack of money, though, than as a matter of style.

It didn't take long for us to have words. It was as if my parents and I were from different countries and didn't understand each other's language. And anyway, my looks repulsed them. They left the next day.

Steal This Book

In the fall of that year, Abbie Hoffman came to the Arkansas campus to speak. I had admired his efforts in resisting the war. Carol and I bought tickets and wound up about fifteen or twenty rows from the stage. However, Carol spent most of the evening out in the hallway with Jayson, as she had on so many other occasions and at movies, because he was active and rarely sat still.

Hoffman showed up late. This was to be expected; he was an anarchist. Why should he show up on time when he believed in disorder?

With a can of Coke in one hand, Hoffman gave a disorganized diatribe against the United States government, attacking everything from the family to the University of Arkansas. Then he mentioned his new book, *Steal This Book*.

Steal This Book was the manifesto I had been looking for. With illustrations, it set forth in readable style how to undermine the system. From getting free food to how to shoplift, this was a bible for the anarchist. I read and reread it.

Hoffman inspired me to put together a small broadside I called "The Critic Advocate." I reprinted pages from *Steal This Book* and wrote articles attacking Nixon, the war, and the hypocrisy of the educational system. Carol and I could afford to print only twenty copies or so at a local church that let us use its mimeograph machine. However, schoolwork started absorbing my time, and "The Critic Advocate" died after a few issues. I was now committed to working as hard as possible to get good grades. It had finally dawned on me that I could impact the system by playing the game. Part of the game was academic achievement.

At the end of 1972, American participation in the war finally ground to a halt. A cease-fire on January 28, 1973, ended direct involvement by American ground troops in Indochina. The last U.S. troops left South Vietnam at the end of March, with a final combat death toll of nearly forty-six thousand. Nixon claimed to have won "peace with honor." But America's longest war had ended in military defeat by a tiny, less technologically advanced country. And, in the minds of Vietnam vets who returned, the war would never be over.

In early January, I received my grades for the fall semester. I had actually made the dean's list. I still looked like a hippie, but my grades were now competing with students who were in law school as a career choice, a way to make money. An idealist could make good marks as well.

That academic year, I studied constitutional law under Professor Mort Gitelman. A free speech advocate, Gitelman worked with the American Civil Liberties Union (ACLU). He fostered lively debates in class on the key issues of the day, from religion in public places to abortion-on-demand. I learned a lot in the class and saw Gitelman as a model for the civil liberties lawyer.

Years later, after I had converted to Christianity and returned to speak at the law school, I stopped in to see my old professor. As I stepped into his office, he said, "I hear you're in the religion business now." I didn't respond and said I just wanted to see how he was doing. He was amiable after that. Although our relationship wasn't quite the same, I still had respect for the man who taught me about the Constitution.

As the school year ended that spring, the United States Supreme Court issued its decision in *Roe v. Wade*. In upholding abortion as a woman's privacy right, a process was started that resulted in the deaths of millions of unborn children. It also embroiled the country in an issue that has divided families and furthered a controversy that Americans will still be wrestling with in the third millennium.

Clinton for Congress

The summer of 1973 was spent in Fayetteville, and I took an extra course at law school. I had made the dean's list again and was looking forward to my last year in law school.

I had worked part-time in the law library, and Carol was working half-days for an attorney in town, but we needed some extra cash. I saw a small advertisement in *The Grapevine* seeking writers. I contacted the editor, Joe Eblen, and went to see him at his house, which sat near the top of Mount Sequoia. Joe was familiar with my writing, as *The Grapevine* had published a few more of my poems and some short stories. One story entitled "The Beheading" was a quizzical tale about a man who is locked in a cell awaiting his execution. He fears the beheading, which we find out in the last paragraph is castration.

My pen name at the time was "J. W. Whitehead." Joe thought it highly amusing that James Whitehead, an English professor at the university, was upset that someone might think he was writing this stuff.

I started working for *The Grapevine* as a writer in September of 1973, doing feature articles at first. Joe gave me some valuable pointers and helped develop my writing skills. I also began doing interviews of local figures of interest. They went well, and I got the reputation of being a tough interviewer.

In late 1973, Bill Clinton, a young law professor at Arkansas, was running for the United States Congress. His Republican opponent was John Paul Hammerschmidt, an incumbent representative who was thought to be unbeatable. Clinton would later lose the election.

I approached Eblen about interviewing Clinton. He was a bit skeptical because Joe and I were both leftists, and Clinton was a moderate Democrat. We didn't want to do an interview that would pump Clinton because we simply did not trust moderates. But it was finally decided that the interview could go forward.

Clinton and I were the same age. I was completing law school, and he had just ended a stint working on the McGovern campaign. He had gone to all the right schools—Georgetown, Yale, and had been a Rhodes scholar at Oxford. He had made all the right connections in the Arkansas political hierarchy and was, unknown to me at the time, beginning his march toward the White House. Clinton was indeed a moderate, and I was a regular reader of *The Daily Worker*, a Marxist newspaper. Circumstances were, thus, ripe for a good interview.

One day in late January of 1974, I knocked on the door to Clinton's office at the law school. He ushered me in, and I told him I worked for *The Grapevine* and wanted to do an interview with him. "This," I said, "will help the students learn more about who you are."

Professor Clinton said he read *The Grapevine* and knew who I was. "Sure, I'll do the interview. Let me check my schedule, and I'll call you in a few days to set up a time." I started to turn to walk out of his office, but Clinton stopped me. "Thanks, John. I look forward to talking with you."

PLEASE RECYCLE THIS PAPER

THE GRAPEVINE ®

Vol. 5 No. 18   Fayetteville, Arkansas   Wednesday, 13 February 1974

CLINTON INTERVIEW
[By J. W. Whitehead]

Photo of Bill Clinton that appeared with my interview
in *The Grapevine* (13 February 1974)

CHAPTER 7

I've never been a quitter.

—*Richard Nixon*

"In fact," Bill Clinton told me, "I think heroin should be legalized."

He's trying to impress me, I said to myself. *He has to be joking.*

I looked every bit the scruffy liberal I was—long hair, old military jacket, obvious druggie. I didn't believe for a second that Clinton would actually stand up for legalizing heroin, but it was clear to me that he surmised *I* thought it would be a good idea and was trying to capitalize on that by ingratiating himself with me.

Our conversation took place as part of a series of interviews I conducted with Clinton for *The Grapevine.* It's almost uncanny to consider the cast of characters who were brought together at the University of Arkansas School of Law back in the early seventies.

One of my classmates was Susan Webber. Two decades later, she would be known as Susan Webber Wright, the federal judge in the Paula Jones litigation. Bill Clinton was a temporary professor at the law school while Susan and I were students there. From the start, Susan and I were opposites—she took his class; I didn't. I interviewed him; she didn't.

Susan was a very good student, possessing the internal fortitude that being a judge requires. On one occasion, Clinton lost his class's final exam papers and he offered to give everyone a B. Susan refused his offer, retook the exam, and earned an A. Even back then, she was wary of Clinton's "deals."

While Susan seemed destined to emerge as a productive member of the establishment, I was the radical who took great pleasure in attacking the law school with acerbic columns and articles every chance I got. Susan and I started out on the opposite side and, I guess, through the Paula Jones saga, ended up that way, too.

Interestingly, future House of Representatives manager Asa Hutchinson, who would prosecute Bill Clinton in the Senate impeachment trial, was also a student at the University of Arkansas School of Law. It wasn't until the early eighties that I actually met Asa, however. The law school invited me to speak, and Asa—at that time a federal prosecutor—came to hear me. Afterward, he introduced himself.

Another figure at the law school—one who seemed larger than life to everyone on campus—was the "god" named Webster Hubbell, who would later be indicted by Ken Starr for his part in the Whitewater scandal. Web was well known on campus. A star defensive player on the Arkansas Razorbacks football team, he was famous for flattening people into pancakes. This was in the days when Arkansas routinely fielded powerhouse teams, so gifted football players carried weighty esteem.

Web didn't look all that different then from the way he looks now, except for the inevitable addition of a few middle-age pounds. He was always a husky guy with thinning hair, though he had a commanding presence.

All in all, it was an amazing assortment of characters—superb student Susan Webber; cavalier, deal-making professor Bill Clinton; long-haired student rebel John Whitehead; big man on campus Web Hubbell; and conscientious Asa Hutchinson. Little did any of us know at the time that years later our paths would converge during a presidential crisis.

The "Arkansas connection," as I call it, continues to amaze me. Call it fate or divine Providence, but our disparate lives were interwoven into unparalleled political crisis and drama.

"The Devil You Know"

In spite of my predisposition against Bill Clinton, I found it hard not to like him. In fact, his were some of the most agreeable interviews I've ever had. He was young and thin, with dark hair and a seventies cut that just began to cover his ears.

Our first meeting took place at a local bar, late at night in early February, 1974. Clinton had just returned from Russellville, Arkansas, where he had been building support for a budding congressional campaign. We sat on bar stools, each of us holding a beer, and Clinton won me over with views that were candid and well thought-out.

Subsequent interviews took place over the next two weeks. During this time, Clinton invited Carol and me to his house for dinner. He served us a salad and red wine, as I remember, and was a good host.

Already, Clinton knew how to play the game.

The context of our interviews was dominated by our nation's worst presidential crisis ever. The nation had learned that the Watergate bugging incident was only part of a massive campaign of spying and sabotage directed by White House officials and the Committee to Re-Elect the President (sometimes referred to as "CREEP"). President Nixon's vice president, Spiro Agnew, had resigned in October of 1973 to avoid a criminal indictment on bribery, conspiracy, and tax fraud charges.

In December, Nixon submitted the first batch of his recorded White House conversations to Watergate Judge John J. Sirica. Although a slew of indictments of key White House officials would follow, the most damning taped conversations wouldn't emerge until late the next year.

Even so, there was enough evidence already presented for Clinton to believe in February of 1974 that Nixon was facing impeachable offenses. I asked him point-blank whether Nixon should be impeached, and he responded without hesitation. "I think there's probably cause to believe that he's committed gross improprieties in office, if not criminal acts," Clinton said. "The questions of impeachment and removal are fundamentally political questions. If I were in Congress now, I would think that the evidence for impeachment was very strong."

Then, not having a clue that two decades later Clinton himself would be an object of the same debate, I asked the wanna-be congressman what he thought the definition of an impeachable offense should be. He replied, "I think that the definition should include any criminal acts plus a willful failure of the president to fulfill his duty to uphold and execute the laws of the United States. [Another] factor that I think constitutes an impeachable offense would be willful, reckless behavior in office; just totally incompetent conduct of the office and the disregard for the necessities that the office demands. Law and order, for example."

I asked Clinton why he thought people were so hesitant about making a commitment toward impeachment. Early on in the scandal, Nixon's favorable ratings remained very high. "I believe one major factor is that they fear the uncertainty that would ensue if the president were removed. It's the old problem of 'the devil you know' is better than the one you don't."

Though Clinton hadn't formally declared his candidacy for Congress, he admitted he was running. I asked him how the present congressman in our district, Republican John Paul Hammerschmidt, had failed. Clinton's response is almost eerie, considering the troubles he would face in the late nineties:

> [Hammerschmidt] has failed by being a passive congressman. I don't
> believe that he has recognized how weak the Congress is or how strong

it needs to be . . . It matters how strong the Congress is, and it matters what the congressmen say and do when the president is abusing his power . . . Hammerschmidt has not been adequately concerned with the national issues until it was too late . . . For example, his attitude on this Watergate business has been deplorable. He said month after month that it wasn't important. He's changing his position now, but for a long time he was saying, "Forget about Watergate and get on with the business of the country." However, that was the very problem because the Nixon people weren't forgetting about it. John Ehrlichman was more concerned with what was in Daniel Ellsberg's psychiatrist's file than with how much oil was in the ground in Texas or how much wheat was planted in Iowa. That's why we're in trouble now. Congress should have done something about this and could have and didn't. That's why I want to run against Hammerschmidt.

Instead of a weak Congress, Clinton wanted to help create a stronger one:

> We need a strong Congress to serve as a limiting institution . . . Congress has to serve as a limiting institution because Congress itself is needed to act as a strong and powerful brake on the abuse of power by the executive and administrative bodies . . . And it's very important to me that I attempt to aid the Congress in assuming its proper role in the constitutional framework.

It is ironic that the very words Clinton uttered to me back in 1974 came back to judge him twenty-five years later. Relevant portions of my interviews with Clinton were reprinted in the *Washington Post* and covered by CNN and other media outlets. It was everywhere. Now, as then, one of Bill Clinton's biggest problems was his use of the language. He creates language traps for himself that lead him to create more verbal ambiguities to escape what he first said.

Eventually, as president, Clinton was forced to admit that he lied in an endless maze of denials and admissions. From his denial of an affair with Gennifer Flowers to an admission that they had slept together "just once"; from his seven-month denial of an inappropriate relationship with Monica Lewinsky to a full admission of the relationship after the infamous "blue dress" left no doubt; from not apologizing to saying "I'm sorry" to everyone from the American public to schoolchildren in Florida to key Democratic personnel to his cabinet and anyone else he believed to be in need of an apology; Clinton uses language like a magician uses sleight of hand.

His tarnishing of the truth virtually forced his former law student, Susan Webber Wright, to find Clinton guilty of civil contempt for his "false, misleading, and evasive answers" designed to "obstruct the judicial process." Of course, this came out after the impeachment trial was history.

But the words that perhaps will most seriously tarnish Bill Clinton's political legacy are the ones he did not say—to Paula Jones. Most likely, if he had merely offered a weak apology to Paula in the summer of 1997, she would have accepted it, the case would have been dismissed, and all the impeachment activities that followed in 1998 and 1999 would never have occurred. Certainly, I would never have become involved in the case. There would have been no Monica Lewinsky scandal or deposition, no impeachment trial, in all likelihood, nothing.

Pure Politician

But back in 1974, neither the young law professor nor I could anticipate such a turning of events. I asked Clinton about one of the most popular movies of that period, *The Candidate*, starring Robert Redford. Redford portrayed a young, idealistic poverty lawyer who started off as a truthful, honest (and appropriately liberal) candidate for public office. By the film's end, he had become corrupt and phony—just like everybody else in Washington (or so we thought).

"What about this happening to you?" I asked Clinton. "Now you could say you are in a 'pure state.' What's going to happen to you later?"

Clinton responded, "What happened to the candidate was he became a product of the modern mass-industrial society, a sort of packaged product. He was nothing more to the people than a PR man's construction. He didn't say anything about anything. I won't let that happen to me. I'm deeply interested in issues. I have enough confidence in myself that I'm not going to get swept away."

Unfortunately, even if Clinton did begin with the right ideals, somewhere along the way he became what he said he would never be. Clinton is now famous for his political finesse, the very skill for which he expressed empathy when it was displayed by Southern politicians of his youth: "Often when [the so-called New South Politicians] have found themselves in a difficult spot, they have been known to give less-than-concrete answers. I personally don't believe that they are selling their souls when they do this. So, you see, I don't view this as a light and darkness thing, either."

"Are *you* a politician?" I asked.

"Yes," Clinton responded.

This was one of Clinton's first political interviews (in fact, it may have been his very first). We were both learning, and consequently covered a wide range of subjects. One thing both of us agreed on was Bob Dylan. Dylan made his early career by taking on the establishment. One of his popular lyrics was "Propaganda. All is phony." I thought that all politicians were the epitome of phoniness; you simply could not trust them.

Clinton could probably tell this just from looking at me and knowing that I wrote for the "underground" newspaper, *The Grapevine*. He fed right into that. "I think [Dylan] is a genius," he said.

Of course, Clinton was running to become part of the establishment, which is why I was predisposed not to like him. Even so, I found he had an uncanny ability to look you in the eye and make you feel like the greatest person on earth. I went into the interviews very critical of Clinton—he wasn't nearly liberal enough for my tastes—but the introduction to my article ended up reading: "To those of us who knew the empty feeling that accompanied the McGovern defeat, Bill Clinton could probably be the reinstatement of the people's candidate."

Even back then, I knew Clinton had sized me up. His comments about legalizing heroin and the current "too restrictive" nature of drug laws were made, I noted, before I had the tape recorder rolling. I didn't take Clinton's heroin comment seriously. Although he may have been moderately liberal, he certainly wasn't stupid. In fact, after the interviews, he called me on the telephone and said, "Boy, some of those things I said; man, I do not want to see in print . . ."

Though I was fully aware of the game he was playing, I still found it hard not to like him. It was this experience that allowed me, some twenty years later, to watch Clinton's presidential crisis develop and have empathy for how his staff supported him. If you're around Clinton, odds are you're going to learn to like him, regardless of your initial impressions or prejudice. If you work for him, you will probably be willing to go to the mat for him in spite of the cost, as so many have done.

There have been few more personable politicians, ever. When Clinton was finally nominated for Congress at the Democratic Convention in Hot Springs, he picked me out of the crowd, waved, and said, "Hi, John."

I was amazed that he remembered me. Not only did he recognize me, *he knew my name.* I was just a student, Clinton was a big-time candidate, but he remembered who I was. This made a deep impression.

We didn't cross paths again until I became Paula Jones's lawyer. I spent many hours ruminating over how Bill Clinton became what he said he would not. How could someone with so much potential and charm and giftedness evolve into what Bill Clinton has now become?

We both emerged from a sixties generation that was intent on bringing about a new age of peace, hope, and understanding. When Clinton was first elected, much was made about the generational differences between him and George Bush, not to mention Bob Dole. This was a changing of the guard, pundits noted, a move from the World War II generation to the baby boomers who followed.

We baby boomers were going to change the world for the better. We would be better people who wouldn't wage senseless wars on foreign nations. We wouldn't let hypocrisy and ambition attack our ideals and principles.

The truth is, however, that we needed more than ideals. We needed the spiritual strength to uphold them—a thought that was foreign to me at the time. I was about to embark on a journey I never could have imagined, one that would bring me face-to-face with this "spiritual strength," a need I didn't even know I had.

PART THREE

TRUE BELIEVER

If there were no light in the universe and therefore no creatures with eyes, we should never know it was dark. Dark would be without meaning.

—C. S. Lewis
Mere Christianity

Four-year-old Jayson took this picture of Carol and me in
December 1974.

My son, Jayson, dressed in the Army outfit
Carol's mother made for him

CHAPTER 8

Where Jesus calls, He bridges the widest gulf.

—*Dietrich Bonhoeffer*

As law school marched to its conclusion, I began to consider my options. During my third year, I had done research part-time for a Chicago law firm. Near the end of my final year in school, I visited the Windy City. But it was clear that the big-city-firm life was not for me. The whole scene turned me off. "Hippie" wasn't the right term to describe me, but "left-wing radical" certainly was. The hierarchical world of suits, with its carefully controlled power politics and blatant displays of wealth, held little interest for me.

What I really wanted to do was civil rights work. I decided to open a small practice out of a tiny house we rented in Fayetteville. Our home sat nestled in a clump of trees near the center of town. A wooden staircase led up to a small attic that functioned as my first office. Carol served as my secretary, and four-year-old Jayson kept us busy, running up and down the stairs and entertaining us through some lean, long, hot days. I had one partner who practiced with me for just a short while. He left because of reasons we'll get to shortly.

An early case provided my first look inside a prison, an experience that I will never forget. A young African-American insisted on his innocence, so I traveled to the Fort Smith, Arkansas, jail for an interview to determine whether an injustice had been done.

If you've never been inside a jail, it's difficult to imagine a more confining or demeaning place to spend your days. You're ushered through numerous barred doors, each of which clangs shut and pens you in with a deafening sound. Along the way, you're frequently held in a sort of pen—the front door won't open until the back door clangs shut. You get the distinct feeling that nobody is going anywhere fast.

With my antiestablishment background, this was a particularly eerie experience for me. All somebody had to do, I thought, was hit me on the head and I'd never get out of there. Paranoia crept up my spine.

Adding to my fear were the heavyweight guards who looked at me with a scowl. These ominous guards patted me down to search me and ushered me through the slow-moving, clanging doors.

The air reeked of racism. Most of the guards were white and had little sympathy for a liberal lawyer who had come to set the black man free. I soon learned of the "triple" standard—whites are treated one way, brown skins slightly worse, and dark-skinned blacks the worst of all. Unfortunately, racism exists even between brown-skinned and dark-skinned African-Americans.

It was a sad place to visit; I couldn't imagine living there, and this indoctrination only strengthened my resolve to dedicate my life to protecting civil rights and the abuses that went on in places like this jail.

I interviewed the young black man through barred doors. His nervousness was patently obvious by the way he spoke in rushed tempo and high volume. He felt like a trapped rat and wanted to get out. My presence raised his hopes, and I didn't want to disappoint him.

My client, whom I'll call "Joe Jones," had been arrested for burglary. Not only did he argue his innocence, he said he had clear evidence of police corruption. As I mentioned earlier in this book, I grew up suspicious of the system and was eager to take on the government.

When we got to trial, it didn't take long for me to realize that the court wasn't exactly enthusiastic about having a civil rights lawyer in town.

"Your Honor," I told the judge, "I'm here today because my client, Joe Jones, has had his constitutional rights trampled."

I knew I was in a mess when the judge's first act was to make fun of me.

"Well now, Mr. Whitehead," the white judge sneered, "I wouldn't want to see Mr. Jones's constitutional rights violated, now, would I?"

It turned out my client really was guilty (I was a bit naive at the time and perhaps too quick to believe him). It was also true, however, that the cops were corrupt. All of those involved—my client and several police officers—deserved to be in jail. But of course, my client, the young black man, is the only one who ended up staying there. I had enough information to make the white cops' eyes grow as big as saucers when I asked them tough questions. You could see the sweat streaming out of their pores when I started naming names, connecting them with people who were known criminals.

Unfortunately, I didn't have quite enough to nail them.

This experience, and several others like it, convinced me of the fundamental corruptness of our judicial system. This is something that most whites could never understand during the O. J. Simpson trial. Our justice system is essentially run by white people. If you have enough money and the right lawyers from the right law firms, you have a much better chance of winning your case.

Through this and subsequent cases, I learned my lesson. When The Rutherford Institute gets involved in a case, most of the time we immediately hook into a local, prominent law firm. I can't change the system, but I've learned how to work it to eke out some sort of justice. That's just the game you have to play. Even if the local lawyers do nothing more than put their names on the case, it gets you in the door, and your case gets considered in an entirely new light.

The Queen of Fayetteville

As a civil rights lawyer, I rarely represented well-financed clients. Some, who knew my proclivities, opted to pay me in a homegrown sort of way, with bags of marijuana and even marijuana plants, which I cultivated in my backyard and carefully dried in our kitchen oven.

Dope became a regular part of my life, often even preceding my morning cup of coffee. What started out as an occasional foray soon became a cruel taskmaster. I was becoming more and more dependent on pot to make it through the day.

Some fellow attorneys, whom I'll call Rick and Tom (not their real names), joined me in my smoking, drinking, and partying and introduced me to cocaine and a few other exotic drugs such as angel dust. Up to this point, my life was driven by defending civil rights and fighting the establishment, but Rick and Tom were driven by their pursuit of ever-new experiences. This is the way many people validate or authenticate their existence. When the world appears meaningless—and the law profession cultivates that sense about as much as any other vocation—it's only new experiences that seem to create meaning out of chaos.

One of the "new experiences" that Rick and Tom dabbled in was gay sex, something you didn't hear about much back in the sixties and early seventies. But as far back as 1965, when I started college, Fayetteville was a progressive town. Located in the Ozark Mountains in the northwest corner of Arkansas, Fayetteville defies the image of a barefooted hillbilly with a pipe in his mouth. Built around the university, Fayetteville is an affluent area connected to vast wealth. The Waltons of Wal-Mart, the Tysons of chicken fame, and other corporate magnates live in the area and are regular contributors to the University of Arkansas. Given this, it's not so surprising that the area would have all the trappings of urban life, including drugs and "experimental" lifestyles.

One Saturday in early October 1974, Rick and Tom invited me to try some new grass, sprinkled with what they said was "dynamite angel dust." I took a few deep drags and felt my mind "loosen" up. As we drove out of town, taking occasional drags on our joints, Rick asked me, "Hey, John, have you ever thought of having sex with a man?"

I started to laugh, assuming he was joking.

"Yeah, right," I meekly offered. I had known these guys for a long time, and back then, gay sexuality was so uncommon and so unheard of that I really didn't take them seriously. I suppose I realized homosexuals existed; I just couldn't imagine that Rick and Tom would be among their numbers.

As we drove, we drank vast quantities of beer. In just a few hours, I personally downed a couple of six-packs. When you drink that much, your body needs relief, and I was in desperate need of a rest room.

With a buzz from the dope and the beer and the pressure on my bladder becoming acute, Rick started speaking more forthrightly.

"You really ought to try sex with a man, John. We're going to take you to see a guy who can show you a good time. You ought to try it."

It finally dawned on me that Rick wasn't kidding.

"Why cut yourself off?" Tom added. "You'll enjoy it, trust me. This guy really wants your body."

I wanted nothing more than to get out of that car and get home to Carol. I was about as miserable and flustered as I've ever been. For the life of me, I couldn't imagine that this was actually happening.

Our car ride ended up at an out-of-the-way cabin, hidden in the woods. Immediately after we stopped, Rick and Tom relieved themselves among the trees. They waited—quite obviously—for me to do the same, but it would have taken an army to get me to unzip my pants and expose myself at that moment, full bladder notwithstanding. I just wasn't going to give them the satisfaction.

Reluctantly, and in great pain, I followed Rick and Tom into the house where I met his highness, the "queen of Fayetteville."

I knew this man! I had seen him many times before, but never dressed like *this*. He was wearing furs and earrings, sucking on a joint, and trying to be provocative as he sprawled out on the couch. This "man" was using feminine gestures, licking his lips, and lightly rubbing his right leg.

"I've been watching you in the bars, John," he said.

Suddenly, the air felt hot and stuffy. It all seemed surreal; it couldn't be happening. I wondered how much of this was due to the "dynamite" angel dust and how much was actually happening.

My only thoughts at this time were, *How am I going to get out of this cabin?* and *How can I convince Rick and Tom to drive me home?* Clearly, they wanted a show, and I wasn't going to give it to them.

The queen licked his lips. "I have the hots for you, John."

"Boy, that's really a nice stereo you have," I offered, trying to change the subject.

"I want to see you naked."

"So, how long have you had this place?"

Enough was enough. I was in pretty good shape at the time, plenty capable of taking on either Rick or Tom. I wasn't sure I could beat both of them at the same time, but I was fed up with this spectacle.

"We're leaving, and we're leaving now," I said forcefully.

"Come on, man. Try it just this once," Rick argued. "It's great."

I raised the volume of my voice even further. "Look, you can't force me to do anything. I want out of this place, *now*." My hands balled up into fists, and I took a step toward Rick.

Finally, my two "friends" relented. We got back in the car, Rick and Tom in the front and me in the rear. As soon as I settled in for the long ride home, I was reminded of nature's urgent calling. It was a miserable and quiet ride back home. My attention was focused almost exclusively on trying to hold off a belligerent bladder screaming for relief. Rick and Tom were obviously having second thoughts about how the afternoon's events might have played out differently.

After we pulled into my driveway, Rick and Tom got out of the car, as if they expected to be invited in. This was rather presumptuous, given the circumstances, but my stubbornness was such that I didn't want them to think they had won. Nonchalantly, I acted as if nothing had happened.

Carol and Jayson greeted the three of us. I made a desperate charge for the bathroom while they casually welcomed our friends. When I got back out, feeling altogether like a new man, Carol shocked me when she took me aside and said, "I invited Rick and Tom to stay for dinner."

"*What?*"

"I'm going to make pizza, and there will be plenty for all of us. Don't you want them to stay?"

Carol's confusion was understandable. Rick and Tom had been friends for a long time; my sudden reluctance to spend an evening with them must have been perplexing. I realized that backing out of the invitation now would be tantamount to admitting defeat, so I gritted my teeth and accepted the fact that we would be having guests.

Several hours later, after Rick and Tom left and Jayson was asleep, Carol and I sat down to talk.

"You're not going to believe what happened to me today," I said.

"What?"

"We spent the afternoon drinking beer and smoking dope, then they took me to a cabin and tried to get me to have sex with a 'queen.'"

"You're not serious!" Carol said in disbelief, but after seeing the look on my face, she was a believer. "Why did you let me invite them in for dinner?"

"I didn't want them to think they had won."

Carol had never met anyone she even suspected of being a homosexual. The whole episode seemed as bizarre to her as it had to me.

But there was even more to come.

Ridiculing Religion

Looking back, I suppose I should have been more on my guard with Rick and Tom. After what I had gone through, it would have been reasonable to suspect they were into other bizarre things besides drugs and gay sex, but I still relied on them for drugs and was back to smoking grass with them just a few days later.

This was a self-indulgent time for me. I was fixated on my own urges and desires, along with my focus on making a living. I took Carol for granted. She stayed home with Jayson while I went out partying. On her own, Carol was powerless to change me.

Back when we were dating, I occasionally obliged Carol by attending church with her on my breaks home from college, but I put my own unique spin on "worship." First of all, I made sure we sat in the back row of the church. Then, when the pastor started speaking, I put my arm around Carol and tried to get her to kiss me.

"We can't do that here!" she whispered forcefully. "We're in church!"

But that simply made the challenge all the more fun. I leaned over and tried to kiss her on the neck. Carol turned away, so I pulled her cheek toward me, trying to kiss that.

On another occasion, the pastor invited the church to attend a special movie. I was a bit surprised, since the movie was directed by John Huston, who had won numerous Academy Awards. It was called *The Bible* and starred some big-name actors. Carol asked me if I wanted to come and was astonished when I enthusiastically responded, "Sure!"

Much to her chagrin, I stopped on the way for a tub of popcorn and two sodas.

"What do you think you're going to do with *that*?" she asked.

"You said it was a movie!" I retorted. "I can't see a movie without popcorn!"

Although we were married in Carol's church, I thought I was

through with that place after the wedding. Even so, her pastor was always trying to get me to pray with him. "Come on, John," he said. "Let's pray together."

"Absolutely not," I said. "I'm not going to pray with you."

Carol tried a "soft" approach: "I think we ought to go to church tomorrow."

"Why?" I argued. "There's no reason to go to church. They're just a bunch of hypocrites. I might go to laugh at them, but that's the only thing I'd do."

I paused. "Nah, I'm not going to church—and you're not, either."

Back at school, though I was determined not to go to church, others were determined to bring church to me. One of them was a young student who regularly stopped by the basketball court at the park to shoot hoops with me. He wasn't very good, but he was always up for a game of one-on-one, which I invariably won.

He had the height of a ballplayer—about six-two—but he was kind of beefy, with glasses, and wasn't at all athletic.

When we stopped to take a breather, he dropped hints. "You know, I think Jesus would have been a good ballplayer."

"Yeah, right," I sneered. "He would have been great in sandals and a robe."

On another occasion, he used a different tack. "I go to this great little church out on Mission Boulevard. You ought to check it out sometime."

"Now why would I do a stupid thing like that?"

Over about ten games, he found a way to lay out the entire plan of salvation in bits and pieces. There wasn't an element I didn't laugh or sneer at, but this guy always came back for more.

Even so, I was adamant in my belief that I had absolutely no need for religion of any kind. God had no place in my leftist view of life.

On Saturday morning, November 23, 1974, Carol, Jayson, and I were shopping at a local store when I noticed a book that was displayed on an aisle rack. The bright red cover with blue lettering drew my attention to a provocative title: *The Late Great Planet Earth.* I picked up the book and saw on the cover that it had sold millions of copies and was on the *New York Times* best-seller list, even though I had never seen it.

The Late Great Planet Earth. It has to be science fiction, I thought. On an impulse, I bought a book that changed my life forever.

Curious Conversion

Hal Lindsey's book gripped me in a way that few books ever have. I read the entire thing in less than twenty-four hours. What fascinated me was Lindsey's premise that the Bible's prophecies came true. Lindsey showed how events that had been predicted actually happened a thousand years later.

For the first time in my life, I started considering the fact that maybe—just maybe—the Bible was a competent source of information. I had questions about Lindsey's apocalyptic view of history, but I couldn't get the book's premise out of my mind.

Not that it was going to change my lifestyle. I was still indulging myself. When Rick and Tom told me they had a drug party planned for the Friday after Thanksgiving, it didn't take me long to consider my options: I could spend the holiday weekend with Carol, my son, and our families in Illinois, eating turkey and watching television, or imbibe in the best drugs to be found in Fayetteville.

"Sorry, honey," I told Carol. "I've got too much work to do this weekend. Why don't you and Jayson go on without me?"

"John," Carol protested, "it's *Thanksgiving!*"

"Do you want me to earn a living or not?"

Still, everything was not quite as it had been. While Carol was packing, I remembered a silver crucifix I had seen her wear. Back then, it meant about as much to me as it does to some of the celebrities and rock stars who wear crosses today. After reading *The Late*

Great Planet Earth, though, I had a sudden urge to put it around my own neck—and this was not a time in my life when I was inclined to deny any urge.

"Carol, do you remember where you put that old cross you used to wear?"

Carol found it at the bottom of a box that had been stored away. I put the cross around my neck simply as a good luck charm, having no idea how crucial a role it would play in my life over the next few days.

"While you're at it," I added, "maybe you could find your old Bible. I want to check out some of the things Lindsey was talking about."

Carol saw me reading the gospel of Matthew that night, but I was far too cynical for her to take any hope from these incipient signs of interest in God. As far as she was concerned, this was simply another "trip" that would soon pass.

Carol and Jayson left Wednesday morning for the five-hundred-mile drive to Illinois, and I worked most of that day and Thanksgiving Day. Late in the evening, I read another portion of Matthew. For the first time in my life, I was reading the Bible as a serious document about the life of Christ.

The next day, Friday, November 29, I worked until about 4:00 P.M. and then got ready for the party at Rick's house. Since Carol had taken our only car, I hitched a ride from our next-door neighbor.

It had been a long week of work, and I was ready to let loose. I could feel the tension flow out of me as soon as I stepped inside Rick's house. A raucous group of friends was already having a good time. Since Rick's wife and small child had left for the evening, we had the house to ourselves, and caution could be thrown to the wind.

I downed my share of beer, smoked a good bit of pot, and carried on in my usual manner.

My first suspicions came early, though. We were watching a football game, and several of the guys started admiring the players' rear ends.

Oh, brother, I moaned inwardly. These guys were just like that Christian who shot baskets with me. They kept hammering and hammering their point home, hoping I'd give in.

My suspicions were reinforced when the party started breaking up unusually early—around eight-thirty. Within fifteen minutes, Rick, Tom, and I were the only ones left.

"Well, maybe I should go, too," I said. "How about giving me a lift home, Rick? I'm tired."

"I'll take you home later," Rick insisted. "Why don't you stick around? I've got some good dope in my bedroom—even better than what we had before. You gotta try it."

Well, that was enough to convince me to stay.

Twenty minutes later, the effects of the pot were kicking in when the doorbell rang. Rick opened the door and in sauntered his highness, the queen of Fayetteville.

Déjà vu, I thought with a groan. Once again, I was without a car and at my friends' mercy.

"Don't worry," Rick said, trying to put me at ease. "We're just going to play some cards and enjoy some grass and beer. Relax."

Normally, relaxation would have been impossible, but the dope was strong. I followed everyone into Rick's recreation room, where we sat down at a table and started playing cards.

This is where things got really weird. I started to feel a sort of humming, dark presence. It was unlike anything I had ever felt before, and a darkness seemed to envelop me.

Of course I suspected the dope, and on closer inspection discovered that the joint was wet and dripping with moisture. To this day, I have no idea what it had been dipped in, but it was strong stuff.

I stared at the dripping joint, which suddenly looked like a phallic symbol. Across the table, Tom smiled at me, and I rubbed my eyes as his nose started to elongate and the tips of his ears grew into points.

Rick didn't look up or move his lips, but in some stange way, he spoke to me. It was a "mind voice," a form of telepathy.

John, there's more to life than what you see. There's a spiritual power higher and stronger than us. He can help you in many ways.

Somehow, I was able to respond, also without using my voice. *Who are you talking about?* I silently asked.

Satan.

The week had been weird enough to begin with. I had just finished a book predicting the end of the world as we know it and the second coming of Christ. Next thing I knew, I was surrounded by a bunch of dope-smoking satanists trying to convert me to their nefarious ends!

I was snapped awake; the effects of the drugs seemed to suddenly wear off as I leaped up from the table, pushed away my chair, and half shouted, "I have to leave!"

In my haste, my good luck charm, the crucifix, flipped outside of my shirt. As if a single puppeteer had pulled three strings at once, Rick, Tom, and the queen forcefully turned their heads away. They could not look at the cross.

With my mind still reeling, I stepped into the living room, grabbed my coat, and walked outside into the freezing November night. I had no way home, but I was willing to walk, even though my house was miles away.

Rick and Tom wouldn't let me go. They followed me outside and Rick called out, "Come back in, John. Let's talk. Just let it all hang out. Let it all go."

"I'm not letting *anything* hang out," I shouted back. "I'm going home."

I continued walking down the driveway and into the street of the middle-class subdivision. Looking over my shoulder, I noticed the sparkling multicolored Christmas lights in Rick's window.

If only people knew what really goes on in this neighborhood, I thought.

I had traveled a couple of blocks when Rick pulled up in his Thunderbird. Tom sat in the passenger's bucket seat.

"We can't let you walk home," Rick said through his window. "We need to talk."

It was cold. I was in no shape to walk several blocks, much less several miles. Reluctantly, I got into the backseat.

No sooner had my jeans met the vinyl than I regretted it. Instantaneously, I was surrounded by that same oppressive strangulation. Even more odd, the smell of sulfur became so strong that it was stifling. I felt I would choke on it and started blindly reaching for the window knob.

You have to let things go, John. Pleasure is all there is to life. If you stick with us, you can do well. You won't have any worries.

My mind was racing. I was dizzy, hot, choking, confused, freaking out.

Throw in with us. You'll have a new life.

The car kept rolling as their minds sent messages reeling into mine. Getting out of the car was out of the question. I felt trapped and can't give a reason for what happened next, except divine intervention. It was totally subconscious, more a reflex action than anything else.

As we hurtled down Highway 71, I looked up toward the sky and said, "Jesus Christ, You are my Savior."

Suddenly I was enveloped by an equally strong but benevolent rush. The most amazing feeling poured over me and through me, like warm milk flowing down my throat. It was as if I could literally feel the Spirit of God rushing through my entire body.

At the same time, Rick and Tom began to moan audibly, as if they were in pain. And to my amazement, I said out loud, "You need to believe on the Lord Jesus Christ. Repent and believe on Christ, and you'll be saved."

There was a pervasive silence, so I repeated myself. "Repent and believe on Christ, and you'll be saved."

I had no idea what I was saying or what it meant, but it came with an authoritative force that took over the mood in that car.

Rick and Tom remained silent. We pulled up to my house on Meadow Street, and I got out. There was no friendly parting. No one spoke a word. I turned to walk into the house, stopping briefly to make sure they were driving away.

I unlocked the front door, walked into the house, and looked at the clock on the wall. It was a little after 10:00 P.M. All of this crazy stuff had happened in less than five hours.

Wild Night

My first thought was, *I have to call Carol.* As soon as she got on the line, I burst out with, "I've become a Christian. I've accepted Jesus Christ as my Savior!"

There was a stunned silence, which Carol broke with, "Are you drunk?"

"No, I'm not. This is for real."

We kept the phone line tied up for more than two hours as I recounted what had happened and how I had suddenly become a Christian, much to my amazement. I'm a practical joker, and for a long time, Carol was certain that this was one of my best efforts.

"Look," I said finally, "I'm flying up to Peoria tomorrow." Maybe I could convince her in person.

As soon as I got off the phone, I felt full of energy. There was no way I could just sit there or sleep, and I remembered a minister I had met. Thumbing through the telephone book, I found his phone number. I had spoken to him some months earlier and wanted to talk to a "professional."

"I have become a Christian," I said. "I believe in Jesus Christ."

"I've never believed in Jesus Christ," he responded. "All that stuff is just a myth."

I dropped the phone, and later found out he was a Unitarian

minister. At the time, however, it was an unnerving conversation.

Not wanting to end the night on such a bizarre encounter, I called my dad.

"Did Carol tell you that I've become a Christian?"

His voice was full of cynicism as he responded, "Sure you are. You're the 'Christian' lawyer who helps all those people get a divorce. Really sounds like a Christian thing to me."

His words really stung. In fact, I looked over at my desk and saw some divorce papers ready to be filed that I had prepared earlier in the day.

After being lifted up so unexpectedly high, I was crashed back down to earth with a spiritual body slam. I still wasn't sure my wife believed me. The minister I called *didn't believe in Christ*. My dad doubted my vocation could ever match my newfound faith—how could I be a Christian and help destroy families at the same time?

My mind was racing so fast that sleep was impossible. I lay in bed, but the wind blowing outside made our old house creak and moan, not unlike the sounds that had emanated from the throats of Rick and Tom earlier in the evening. Jayson's Siamese cat kept rubbing against me, so I put it outside, but that only added to the cacophony of sound. The cat clawed at the windows. Together with the wind, it sounded like the entire house was poised to collapse on me.

This was my personal horror movie. Only this time, I wasn't in a theater watching it; I was starring in it.

And this was real.

To settle my nerves, I took out the Bible Carol had left for me and started reading the Psalms. David's words had a soothing effect, so I kept reading until I saw the sunlight hitting the street in front of the house.

It had been an unbelievable night, but looking back, I think that anything less wouldn't have sufficed. I was so cynical that I needed something life-shattering to shake me up. I was too hardened to respond to a soft invitation. If God hadn't hit me on the head as force-fully as He did, I never would have left the life of self-indulgence and drugs that was slowly destroying me.

I knew I had changed when I got out of bed and went to my upstairs office. Taking out a large stash of marijuana, I carried it into the backyard and set the entire bag on fire. Watching the flickering sparks fly off into the early morning sky, I felt no longing for my usual morning "high." I was happy to watch it burn.

Convincing the Skeptics

That day I flew to Peoria. Carol met me at the airport, and for the next several days she watched me skeptically, asking herself, *Was his conversion real or simply another trip?*

Her initial suspicion was that I had freaked out on a bad acid trip, so she kept waiting for me to come down or for the effect of the drug to wear off. It took a number of days for her to believe that I was per-manently changed. My willingness to go to church on Sunday—as well as talk to the pastor—finally convinced her. This was real.

When Carol and I got home from church, my parents were less skeptical, but they still didn't know how to react to the "new" me.

"So, now you've become a Jesus freak," my mother said.

At the time, I didn't know what a "Jesus freak" was, but I could tell from her tone of voice that in her mind this was simply another tangent I had gone off on. They fully expected me to join a religious commune or cult or—even worse—take Carol and Jayson, whom both my dad and my mother adored, with me.

To them, I had simply gone from being a problem child to an adult religious nut.

Back in Fayetteville, the reception to my conversion met with no better response. My law partner watched as I put Carol's Bible on my desk.

"That thing makes my skin crawl," he said.

He was gone within a week.

Tom contacted me one last time. He said he needed to pick up some records he had loaned to me. We sat in my living room, making awkward small talk for a while, neither of us even getting close to mentioning "the night." It was clear to him that I was no longer going to be part of the old gang and the drug scene.

I knew I had found something fascinating and real, but Tom was convinced that I had lost something crucial—my mind! Neither he nor Rick ever spoke to me again.

Now that we were back home, Carol and I needed to find a church in Fayetteville. My first thought was to go to the church that my basketball buddy had talked about so often. I hadn't seen him in a while and eagerly anticipated the look on his face when he saw me walk through the door.

Unfortunately, that never happened. When Carol, Jayson, and I arrived at the Mission Boulevard Baptist Church, I asked one of the church members about my friend. Her face grew dark as she said, "He passed away some weeks ago."

"What happened?"

"Didn't you know? He died of cancer."

My friend had never even hinted that he was sick. He was only in his early twenties, just beginning his life.

How sad, I thought. *I only wish I could thank him for taking the time to talk to me.* I also wanted to apologize for all the cynical statements he had suffered through because of me.

My basketball buddy was dead, but his pastor was very much alive, and Pastor Brian Disney and the members of his church gave gracious amounts of time to both Carol and me. Pastor Disney personally conducted Bible studies with just me, explaining the elementary aspects of the faith, and giving thoughtful answers to the plethora of questions I threw his way.

More than anything, his interest showed me that somebody cared.

Up to this point, my faith had either elicited guffaws of laughter or looks of disbelief. Finally, somebody was taking me seriously and was genuinely pleased with what had happened to me. His care and concern meant a lot to me.

On December 29, exactly one month after my salvation experience, Carol and I were both baptized in a cold Arkansas creek. As I came out of the water and walked, dripping wet, to shore, I noticed a dead rabbit lying on the rocks.

That's me, I thought. *That's what I used to be. Now I can be a better person and do some of the things I started out to do.*

A new journey had begun.

Me and Carol (holding Jonathan) and Jayson with Dr. R.J. Rushdoony at
Westwood Chapel (Spring 1977)

CHAPTER 9

Religion is a search for the truth about man's existence and his relationship with God and his fellow man, and once you stop searching and think you've got it made—at that point, you lose your religion.

—Jimmy Carter

A hideous creature sauntered in front of me. It had hooves where feet should have been, and its long tail swung back and forth. Its movements were deliberate—robotic and awkward. Electric bolts cascaded from its head, outlining its body like a bright neon light.

The creature stopped and turned toward me. His menacing stare went right through me, and then to my horror he reached out his grotesque arm to grab me.

I awoke sweating, my heart pounding. The creature had looked so vivid, so real. In all my years at the movies, I hadn't seen anything that shook me in quite this way. And then a thought struck me: *Was it a dream or a warning?*

Did Satan really walk about looking for someone to devour? And if so, was I next? What was I doing that was worth opposing? And the biggest question: Why me?

It was January of 1975. My recent conversion had spawned an insatiable thirst for reading and studying the Bible. Fully half of every day was spent exploring the truths held in that small book.

I wanted to search out the depths of Christian experience, which is why I was willing to go back to Carol's church in Peoria, where we had gone for Christmas. Carol grew up in an energetic Pentecostal church, one that verged on being a "Holy Roller" congregation. I was new to the faith, and this assembly certainly seemed to be vibrant and alive.

The elderly pastor, Dr. B. G. Drake Sr., preached on the "anointing," which he said is accompanied by "speaking in tongues." *Glossolalia* is practiced in several religions, and it finds its most welcome home among Christian circles in Pentecostal denominations, where it is seen as a sign of being "baptized" in the Spirit.

According to Dr. Drake, the gift of tongues was a requirement for becoming a whole Christian. I certainly wanted to be an exemplary follower of Jesus, so I approached Dr. Drake after the sermon and asked, "How does one get this gift?"

"Stop by my home this afternoon. I'll pray with you about it," he said.

Several hours later, Dr. Drake explained that the gift of tongues is given through prayer. All I had to do was ask, and God would provide the gift.

"Well, what does it sound like?" I asked.

Dr. Drake thought for a moment. "When Mrs. Drake was anointed, she trilled like a dove."

"A dove?"

"Yes, you know those high-pitched sounds doves make?"

Carol and I got down on our knees, and the pastor and his wife stood above us, placing their hands on our heads. Dr. Drake's prayers were fervent proclamations and forceful entreaties; his wife let loose with that "trilling" voice the pastor had told us about.

I waited for something to happen. Through drugs, I wasn't all that unfamiliar with unusual thoughts or sounds or sights, but nothing happened.

The pastor kept praying, even more fervently now; occasionally, a droplet of sweat rolled off his face and onto me. His wife's trilling increased in both tempo and volume and after a while—in all honesty—it seemed a bit hopeless. Apparently, God chose not to "anoint" us.

I left the pastor's house a bit skeptical and returned to focusing my mind, rather than my tongue, on God. I bought every Hal Lindsey book I could find and continued studying the Bible with a voracious intellectual appetite.

The more I studied, the more confused I felt about my chosen vocation. As is often the case with zealous new believers, I became passionate about not separating my religion from my work. I funded the bulk of my previous advocacy practice through lawsuits and divorce cases. A "Christian" lawyer helping people get divorced seemed questionable, at best. More than anything, it held little interest for me. In my heart, I wanted to use my legal training as a form of Christian ministry, whatever that happened to be.

But how?

I asked around, telling people of my desire to study further, and several suggested I check out some seminaries in Dallas.

There was one other factor to consider, of course. During this transformation, my family and I were going broke. My mind may have been expanding, but my wallet was as thin as it had ever been. I couldn't just go to school; I'd have to find a job. When an old friend who lived in Dallas helped me locate a summer position as a bankruptcy lawyer, everything seemed in order.

"I think God is opening this door," I told Carol. I closed my law practice in Fayetteville, and we rented a U-Haul truck to transfer the few belongings we had accumulated to Carol's parents' garage in Illinois. Within a few days of unpacking, we repacked a few necessities—leaving behind everything that was not absolutely essential—and headed for Dallas.

Dry Wells

Facing a new beginning with new faith, we should have been optimistic, but we felt more like vagabonds than pioneers. I began to wonder if my little family was like the Hebrews I had been reading about in the Bible. Under Moses, they wandered in the desert for forty years, never to see the promised land. Would we do the same in America?

To make matters worse, finding a summer position proved easier than choosing a seminary. After visiting several schools, I had the same feeling as when I was interning as a social worker in Little Rock—somehow, institutionalized evangelicalism was taking the vitality out of the Christianity I was studying in the Bible.

There *had* to be another way, at least for me.

I was still searching for something definitive in my Christian experience. We visited another charismatic church and were told once again that the gift of tongues was essential to realize a complete spiritual life.

"After tonight's service," the pastor said, "I'm holding a prayer session at the altar. Anyone who wants to receive the gift of tongues can come forward and do so."

It was a seductive message. The pastor drove a late-model car and dressed like an executive. We drove a ten-year-old car that Carol's dad had bought for us at an auction, and I usually shuffled around in old, worn clothes. Maybe this guy was onto something that had eluded me.

I squeezed Carol's hand. We were going to give it another try.

Minutes later, I found myself on my knees, sunk into a plush red carpet. This time there was no pastor's wife trilling, but there was a rock band trying to drum the Spirit into us. I'm not sure who was louder—the pastor and his assistants who called out fervently in prayer, or the electric guitar that laced its music into my soon sore ears.

We left with headaches but without the ability to speak in tongues. Twice we had heard that we were incomplete Christians without this gift. Twice we had experienced pastors praying for us to receive the anointing. Twice we had been found wanting.

That was the last time I ever sought solace in tongues.

The oil-rich country in Dallas was, spiritually speaking, proving to be a dry well. Not only was it not spiritually fruitful, but we were bogged down financially. After yet another day of frustrating seminary searching, I returned home to our little apartment to find that our clothes were hung outside to dry.

"I didn't have enough money for the Laundromat," Carol explained.

"Where did you wash them?" I asked.

"In the bathtub."

The only problem, though, was that the humidity in Dallas that summer was so high that the clothes wouldn't dry, no matter how long they hung out.

As a credentialed lawyer, it was both humiliating and frustrating to be in such poor financial straits.

While reading one of Hal Lindsey's books, I noticed an address for a school Lindsey had started. Believing that Dallas had nothing to offer us at the time, I sent a letter to the Light and Power House in Westwood, California. I had neither a street address nor a zip code. My envelope read simply:

The Light and Power House
Westwood, California

Somehow, the letter got there. Three days later, I received a reply. Entrance was relatively easy—no exams, just the completion of a simple application and a minimum fee, one that even I could afford.

We decided to go for it.

Go West, Young Man

It was mid-August of 1975. The heat, which had been unrelenting in Dallas, proved absolutely vicious in New Mexico and Arizona. Our 1965 Dodge didn't have air-conditioning, and it was packed full, with just three tiny spaces for us to sit in. There was no airflow at all—not that 110-degree air would actually cool us, anyway!

For several days, I sweated through my clothes and gripped the scalding-hot steering wheel, dreaming of cooler days.

"As soon as we get to Los Angeles, the first thing I'm gonna do is drive to the Pacific Ocean, take my shoes off, and walk into the water," I told Carol.

"That sounds great," Carol said.

"Yeah!" young Jayson agreed.

Finally, after three blistering days inside the car, we saw the signs for Santa Monica beach. I parked our car, ripped my shoes off, and raced Jayson to the ocean. I was so glad to be in California, hoping for better days ahead.

The "better days" were still a long way away, though.

Pets Yes, Children No

In the end, Los Angeles wasn't any kinder to us than Dallas had been. Because the letter from the Light and Power House had arrived so quickly, we took it to be a sign from God that He was going to bless our move, that everything would fall into place.

We couldn't have been more wrong.

One of the great ironies was that we couldn't find an apartment that would accept Jayson. If he had been a dog or a cat, there wouldn't have been a problem—pets were acceptable, but kids were an entirely different matter.

Near the end of places we had circled in the newspaper, we finally came across a place with one double bed, which the three of us shared. It certainly wasn't a steal, but it was the only thing we could find. It was late at night, and we were all totally worn out.

As soon as we got settled in, the faint odor that we had begun to notice increased immeasurably. The smell of (ironically enough) animal feces was so strong that we immediately got up, despite our fatigue, and headed for a cheap motel.

We were getting desperate. Our money was running out, and I needed to find a place for my family. I was willing to do *anything* legal just to scrape together enough cash to find a suitable place to live.

Since I had come to attend Bible school, my natural thought was to go from church to church. Because I was a lawyer, I was granted interviews with some very busy pastors.

One of them had what looked to be a two-thousand-dollar desk and an impressive office. It was a little embarrassing coming "hat in hand," so to speak, but at first the pastor seemed respectful enough. Less than five minutes into our conversation, however, his intercom buzzed.

"Mr. Franklin is on the line," his assistant said.

"Sorry, I have to take that," the pastor apologized.

I then listened to something that obviously had to do with a construction project.

"Now, what were you saying?" he asked me after hanging up.

No sooner had I started into my tale than his door burst open. "Pastor, I need to get your signature on these letters right away. Mail call is in thirty minutes."

"Just a moment, John," the pastor said.

There was another five minutes of small talk as he signed his letters, then buzzed his assistant to pick them up.

"Don't forget your three o'clock meeting," she reminded him.

"That's right! I'm sorry, John. It was great meeting you, but I have to go."

That was pretty much a representative meeting. One busy evangelical leader after another had little time for an individual in need. As I left the church, I was in sort of a religious shock. The culture I was witnessing seemed so foreign to the one I read about in the Bible, a culture in which Jesus took time out to talk to the woman at the well and extolled the Samaritan who stopped his business long enough to help a poor traveler in need.

I gave up on the churches and scoured the city, frantically looking for an apartment we could afford on our limited budget. Every night that we stayed at a cheap motel further depleted our ability to find a more permanent place to stay.

"John," Carol finally offered, gently, "we've only got a few days left before we completely run out of money."

"I know."

"If we sell the possessions we stored in Peoria . . ."

I sighed. Talk about "burning bridges." We were literally going to get rid of everything that didn't fit in a small sedan. But we didn't see any other choice.

"That means you'll have to go back."

Carol nodded.

What else could we do? We had prayed for God to provide a place, but couldn't find one. I had approached busy pastors for help, only to find their interest wane when they realized this was one lawyer who wasn't rich but who, in fact, needed a helping hand. Every day that we hesitated brought us one step closer to complete destitution.

"I can't imagine being apart from you and Jay for so long," I offered. Carol felt the same way. Though my earlier days had caused marital tension, we had never been separated for more than a few days at a time. Now, we were looking at several weeks apart, at the least. That's how long it would take for Carol to sell our possessions and for me to find an apartment.

Good-bye

The next day I awoke with the thought, *Tonight I'll be absolutely alone.* Los Angeles is a big city, and I didn't know anyone. The two people I did know were about to board an Amtrak train and travel halfway across America. I had my share of second thoughts but couldn't come up with any other solution.

Jayson started whimpering at the train station. The one good thing about the hot drive to California was that it had given us long blocks of time together, and Jayson didn't want those days to end. Nor did I.

But they had to.

Carol finally pulled my four-year-old son from my arms.

"Come on, JayJay," she said. Jayson hugged me tighter, his tears wetting my neck and shoulder.

Finally, I uncurled his fingers from around my neck and passed him on to Carol.

"I'm going to miss you," I told Carol. She no longer hid the tears but let them flow freely.

"I'll miss you, too. I don't want to go."

"I wish you didn't have to. I promise you I'll find a place for us to live. I'll call for you as soon as possible."

"I know you will."

One more long kiss, one last clench of hands, then Carol and Jay turned and boarded the train, waving through the window on their way to find a seat.

I stayed on the platform and watched until the train took my little family away.

Dorm Life

Now that I no longer had a family staying with me, I was able to move into the Light and Power House, which was just that—a *house*. I assumed "house" was just a quaint name for a ministry building, but this was an older, large (three-story) home, situated on a small hill overlooking Westwood Village (near UCLA). Typical for California, it was adobe style and the color of sand.

What the house lacked in comforts was more than made up for by the engaging people who occupied it. It was a relief to find a group of Christians who approached life intellectually. Nobody was trying to get me to speak in tongues. Nobody kept interrupting our discussions to take phone calls or address "pressing church business." It was just a group of Christians eager to study, grow, and learn.

As the only lawyer-in-residence, I received a certain amount of respect right away among the other sixty or seventy students. Not everyone lived at the house, nor did everyone qualify as a full-time student. Classic definitions didn't fit this place.

The class structure was loose and flexible. There were no tests, but we did have to write papers, though I soon learned that brevity was a sacred virtue here. For my first paper, I turned in a thirty-page thesis with well-documented footnotes. At first I thought my instructor was impressed, until he remarked, "Next time, five or six pages will do, John."

The predominant structure of the school was a brief period of instruction, followed by lots of discussion. Everything got talked out, and professors challenged us to think carefully through every topic. I was very impressed with the teaching.

Hal Lindsey was by now a superstar, with several of his books selling millions of copies. I eagerly looked forward to his first lecture, which was held on a Saturday night. As we waited, in walked a man wearing a black leather jacket. I knew without asking that this was Hal Lindsey. He had an influential presence about him and was shown deference by most of the people in the room. What he lacked in height, he made up for in stature. For a man his age, he was in tremendous shape and obviously worked out.

He had been told about me, so one of his first comments to me was, "How'd we find you?"

I told him my abbreviated story. He nodded and seemed thoughtful, but didn't say much else.

Though the meeting itself might sound anticlimactic, for me it was anything but. This was the man who had, more than anyone else, led me to God. He was the one who pointed the way and gave me a respect for Scripture that I had never had before. It was a tremendous thrill to meet him and shake his hand.

I met another very influential man during this time, but in this case it was only through his books. It was at the Light and Power House that I was first introduced to Francis Schaeffer's writings. An entire class was devoted to discussing Schaeffer's ideas and theses, so I combed through copies of *The God Who Is There, He Is There and He Is Not Silent,* and *Escape from Reason.* This was my first—and probably my best—training in apologetics. At the time, I had no way of knowing that Dr. Schaeffer would soon become a close friend and colleague.

Living with bright professors and students was invigorating, creating a sort of communal experience. In between classes, students played Ping-Pong, strummed on a guitar, or joined a small group singing songs. Even communion was informal—a bit of cracker dissolved on the tongue and a drink from a cup of wine passed from person to person.

The area of the house I lived in was called "the pit." After being married for eight years, it was a bit crazy living with a bunch of single guys. We got to know one another well, and I soon realized that even Christians have their own issues to work through. One particularly devout student—who may have had the best prayer life of any of us—had a rather unique way of voicing his displeasure. Whenever he got really angry, he turned around, dropped his pants, and "mooned" the rest of the room. Another student kept a pet raccoon on the ledge outside the window.

Our studies were interspersed with typical horseplay. I was sleeping soundly in one of the bunk beds one night when I heard a loud crack and then a huge *thump,* followed by a loud litany of obscenities. I awoke to discover that one of the guys had crashed through his top bunk—and it wasn't an accident. Earlier in the day, one of the housemates had sawed through most of the boards underneath the bed. All it took was a little bit of weight for the bunk to give way.

This craziness was exactly what I needed. I missed my family deeply, and an occasional laugh provided healing balm for a hurting heart. Without these shenanigans, I would have been so lonely it would have been difficult to get through the day.

Some of the guys routinely tracked me down on a Saturday night. If left to my own, I usually studied. "Come on, John," they urged. "It's Saturday night. Let's go get something to eat."

Eating on such a tight budget required some ingenuity, as you'll soon see.

Poaching Pizza

Carol and I spoke on the phone almost every night.

"Good news, John!" she told me just a few days after she had left. "I got a job."

While we needed the money, Carol getting a job seemed much too permanent for my taste, even though I knew there was no other way. It was her wages that paid for my room and board at the Light and Power House.

She also enrolled Jayson in kindergarten, another sign of permanence that only deepened my resolve to find a place where we could stay—*together*.

David Harrison, the live-in manager at the house, had a wallet about as thin as mine. When he asked me to go out to eat, I knew what he meant—we were going to "poach pizza."

If you've never poached pizza, here's how it works. First, Dave and I walked into a crowded pizzeria and ordered two beers. Those drinks were the only item we'd spend money on all night. The restaurant in Westwood Village that we frequented was always packed, providing ample fodder for starving students. We kept one eye on the television, and one eye on the kitchen door.

As the pizza went out from the kitchen, we made a mental note of what it was and where it went.

"Dave!" I whispered. "A supreme!"

His eyes grew big as we saw the waitress place that extra-large supreme pizza, with a thick crust, in front of just two people. No way were they going to eat all of it.

We bided our time until thirty minutes later, when Dave saw the couple getting up to leave. He gave me a gentle nudge, we slipped off our stools, sauntered toward the back, and slipped into the booth just after the couple slipped out.

We turned pizza poaching into a science. Most people left behind at least a few pieces, and many times it was still warm. If they left any beer in a pitcher, we really felt we had scored. Surprisingly, customers almost never look behind.

It was just crazy enough to make it safe. If somebody saw us actually do it, they couldn't believe it and assumed we had been with the earlier party all along.

When I told Carol about it, she reacted with disgust. "Ooooh, that's sick," she said.

"Hey, nobody touched it," I protested. "Besides, it's *free.*"

She couldn't argue with the price.

These free meals allowed me to save what little I had, counting down the days until Carol and Jayson could join me again.

Two months of bachelor living were more than enough for my tastes. I finally found a small apartment in a black and Hispanic neighborhood in Culver City. It was clean, and with an outside gate, relatively safe. But even more important, it was within our price range.

I eagerly called Carol. "I found a place!"

"That's great. Where is it?"

"Culver City, near Westwood and Los Angeles."

There was a pause. "Is that an okay neighborhood?"

I changed the subject. "The apartment's clean. There's a gate out front!"

Carol read my words exactly. "That's okay. As long as we're together."

Since Carol had already sold our possessions, it didn't take long to pack everything up. In fact, she and Jay were on an Amtrak train the next day.

I was at the train station early the next morning, multiple emotions running through me. As I paced across the tile floors, the events of the past year raced in and out of my mind. I was elated that Carol and Jay were coming back. I was encouraged by the learning experience provided by the Light and Power House. But behind the rosy feelings was the constant, nagging shadow: *What's next? What will our future be?*

Culver City

Culver City proved to be a positive experience for all of us. It was the first time we had lived in a minority neighborhood, populated by low-income blacks, Hispanics, and a few whites. Jay became wonderfully color-blind in his choice of friends, an experience that was well worth the rent.

Living there further sensitized me to the plight of the dispossessed in our society. Two little black kids, Pookie (a girl) and Rodney, her brother, became frequent playmates of Jayson. Even though they were just four and six, their parents often left them alone for long periods of time. Soon, they were regular visitors in our apartment, usually barefoot and hungry, wearing only faded T-shirts and shorts. Watching these little kids get so excited about something as simple as a cookie reinforced my resolve to somehow help the disadvantaged.

Finally, the figurative clouds over our heads started to clear. It was as if the sun had broken through and shed some warmth and light into our lives. Carol landed a great job at a large law firm in downtown Los Angeles. As secretary to a partner, she earned a decent salary and had access to a typewriter and a copy machine—which would prove invaluable in the near future, though neither of us knew it at the time. As for me, I got to spend more time with Jay than I ever had before, and after the separation, nothing was sweeter. Carol rode the bus to work, and I dropped Jay off at school before going to classes at the Light and Power House. Jayson was in a half-day kindergarten at a small Christian school, and I picked him up every day at noontime.

After fixing lunch, the two of us watched reruns of *The Courtship of Eddie's Father*, after which we walked to a nearby park and played football with other kids.

And then I met a woman whose plight launched me into a lifelong obsession.

Chin Up

I was lounging around between classes in mid-November when one of my fellow students grabbed my arm.

"John," he said. "I want to introduce you to Mary Chin. She needs a Christian lawyer."

Mary was a substitute teacher in an elementary school in Los Angeles. An intense, though slight, Asian woman, Mary wore a small gold cross around her neck. One day, a student asked her what the cross was all about.

"To me, this symbolizes that God loves us," Mary replied. "He sent His Son to die on the cross so that we could all have eternal life. I believe Christ is a real person, and I talk to Him every day through prayer."

That was it. Three short sentences, less than fifty words, but it created a maelstrom.

The principal got wind that "religion was being taught in one of his classrooms," so he called Mary to his office and read her the riot act.

"Mary, we have separation of church and state in this country," he lectured. "It is illegal to discuss your religious beliefs in the classroom. I must ask you to stop."

Mary was frightened, but something in the principal's words didn't seem right to her. "Don't I have any rights to free speech?" she asked. "All I did was answer a student's question. I didn't try to proselytize. I was just honest."

"Mary, you crossed the line, and I will not tolerate that in this school. You must not say anything like that again, understood?"

Mary was understandably upset about the incident. Through a friend, she heard that a lawyer was attending classes at the Light and Power House.

When she recounted the details to me, I wasn't sure how to respond. I certainly wasn't surprised. In law school, we were essentially taught that if religion in public places was not unconstitutional, at the very least *it should be.*

Without giving Mary any assurances, I said simply, "I'll check on it, Mary, and get back to you."

That afternoon, I found a law library and literally buried myself in books, reading up on religious freedom. It was intoxicating. My faith, training, and vocation were coming together in a cohesive unit. Over the next several days, I read hundreds of pages of law review articles and constitutional law treatises. There were a number of unanswered questions, but one thing was patently clear: Mary was right and the principal was wrong. Both history and the law supported Mary's position.

The principal agreed to meet with me—on his turf—and my financial situation was such that I just barely succeeded in dressing like a lawyer, wearing an old tan polyester suit with an out-of-date tie.

"We've got a problem here," I told him, then proceeded to lay out Mary's case according to established precedent and case decisions. No longer facing a substitute teacher who was ignorant about the law, the principal offered little resistance.

"You are ill informed about the true nature of the separation of church and state," I explained.

He agreed.

Walking out of his office, my chest was swelling with the satisfaction of being back in the legal saddle again. *This is where I belong!* I told myself. I knew I had found my calling, the cause and mission to which I would devote the rest of my life.

Feeling bitten by the religious rights bug, I started slacking off in my classes at the Light and Power House and spending more time in various law libraries. My intellectual adrenaline was flowing freely, and it wasn't long before I had amassed a considerable collection of materials and enough knowledge to start writing articles. I was zealous for religious people to learn their rights.

The more I studied, the more I realized that the piecemeal approach represented by magazine articles wouldn't suffice. Rights were being abrogated on all fronts, and nothing less than an entire book addressing the subject in a comprehensive way would suffice. Decades of myths surrounding church-and-state issues had erected a formidable wall—one that I was eager to tear down.

Into this solo pursuit came a man who would provide focus, intellect, and a personal library that helped my dreams take concrete shape—Dr. R. J. Rushdoony.

Rush to Judgment

This guy looks like Moses, I said to myself.

A man of moderate height with a graying beard, Dr. Rousas John Rushdoony had a deep, baritone voice, though he spoke in a near-monotone. What he lacked in animation, however, he adequately made up for with a commanding intellect. In January 1976, he spoke at the Light and Power House. At the time, I knew nothing of the man or his somewhat controversial beliefs. But as he spoke about the law and his perspective on it, I decided he would be a valuable person to know.

"Hello, Dr. Rushdoony, my name's John Whitehead. I'm a lawyer and spend a good bit of time studying church-state issues."

"Really?" he said, showing genuine interest. "Why don't you come and hear me on Sunday morning?"

Though Rushdoony lived more than three hours north of Los Angeles, every Sunday he drove down to Westwood Chapel—a mortuary—to speak to a small group of people who used these facilities as a church meeting place. Westwood Chapel, of course, is famous as the depository of Marilyn Monroe's body where, every week for years, Joe DiMaggio faithfully delivered a rose into the slot at the foot of Marilyn's remains.

Dr. Rushdoony (or "Rush," as his friends called him), is an ardent postmillennialist and what is commonly referred to in evangelical circles as a "reconstructionist." Simplified, this belief states that Christians will slowly but surely assume control of civil society until they finally triumph over evil in this world. When unrighteousness has been virtually eradicated, Christ will return triumphant to the earth, His way paved by the faithful Christians who have "reconstructed" society for Him.

Any time you talk about building a "Christian-ruled" kingdom—especially one destined to take over the world—you are going to raise controversy in both religious and secular circles. But Rush's system of belief went even beyond these bounds. Because he holds that Old Testament laws are still in effect, he believes that in the reconstructed era children could, under certain conditions, be executed for violating their parents' commands. (Noticing how "grandfatherly" he was around children made it hard for me to believe he would actually follow through on this belief.) He also believed that the Old Testament dietary laws were to be followed, which meant no ham, shrimp, oysters on the half shell, or other delicacies.

I had difficulty reconciling his silly-putty way of handling children with his stringent theological beliefs. On one occasion, as two kids sat contentedly on Rush's knee, somebody from the Light and Power House asked him what would happen to a Hindu under a Christian-controlled regime (such as Dr. Rushdoony imagined).

"As long as he didn't practice his faith, the Hindu would be fine," Rush replied.

"But what if he practiced his faith?"

"Then he'd be guilty of violating the laws of the state."

"And?"

"And be subject to capital punishment."

There was a long silence after that.

My faith was a little more than a year old when I first met Rush, and with his prodigious intellect, he seemed the next logical step following my Hal Lindsey introduction. Without a doubt, Dr. Rushdoony is one of the most well-read people I have ever known, routinely devouring hundreds of books every year. Though his beliefs are controversial and somewhat fantastic, he had a quick, reasoned answer for every objection that was raised—at least, it seemed so to me at the time.

The main thing missing in my evangelical faith was any kind of system or structure. I didn't have a strong denominational affiliation, nor any particular creed that placed me within a more specific point of the greater Christian church. Rush's system provided what was wanting. Out of his mouth, the idea of Christians taking dominion over God's earth made perfect sense. I truly believed that Christians were one day going to control society, establish right and wrong, and define goodness. Of course, this meant that Christians would rule over people as well as creation, but who was more qualified to rule—I thought then—than somebody who was a faithful Christian?

In addition to being brilliant, Rush was also very kind. Though he didn't know me well at all, when I spoke to him after church one Sunday and mentioned that I was writing a book on the history of church and state and the First Amendment to the Constitution, he immediately offered the use of his vast library.

Next thing I knew, I was sitting next to the man himself in Rush's white Lincoln Continental, heading north toward the Redwoods. Chalcedon, Dr. Rushdoony's organization, is located in Vallecito in Calaveras County, the setting of the celebrated story of Mark Twain's jumping frog.

Rush's home is out in the middle of nowhere. There was no way you could come across it by accident, and it is miles removed from any threat of civilization. Even so, Rush was not one to take his theology lightly, especially when it comes to man's sinful nature.

As we pulled up to Rush's house, he locked and double-checked every door on the car.

"Why do you do that?" I asked. "There's no one out here except a few coyotes and maybe a bear!"

Rush seemed offended by my question. He promptly and firmly replied, "Because man is a sinner."

It was quite clear to me that the only possible sinner in this case was *me*. Not quite the welcome I was expecting!

Rush's library was located in a separate building. His books numbered in the thousands, and many of them were rare and/or out of print. I spent an entire week reading up to nine hours a day, and barely made a dent in what was before me. There were books on every subject imaginable—the natural world, politics, medical surgery, farming, theology, you name it. I rarely saw Rush without a book. One time when we traveled, I noticed that he carried two suitcases. One held his clothes and personal belongings, and the other was reserved exclusively for books.

Because he believed that Christians were truly going to take over the world, Rush believed that we had to be ready to rule in all sectors of society. Thus, if you asked him a question about obscure NBA rules or farming in Vietnam, he could answer it (those are two real-life examples!).

Each night, I ate dinner with Rush and his wife, Dorothy, and their half-blind German shepherd, Juno. Thus it was only natural that when Rush drove me home a week later, I invited him to stay for dinner, hoping to partially return the favor.

After we arrived at our little apartment in Culver City, I sat listening to this gurulike man speak in my own living room. I was thrilled at the thought of having him stay for dinner and getting to know Carol better, so I excused myself to peek into the kitchen and see how dinner was going.

Carol popped open the oven to check on the meal. In abject horror, I watched her pull a sizzling ham out of the oven.

"You can't serve that!" I protested.

"Why not?" Carol asked.

"Rush won't eat pork! It's forbidden in the Old Testament."

I realized that I should have warned Carol ahead of time, but she was typically flexible. "That's all right. I'll just put the ham in the refrigerator and make some hamburger steaks."

I fervently hoped that the smell hadn't reached and offended my new mentor.

Christian Lawyers

With the research from Rush's vast library fresh in my mind and notebooks, and feeling that I had gained a good foundation in my biblical studies at the Light and Power House, I quit taking classes at Lindsey's school and instead took a part-time job with some attorneys in Los Angeles. On the side, I started writing my book.

At first I felt quite alone, one man bucking the system to reestablish religious rights, so I was thrilled when a prominent Los Angeles attorney invited me to travel with him to Chicago to attend a meeting of attorneys gathering under the umbrella of the Christian Legal Society. He paid for my flight and several nights at the Palmer House Hotel. Aside from my ratty suit, I felt first-class for the first time in my life.

It went downhill from there, unfortunately. "John, what's this?" one of several lawyers asked me. He noticed that my old (but best) dress shirt was so threadbare you could see through it—not the typical attire for a lawyer, by any means.

After several similar conversations, I called Carol that evening and said, "I've got to splurge on some new dress shirts."

I went to Chicago eager to talk about important church-state cases, keen on standing up for people like Mary Chin who were being handcuffed by ignorance and sometimes outright malice toward religion. Though I was an advocate looking for like-minded zealots, I found, much to my dismay, that I was surrounded by a group of "discussers."

The workshop schedule alone was enough to sober me. "Is It Biblical to Sue?" one class asked. Another addressed, "Should Lawyers Be Involved in Lawsuits?"

These were questions I had answered long ago, and I saw little benefit or need in endlessly debating them. Having grown up with a leftist, ACLU-type background, I went to law school specifically to prepare to sue people and fight for justice. These lawyers, however, too often simply wanted to get together with other Christian lawyers and occasionally contribute a friend-of-the court brief, or perhaps discuss papers on various legal and nonlegal matters. To me, they certainly weren't out to challenge the status quo.

In spite of my disappointment, I tried to fit in. I thought if I joined them, perhaps I could encourage them to become a little more active. With the L.A. attorney's backing, I was hired as a constitutional consultant. The pay was not great—somewhere around a thousand dollars a month—and the work was time-consuming, writing briefs, brochures, and letters, attending meetings, and advising lawyers across the country.

At one meeting, I laid out the case for a much more proactive approach.

"We need to take a more activist stance," I urged my fellow lawyers. "Christians and other religious people need an advocate group that will fight for their causes, just like the ACLU fights for their various factions."

As I looked around the room, I saw that I was practically the only person who believed this, but I continued to advocate for a different approach.

"We need to educate laypeople about their rights under the law. There's no reason we can't put together a packet that a concerned Christian could use to take on the school board—and win. We also need to take on *pro bono* [at no charge] cases that will defend religious freedom."

"You mean to *sue people*?" I was asked.

"Absolutely," I replied.

My tirades were tolerated but not appreciated. At one of my last meetings, I spoke up in exasperation and said, "I simply cannot endure another discussion on the topic, 'What is a Christian lawyer?' Isn't it time to move on to more substantive work?"

Rather than continue to quarrel, we decided to part ways. CLS was never going to be what I wanted it to be. Some other organization would have to pick up the mission.

Fireworks

After Carol had retyped my four-hundred-page manuscript four times (this was before computers were readily available), my first book, *The Separation Illusion,* was finally ready for publication. What followed is typical for many would-be writers—extremely disinterested publishers. I had poured massive amounts of time and energy into a subject—church-state relations—that fascinated me. We were living in a moment in history in which clarification was urgently needed. Religious rights were being trampled without so much as a whisper of protest. Christians just rolled over and allowed themselves to be steamrollered by lawyers who were tearing the Constitution to shreds in pursuit of their religion-free society.

But what fascinated me alternately bored or irritated Christian publishers. The worst sound in the world when you're shopping a book around is silence. Some of the publishers didn't even bother to respond. I followed up with one when I noticed that he was present at a meeting that I was attending.

"Did you receive my manuscript, *The Separation Illusion*?" I asked.

"I certainly did," he responded. "I read it, too."

"And?"

"Who are you to say these things?"

I had actually had the nerve to praise George Washington—not your typical evangelical Christian, certainly, but a man who I believe possessed some keen political insights regarding the effect of religion on secular society.

"Are you aware that George Washington had syphilis?" he inquired.

Regardless of the truth of this—which I wasn't at all sure of—I didn't see what it had to do with Washington's desire to shape our young republic. This experience taught me how prejudice can get in the way of finding a Christian publisher. One relatively tangential sentence can kill a book's chances.

His question, "Who are you to say these things?" intrigued me. I was attending a conference at which many "super Christians" were speaking—Chuck Swindoll and other equally well-known names—and soon realized that regardless of whether what I was saying was true, I'd have a difficult time being heard because of who I was *not*—a well-known preacher. Being a Christian lawyer certainly wasn't enough to open any doors.

After I had exhausted all the possibilities I knew, I asked Dr. Rushdoony if he had any contacts. He personally sent my manuscript to George Mott of the now-defunct Mott Media. With little fanfare but great relief, the manuscript was accepted and scheduled for a spring 1977 publication.

Carol, Jayson, and I spent July 4, 1976—our country's two-hundredth birthday—at Disneyland. That night, as the fireworks went off, I sat on a bench near a statue of Walt Disney. As Jay ooohed and awed over the fireworks, I couldn't help but compare the beautiful chaos of the explosions with what was happening in my own life. I had no idea what shape the sparks would take, but with the publication of my book and the focus my life had taken defending religious rights, I knew it would be exciting. I just didn't realize how difficult it would be to fit within mainstream evangelicalism.

I should have wised up after listening to the reaction to an interview given by Georgia Governor Jimmy Carter. In the midst of his presidential campaign, Carter spoke candidly to *Playboy* magazine.

Known as a born-again Christian who lived by high morals, Carter worked hard to connect with this skeptical audience. Though he stated he had never been physically unfaithful to his wife, he also said that a man in his situation should "not be condescending or proud" in light of the "relative degree of sinfulness," explaining that he had lusted in his heart "many times" and thus technically fell under Jesus' denunciation of adultery.

Much to my surprise and dismay, evangelical Christians attacked him without mercy, even though few of them could honestly disagree with what he was saying—a clear and fair interpretation of Scripture. Nevertheless, many Christian spokesmen read Carter's words out of context and lambasted him for his remarks. They attacked him out of ignorance, which only seemed to increase their malice.

As the fireworks exploded over my head, little did I know that the same explosions that rocked Carter, our nation's thirty-ninth president, would also blow up in my own face. As I sought to answer truthfully questions put to me in the wake of the Paula Jones case, evangelicals I had never heard of came out of nowhere to lambast me.

In many ways, I'm thankful that I didn't know then what I know now. I was just at the cusp of my career, ready to launch out and make my (unknown to me at the time) controversial mark.

My second son, Jonathan, and me at Santa
Monica Beach (August 1977)

My daughter, Elisabeth, on my
shoulders (May 1981)

CHAPTER 10

I am the Antichrist.
*—Johnny Rotten,
lead singer, The Sex Pistols*

Fortune cookies with Bible quotes inside? "Jesus" refrigerator magnets? Coffee cups with the slogan "Things Go Better with Jesus"? And then, to top it off, two men in white tuxedos with canes and top hats dancing down the aisle singing "Tea for Two"?

This bizarre display at the 1977 Christian Booksellers Association in Denver constituted my first exposure to commercialized Christianity. *What does any of this have to do with Christianity?* I asked myself. *Jesus wore only one set of clothes and took money from a fish's mouth to pay His taxes!*

My publisher had sent me to Denver to promote *The Separation Illusion*. I wondered how such a serious book could find its way in a market that catered to such fodder.

While the book never became a best-seller, it did lay out much of my mission at the time. In the book, I argue that the people who founded America never intended that religion be separated from American public life. The founders would certainly have considered it absurd that Christians would not be allowed to talk about a cross hanging around their neck, or that a little girl who wrote "I love

Jesus" on her valentines would be told that her reference to Christ was "illegal."

For decades, a certain segment of our society has worked tirelessly to "sanitize" the schools and public places of religion. Some of them fear a dominant Christianity because they've seen the historical effects of misguided Christianity. Others aim to construct a form of religious apartheid because they are offended by Christian principles. Still others—including many Christian believers—think religious beliefs should be kept private and not "imposed" on others. A few even believe that all religion is superstition and that society would be genuinely better off in its absence. The cumulative efforts of these groups have steadily eroded the rights of religious people.

My book was somewhat apocalyptic. If I had to write it over again, I'd temper my zeal and soften many of my overstatements, but the basic thesis was and is sound.

The publication of my first book came shortly after the birth of my second son, Jonathan Mathew. Our family had been put on hold as a result of my conversion, but Carol and I didn't want Jayson to be an only child. Since we couldn't afford insurance, we found a doctor who delivered babies by natural childbirth in his office for a fraction of the usual cost. We took Jonathan home with us two hours after he was born.

This was the first birth I actually got to participate in, which led to a somewhat embarrassing mistake. I thought I was calm, but my heart was racing, and in my excitement I filled out the birth certificate wrong, entering Jayson's middle name and birth weight instead of Jonathan's.

"John, what did you *do*?" Carol asked me when we received the birth certificate in the mail.

I was as surprised as she was, and we had to go to court to correct the error. The Los Angeles judge glanced at the paperwork, then asked us, "Now tell me, what happened that leads you to want this birth certificate changed?"

"I was nervous?" I offered.

The judge chuckled and approved our request.

Nineteen seventy-seven also brought another momentous personal event—my fight to defend religious rights was about to reach a new platform.

God and Caesar

"John, I'd like to talk to you for a minute."

"Sure, Rush."

"There's an attorney in Cleveland I'd like you to meet. His name is David Gibbs, and he has just started an organization called the Christian Law Association."

"What do they do?"

"They work to preserve the rights of Christian schools to operate."

I was familiar with their concern. From the mid-seventies until the early eighties, a tough battle ensued between Christian schools and some churches over the issue of licensing. The idea, simply put, was that by accepting a governmental license, a Christian school was putting itself "under Caesar." By implication, it was also placing its parent ministry (the church) under that same restriction, thereby rendering what was God's to Caesar.

This was more of a theological concern than one with practical implications. I wasn't convinced by these Christian schools' logic. In fact, I thought it was a fair question to ask why churches were getting involved in running schools in the first place. But that wasn't the point. These Christians had a right to believe what they believed. If they thought they were compromising their faith by accepting a government license for their school, they should be free to operate without one.

It was a natural jump for me to go from working with the Christian Legal Society to the Christian Law Association (CLA), even though it meant leaving the little congregation served by Dr. Rushdoony in Los Angeles and moving out to Cleveland. I joined David Gibbs's law firm, with the assurance that I would be handling mostly church-state issues.

My new boss was a rather large man who, it often seemed, talked more like a used car salesman than a lawyer. Though he tried cases, his gift was speaking in churches and raising money on behalf of the CLA. He is an enormously gifted storyteller, and I marveled at the response he received after speaking at a church in California. A wave of people went up front to meet Gibbs, many of them even asking him to sign their Bibles.

David lived a frenetic life; as his colleague, I soon joined him in the mad dash from courtroom to speaking engagement and back again. He had to be in the courtroom to defend his cause and have a reason to raise money, but he had to keep speaking to raise the necessary funds to support his courtroom work.

Unfortunately, lawyering and raising money are both full-time jobs, so Gibbs was always trying to make up time on the roads. With me in the passenger seat, his Mercedes regularly clicked along at speeds that greatly exceeded the speed limit. There were times when my fingers were so white from holding on to the handle of the car door that I thought medical personnel would have to amputate my limbs to free me from the automobile. David had a CB radio going all the time, allowing him and the truckers who followed him down the road to evade the "smokies" and their dreaded radar.

I signed on to work with David Gibbs and CLA in part because I was eager for courtroom experience, but all I saw was paperwork. For six months, I accepted writing briefs as part of paying my dues, but it was getting tiresome seeing other lawyers take my work and words before the judge while I had to sit there silently, often knowing far more about the issues than did the lawyer arguing the case.

"David, please, just let me question *one witness*," I finally pleaded.

"Don't worry, John," he assured me, "your day will come."

But nothing changed. In one particularly embarrassing incident, the lawyer arguing our case was stumped by a judge's question. He excused himself so that he could ask me what the answer was.

It was tremendously frustrating.

In 1979, I was given a distinctly "weighty" case. (The tough-sells inevitably came to me.) "I'm sure you can find a way to make a valid argument," Gibbs told me.

In this case, I was asked to argue a lawsuit being leveled against the Smithsonian Institution. The plaintiff argued that the Smithsonian was teaching evolution and therefore establishing a religion, contrary to the First Amendment. Our client, a citizen in Virginia, believed evolution to be a mere theory and was greatly concerned that evolution was being taught as a fact by the Smithsonian exhibits.

After reviewing the preliminary papers, I knew I'd have to fly out to Washington, D.C., to view the exhibits for myself. Looking down from several thousand feet as the plane made its approach, seeing the White House and the Capitol, not to mention the Lincoln Memorial and the Washington Monument, I was smitten. I had spent countless hours studying the fundamental issues of America's founding, having read many of the works by men who were honored with these reverential sites. To top it off, I found the Virginia countryside, with its gentle rolling hills and lush green mountains, intoxicating as our client drove me from Dulles airport to downtown Washington, D.C.

This would be a great place to live, I thought.

The exhibits in question at the Museum of Natural History clearly taught evolution. Some of the plaques showed fish growing legs and crawling out of the water. While I thought these appeared somewhat ridiculous, I had my doubts about how they constituted an establishment of religion. The plaintiff's contention was that if government can't teach Christianity, it shouldn't be able to teach any other religion, either.

This put me, ironically, somewhat at odds with the plaintiff's position, as I was advocating for a more accepting view of religious rights. But you don't always get to choose your cases—at least, not when you work for someone else—and I always enjoy a good intellectual argument. I thought it would be fun to see if I could actually prove that the unquestioned acceptance of evolution was a religion—which, in my opinion, it is.

I wrote the brief, opting to take the position that this exhibit was nothing more than an establishment of the religion of humanism. David Gibbs argued the case.

Sometimes, you know right away how the judge is going to rule, even before the arguments are presented, and this was one of those times. Gibbs could hardly speak ten sentences without being interrupted, sometimes quite gruffly, by the judge, while the Smithsonian's lawyer was given free rein to develop his argument and state his case. The tone in the judge's voice was laden with condescension whenever he addressed Gibbs, and I knew we didn't have a chance.

We lost the case, but I nurtured a dream. Cleveland wasn't working out. While I appreciated the opportunity of working with David Gibbs, I realized I would never get the courtroom experience I so eagerly desired. Besides, when I flew back onto the snow-covered ground of Cleveland and felt the bitter wind that blows off Lake Erie, the pleasantness of northern Virginia loomed especially large in my mind.

"Carol," I said when I got back, "what do you think about moving to Virginia?"

Even though Carol was now pregnant with our third child, she didn't complain. She knew I wasn't happy in Cleveland, and Virginia would complete the countrywide tour we had embarked on. I went to school in the South (Arkansas), studied theology on the West Coast (California), worked in the Midwest (Ohio), and appeared headed to the East Coast.

Now all I needed was a job!

Nobel Aspirations

In the midst of our preparations for the move, I received a late-night phone call. Carol and I were both in bed, and I had just drifted off to sleep when the silence was pierced by the phone's ring.

"Hello?" I mumbled into the receiver.

"I'm looking for John Whitehead."

"I'm he."

"My name is Peter Nobel. I read your book *The Separation Illusion* and have tracked you down because my wife and I were arrested this evening. We're now out on bail."

Feeling suddenly awake, I asked, "What did you do?"

Usually, when a call comes after midnight, the answer is always, "I was out drinking." But this was altogether different.

"We teach our children at home. Michigan officials claim we are an unlicensed school and thus have committed a misdemeanor."

"*You were arrested for teaching your children at home?* That doesn't make sense."

"It's true. Will you take our case?"

"I think I can help you, but let me call you back in the morning."

The Nobels lived in Michigan and had seven children, all taught at home. Ruth Nobel had an education degree, but she did not have a teacher's certificate.

"Why not?" I asked her the next day.

"Because I believe that to take a certificate from the state would be wrong," she explained. "It's a matter of conscience for me. God has ordained that my children's education is my responsibility; I don't need the state's approval."

I thought the case looked strong and winnable, but I also realized that the Nobels fit what quickly became the standard profile of future clients: poor and unable to pay my fee. To help them, I'd need to supply my own funding. I wasn't able to raise much, but I did get enough to fund my way out to Michigan. It was low-budget lawyering, to be sure. I stayed in the Nobels' house and ate their food to cut down on expenses. They lived out in the country in a worn-looking house. Peter worked during the day, and the family raised pigs for extra income.

Since the house (with seven kids) could get somewhat loud, I frequently took morning walks for some peace and quiet. I started talking to the pigs as I watched them grovel and grunt, growing particularly attached to a small one named "Tar Baby."

Though the house was somewhat old and crowded, there was no question that the children were getting a quality education. Ruth was very organized. Each child had a desk and bulletin board, and Ruth kept a file on each student's progress. Additionally, she showed me the kids' standardized test scores, all of which were well above average.

I returned home to prepare the case as well as to welcome our third child, Elisabeth Anne, into the world. As soon as the doctor held her, I saw from his expression that he was concerned.

"What is it?" I asked.

"Her skin looks jaundiced," he replied calmly.

I noticed the distinct orange tint of her skin. "Is that serious?"

"No, I think we can handle it, but we'll have to put her under the lamp and run some tests."

After further investigation, we found that Elisabeth's orange tint had nothing to do with jaundice. It had more to do with the fact that Carol and I had been drinking fresh carrot juice every day! Elisabeth soon looked like a normal baby girl.

Just two months after she was born, we packed all our belongings in a large U-Haul truck and hit the road once again, this time headed to Virginia.

I didn't know it then, but we were just a few months away from making history.

"Why Are We Here?"

Once settled in Virginia, I continued making headway in the case for the Nobels. After reviewing everything I had, I believed the case was a slam dunk, so I phoned the local prosecutor, a young man still in his thirties. His office was being pestered by the local public school hierarchy, which viewed homeschooling as a major threat. They believed that teaching kids at home would ultimately destroy public schools. None of their fears have materialized, even though the practice of homeschooling is reaching record levels.

After I got him on the phone, I said, "Hey, listen, here's what our case is—" I then spent a few moments outlining our strongest contentions. "I honestly think we're going to win this thing, so why fight it? Why go through all this? Let's just settle it."

"You mean you want me to drop the charges?"

"That's right. You won't win, so you might as well let it go."

The prosecutor was an obstinate man, and though I don't mean to be uncharitable, in this instance I think he displayed his ignorance. He didn't understand what was coming. If he had studied the case, he would have come to the conclusion that losing was probably inevitable.

Most prosecutors are far more hesitant to go to trial. I've dealt with a number of prosecutors who have never lost a case—that's because they go to trial only when they know they will win. It's cheaper that way.

"I can't do that, John. The Nobels are breaking the law. They're *lawbreakers,* and I have to prosecute them."

In his opinion, I was representing a bunch of kooks.

This case was going to trial.

On one level, I felt sorry for the Nobels. They honestly thought they might go to jail—that was certainly the prosecutor's and local public school authorities' intention. You hate to see your clients feeling that pressure.

On another level, however, I realized that this was my chance. I had written numerous briefs before, but now I'd get to argue the case. It was the first time I'd ever be on my own.

I was determined to be well prepared, so I contacted two expert witnesses. One was an authority on testing, who performed an independent academic and social evaluation of the Nobel children. The other expert witness was prepared to testify on problems inherent in modern public education, arguing that home education is a viable alternative.

In the weeks that followed, I traveled through a range of emotions—excitement, nervousness, anticipation. It usually takes two or three trials to build a foundation for confidence, but I felt good about being thoroughly prepared. I knew my case, had excellent expert witnesses, and had studied the law inside and out.

Before the judge, I laid out my case: Mrs. Nobel had a First Amendment free exercise religious right not to accept a state certificate. This, to my knowledge, was the first time anyone had ever defended homeschooling using this argument.

Furthermore, I argued that Mrs. Nobel had surpassed any standards set by the public education system. My expert testified that the Nobel children were better adapted to life than most students in the Michigan public schools. Given this, any requirement of a certificate for Mrs. Nobel would be superfluous.

"The fact is," I argued, "the Nobels *are* educating their children and they *are* running a school, a very effective one at that. It certainly looks like a school—the children sit at desks, and there are bulletin boards. It operates like a school—there are regular set hours, with standard breaks. They even have P.E. [physical education] breaks in the afternoon. And the kids are regularly tested and exceed national standards. How can this *not* be an acceptable school?"

The prosecutor wouldn't back down from his original argument, that the Nobel children weren't being "properly" or even adequately educated. When he brought up the subject of socialization, I brought in my expert who testified that the Nobel children's test results showed them to be far more socialized than most children their age.

When he persisted, "How can you call this a school?" I smiled. He had fallen into my trap.

"Bailiff," I said, "could I have your help for a moment?"

I went outside the courtroom and nodded to Mr. Nobel. Together he, the bailiff, and I carried in several boxes of books.

"This is what the Nobels are using this year to educate their children, Your Honor," I said. The three of us took the books out of the boxes and stacked them at the front of the courtroom. They went from the floor to the top of the judge's bench.

The judge loudly proclaimed, "I'm calling a recess. I'd like to see the lawyers in my chambers." He seemed completely out of patience.

The judge, the prosecutor, and I filed in to the judge's chambers and took our seats. The first words out of the judge's mouth were directed toward the prosecutor. "Why are we here?" he asked.

The prosecutor knew he wasn't doing well. He literally stuttered, displaying a total lack of confidence, and stammered out, "Well, your honor, a law's been broken and I have to prosecute this."

"You may know why we're here but *I* still don't know why we're here," he snapped. "You're wasting my time. I've heard all I need to hear. I'll make my ruling soon."

I walked out of his chambers feeling confident, knowing we had a really good chance of winning this case. You can never take a decision for granted; sometimes, judges seem to relish giving off false signals and rendering a surprise decision, but in this instance, I really believed we had won.

The Nobels were upbeat. I was so proud of Ruth. She performed brilliantly on the stand. "You did great, just great," I encouraged her.

Two months later—an unusually brief time—a reporter called me on the phone to ask for my reaction to the Nobel decision.

"You won!" he said.

Right away, I called the Nobels. They were ecstatic.

When I finally got a copy of the decision, I read that the judge agreed the Constitution protected Ruth Nobel's freedom of religion to teach her children at home. This was an enormous victory, the first homeschool case to be decided on the basis of the free exercise clause of the First Amendment.

The Nobels couldn't pay me, but in their Christmas card that year they included a check for $100—quite a sacrifice for them—and a tempting offer.

"If you want Tar Baby," they wrote, "he's yours."

"Hey Carol," I called out, "look at this. We can get a free pig, start a pig farm, and raise some money on the side!"

"In this neighborhood, John?" Carol asked.

"Does that mean no Tar Baby?"

"The only pork coming into this house is a ham that's ready to be cooked."

Having fallen in love with Tar Baby, I certainly didn't want him sold for bacon, so I turned down the kind offer from this generous family.

We celebrated a wonderful Christmas, with three children and an important victory under our belts. Having put at least $25,000 worth of free time into this case, I'd certainly need more than $100 (plus a pig) in payment for my future services, but it was a start.

There would be many more challenges in the days to come.

Chuck McIlhenny, me, and Tom Neuberger in front of City Hall
San Francisco (1979)

Dr. Francis Schaeffer

CHAPTER 11

If defense of human rights is subversive, then I am subversive.

—Salvadoran Archbishop Oscar Romero

One of the factors sealing our move to Virginia had been an amazing phone call. I'm not much for signs from heaven, but this was too big a coincidence to ignore.

As we considered our options, while still in Cleveland, I picked a Realtor out of the phone book—Bill Blake—and made a long-distance call. After I introduced myself and told Bill we wanted to check on houses to rent in the northern Virginia area, he shocked me by asking, "Are you the same John Whitehead who is handling the Chuck McIlhenny case?"

I just about dropped the phone. "Indeed I am," I replied.

Charles McIlhenny, pastor of the First Orthodox Presbyterian Church of San Francisco, had fired his church organist, Kevin Walker, after discovering that Walker was gay. Pastor McIlhenny believes the Bible prohibits homosexual activity and that Walker's lifestyle was at odds with the teaching of the church.

Walker responded by suing First Orthodox Presbyterian Church under a San Francisco law that prohibits discrimination on the basis of sexual orientation.

McIlhenny asked around and was told to get in touch with me. As he presented his case over the phone, I prompted, "Now, explain your reason for firing Mr. Walker."

"The organist is in a leadership position, and he's playing hymns before God. This man is in open sin against God. I could not let him be in that position. I've told Kevin that he is welcome to attend church, but he can no longer play the church organ."

"What if the government insisted that Kevin not be fired?"

"Allowing Kevin to play would violate my religious beliefs."

This was a textbook, bellwether case.

"I'll take it," I said.

My heart sank when Pastor McIlhenny told me the church had just twenty-eight members. *There's no way they're going to be able to pay my costs*, I thought, but I couldn't have been more wrong. The church raised well over $100,000 to pay legal expenses. Since I was already representing the Nobels—for practically nothing—it would have been difficult to take on another nonpaying client. Their ability to pay me allowed us to make the move to Virginia.

Carol was generous in allowing me to pursue my dream, as she was forced to cope with less than a comfortable life because of it. Since McIlhenny's church was located in San Francisco, I was often on the other side of the country. Because our old Chevy van had quit running, we had only one car (a Volkswagen Beetle). Whenever I flew out to San Francisco, Carol had to pack up the kids (sometimes early in the morning, sometimes late at night), and drive an hour or more to reach the airport. We kept a blanket in the little cubbyhole behind the backseat for Elisabeth to sleep in.

These were tough days, but both Carol and I believed in what I was doing.

Punishing the Church

I spent so much time with Pastor McIlhenny preparing for the case that we became good friends. We had many late-night talks about theology and Rushdoony's reconstructionism. With McIlhenny's persuasive arguments, I was won over and became a Presbyterian.

But more than anything, we were focused on winning the case. Both of us realized the precedent-setting nature of this lawsuit, and we were determined to win.

My deposition with Kevin Walker occurred on September 21, 1979. This deposition would lay the groundwork for my arguments and go a long way toward securing victory—if I could find the right platform, of course.

One of the challenges Kevin was making was that the church was threatening his livelihood. This was a serious charge, so I needed to put it in a new light.

"You said you were employed by the First Orthodox Presbyterian Church," I said.

"Yes," he answered.

"Did you consider that job as a source of livelihood?"

"Yes, sir."

"What was your salary?"

"Ten dollars per Sunday."

"Ten dollars per Sunday, which would entail . . ."

"One service in the morning."

"Approximately how many services per month?"

"Four or five."

"So you would make forty to fifty dollars per month?"

"Yes."

"And that is a source of livelihood?"

Later, Kevin admitted that once the church terminated his position, he didn't try to get another job for some time. In other words, he felt no compelling need to replace this source of "livelihood." And for good reason. The church had employed him for just slightly more than four months. This was not a long-standing employment.

I then asked Kevin his opinion of "sexual orientation." Since he had sued the church for discrimination on that basis, I wanted to know just what he thought "sexual orientation" protected. In Kevin's mind, sex with minors or animals constituted "sexual orientation."

I then asked Kevin, "And you would also admit that this case we are working on right now is important to the homosexual community?"

"Yes, sir," he said. A few minutes later, he admitted he was a member of Gay Rights Advocates, a nonprofit legal organization set up to defend homosexuals.

Walker's lawsuit requested damages for psychological injury, so I began to explore this. "Did you seek psychiatric help?"

"No, sir. I did seek certain reassurance from my friends . . ."

"Did you lose sleep, have insomnia, bite your nails? What type of anxiety? I am trying to find out what your psychological injury is."

"My anxiety is pretty well under control except that I would think about it a lot. It was—it's on my mind a lot. It did not cause me to lose sleep. Perhaps it affected the quality of my sleep."

Another issue that came up was Kevin's "qualifications" for the job. Of course, he knew that he needed to be a Christian. During the job interview, Kevin had told Pastor McIlhenny that he was a "fundamentalist" Christian and admitted to me that he is aware of how fundamentalist Christians view homosexuality (though he doesn't hold that view).

It was a long and contentious day as Walker's lawyer from the Gay Rights Advocates regularly interrupted and challenged my questions. The real breakthrough came near the very end of the deposition.

"In the fact that you have sued a church for damages," I asked, "aren't you attempting to punish the church . . . for holding a particular religious belief?"

"Yes," he said. I tried not to smile.

"Are you not attempting to force the church to adopt the religious beliefs of those churches that believe that the practice of homosexuality is not a sin?"

His lawyer offered some clarifying details, but Walker ultimately answered, "Yes."

"Would you like to see the defendant church here change its policy on the practice of homosexuality?"

"Most definitely."

In this, Kevin was admitting that his lawsuit was about far more than being out ten bucks a week. It was about punishing a church for taking a stand against homosexuality. This was advocacy, pure and simple.

As soon as the deposition was over, I prepared papers to file a Motion for Summary Judgment, arguing that a trial was not necessary in the case, since it was a matter of law that the First Orthodox Presbyterian Church had a First Amendment right to choose an organist based on that person's religious views.

The motion was denied, and a trial was scheduled for January 1980. Some friendly lawyers called me up a couple of months before the trial and warned, "John, we just want you to know. Your judge has long, blond hair—"

"And?"

"He's rumored to be gay."

I sighed.

"That might make the case a bit tougher," one said.

"Yeah, it might," I admitted. Not that I believed he would be unfair, but having a gay judge in a gay discrimination case was nonetheless something to think about. I'd have to shape my arguments accordingly—and carefully.

The day before the trial, I got another call. The judge had removed himself from the case in order to attend a cooking class in Los Angeles! His replacement was a Roman Catholic.

Weeks of preparation had to be altered substantially. I immediately changed my oral argument to include examples from Roman Catholic liturgy. Tom Neuberger, a good friend and attorney who was ably assisting me, took the opposing side to help me develop my argument and fine-tune my presentation. In fact, without Tom's help throughout this case, I couldn't have provided the level of legal representation that was needed.

The next morning, there was a veritable horde of reporters and advocates hoping to attend the hearing. Who would have thought that a lawsuit against a tiny congregation of twenty-eight people and a job that paid ten dollars a week could become a case of national concern?

Inside the courtroom, I stood and presented my arguments, which now included analogies familiar to the judge. "Forcing the First Orthodox Presbyterian Church to hire a gay organist is tantamount to forcing a Catholic priest to hire a gay altar boy to help with Communion," I said.

After weeks of preparation, I had just minutes to make my case. The lawyers for Kevin Walker, members of a gay rights advocacy group, presented their side as well. The judge seemed fair to both sides and asked intelligent questions of each of us. The hearing was over in less than an hour.

At that point, all we could do was wait. We had given it our best shot.

As we left the courthouse, a young man stepped in front of me.

"Hi, I'm Mike Farris," he said. He was dressed in a sharp suit with a professional, conservative haircut. Mike struck me as the classic "eager beaver" type. Though he lived in Seattle, he had flown down to San Francisco just to see me.

What this signaled to me was that, finally, religious rights were getting some attention. Pastor McIlhenny and I had made the cover of a few religious magazines and had attracted enough attention that a young lawyer would fly south to meet me for the sole purpose of asking if he could work with us.

While we certainly could have used another lawyer, I didn't have any money to pay someone else's salary. Carol and I were barely scraping by as it was.

"Mike, go for it," I said, encouraging him to work along the same lines—on his own. I was delighted to have somebody else work on behalf of these same issues. At the time, however, I didn't have an organization he could join.

The notoriety surrounding the McIlhenny case certainly changed our lives. Not only did it feed my family, but it garnered the attention of other nationally known Christian leaders. Shortly after I got back from the hearing, Farris called, inviting me to meet with him and Tim and Beverly LaHaye at Dulles Airport.

"They're thinking of starting a legal organization," he explained. "You'd be the natural person to head it up."

Though I felt some vindication that my cause was gaining notice and support, as I listened to the LaHayes it became readily apparent that their aims were slightly different from mine. Tim wanted to have all the public schools overruled because he believed they now, by virtue of what they taught, constituted the establishment of religion.

"That won't work, Tim," I protested. "You'll be thrown out of the courtroom without ever being heard."

He was adamant, however, in pursuing this argument. As I spent more time with other Christian leaders, I went through this same scenario. I have respect for Tim LaHaye; he has written some good books, and his wife, Beverly, has accomplished many good things through Concerned Women for America. But they weren't lawyers— and Tim was trying to get me to buy into his legal strategy, one that I knew wouldn't work.

Though the meeting failed to establish a cooperative effort with the LaHayes, it began a friendship with Mike Farris, who eventually moved out to Virginia and ran an unsuccessful campaign for lieutenant governor. After the film version of my book *The Second American Revolution* was released a couple of years later, Mike came up to me and said, "I must have watched that thing a hundred times." We sat and watched it together, and Mike could recite the dialogue by memory. "I could do almost the whole movie verbatim," he said.

On another occasion, Mike called and asked me out to dinner. I took Jayson with me, and we ate at a local hot dog joint in Manassas, *Third Base,* which had the best chili dogs I've ever eaten. Jayson was awed by Mike's proficiency at Pac Man, a popular video game at the time. Since he never got "killed," Mike could play for hours on the same quarter. He was the first guy I had ever met who would have to walk away from the machines, not because the game was over, but because he had to be somewhere else.

Eventually, Mike formed his own group to defend homeschoolers.

Fateful April

April 1980 was fateful for two reasons, one of which I took little notice of at the time, not realizing I would one day become involved in the biggest sexual harassment case in our nation's history. The Equal Opportunity Commission issued regulations prohibiting sexual harassment of women by their superiors. Although women had been sexually harassed in the workplace since the first woman ventured outside the home to earn a living, the United States was just beginning to understand its obligation to eradicate this human rights violation. Seventeen years later, I would help prosecute the sexual discrimination of a young woman who was harassed by a man who became our nation's forty-second president.

Also during April 1980, the San Francisco decision came down. We won! The judge ruled that the First Orthodox Presbyterian Church had a First Amendment right to hire an organist of its choice. In the judge's opinion, the sexual orientation law did not apply to the church in this situation.

The gay community unleashed a veritable maelstrom in response. There were regular threats against Pastor McIlhenny, his wife, Donna, and their three children.

"Chuck, you've got to get out of San Francisco," I urged.

"John, we really believe God has called us to stay here as a witness to the gay community. We're not leaving."

Chuck paid the price for his courage. The next time I talked to him, his voice had a new tone of resignation.

"What happened?" I asked.

"They set my house on fire."

"Chuck," I urged once again, "you've got to get out of there."

"We're staying," he insisted.

Several weeks later, his house (which was connected to the church) was set on fire once again.

I admired his courage. To this day, Chuck and his family still live in that house in San Francisco, and he is still the pastor of the First Orthodox Presbyterian Church.

Aching Advocate

As the year dragged on, I watched the news reports with rapt attention as Lech Walesa challenged totalitarianism in Poland through the Polish Solidarity Union. His successful stand against the Communist Party was one of the first real signs of a crack in the oppressive hegemony of Eastern Europe since the Second World War.

Flush with Walesa's inspiration, I redoubled my efforts to do all I could to stand up for freedom and justice in this country. I began accepting cases left and right, even though virtually none of them brought in any income. I remembered David Gibbs's example and decided to go on the road to support my legal habit with speaking engagements.

While the churches were initially very welcoming, the response was tepid, at best. After I had spoken, few people saw any urgency or need to mount a legal or even educational effort to maintain our freedoms. In fact, my message seemed somehow "countercultural" to many congregations, which were focused primarily on theological concerns and had little interest in the so-called "secular" concerns of the law and legal system.

I'll never forget one church. Just before I was to speak, a woman sang an oppressively pessimistic song, with words that essentially said,

"The end times are upon us. We're all finished, life is over, there's no hope . . ."

Oh, great! I said to myself sarcastically, sitting in the pew. *My message is really going to go over well in this congregation!*

Their philosophy was focused on the end times; they had little patience for a lawyer who talked about improving or influencing a democratic society that they believed was destined to get worse and worse until Jesus Christ returns.

I routinely followed up my talk with question and answer sessions, and on this occasion the pastor was the first one to stand up. "God bless you for your efforts, young man," he said, "but Jesus is about to be back tomorrow. Don't worry. The Rapture's coming!"

This was followed by a chorus of "Amens." Everything I had said in the previous hour was wiped out with one simple comment.

To make matters worse, the pay was nothing short of pitiful. The so-called "love" offerings churches gave me barely covered my travel expenses. On numerous occasions, a pastor or church leader would say, "We'll send your honorarium in the mail," but the check never came. It was only through the generosity of a few friends that my family was able to keep eating.

A conference in rural Virginia at an old Baptist camp led Carol and me to seriously reevaluate what I was doing. It was midsummer, so I had the air-conditioning in our big red van going full blast for the three-hour trip. The humidity around our nation's capital is such that, historically, it resulted in Congress leaving during the summer. Nobody wanted to stay in the Washington, D.C.-northern Virginia area during the summer if they didn't have to!

Along the way, I got a flat tire. The only clothes I had with me were on my back, the three-piece suit I was wearing. I took off the coat but still had to work in slacks and a dress shirt. Within minutes, my knees were dirty, my shirtsleeves were ringed with grease, and I was soaked with perspiration.

The dirty work completed, I got back in my van and completed the drive to the campground, where I was greeted by about thirty pastors. They commiserated over my misfortune, and then gathered to hear me speak. Their response was far cooler than their welcome. Afterward, walking me to the car, the guy in charge said he'd send me an honorarium for my efforts, and several weeks later I received a check for $100.

That afternoon, Carol and I went for a long walk. I had given up an entire weekend, driven hundreds of miles, wrecked a suit, and was given just enough money to basically cover my gas. This just wasn't working.

"I still have the dream," I told Carol, "but we have to eat, and we can't ask any more of our friends. They've given enough already."

There was a long pause, which I broke with, "Maybe my mom is right. Maybe it is time to get a 'real' job. The churches just aren't interested. Instead of fighting for the cause, the cause seems to be fighting me."

Carol was supportive and listened patiently, while I thought through the issues by talking out loud.

"I have a small base of paying clients," I explained, "but I think I could expand it. We could focus on that."

The next day, I drove to my one-room office in Washington, D.C., which the National Association of Evangelicals rented to me cheaply, to start cleaning it out. As far as I was concerned, I had given this religious rights business my best shot. I still hoped to take on an occasional case in the future, but the idea of making a ministry out of it just wasn't feasible.

As soon as I walked in, one of the NAE secretaries gave me a call slip: *Franky Schaeffer called.*

I was intrigued. Franky's father, Dr. Francis Schaeffer, had made a huge impact on my thinking, and his books were literally shaping the church. He was the hottest thing going in evangelical circles—and so was his son, Franky. I was immensely curious, wondering why Franky would call *me*.

I called him back as soon as I got home.

"Hi, Franky," I said. "This is John Whitehead."

"Hey, man. It's good to talk with you. I read your brief in the San Francisco case and tracked you down. I want you to work with my dad and me."

I couldn't believe what I was hearing. Just as I was ready to take a step back, this was a major move forward. "I would be honored to work with you," I said.

There followed a lengthy discussion on virtually everything I had been working on. We discussed the role of the Supreme Court in its *Roe v. Wade* decision; the new definition of "privacy"; and religious rights. Franky, always the entrepreneur, finally burst out, "You've gotta write a book on this, John. You could call it *The Second American Civil War*. My dad and I will help you get it published."

"Well, let me think about it," I said. Just hours earlier, I was prepared to abandon my work and build a private practice. Franky was asking me to jump back in, headfirst, to the heretofore thankless task of defending religious rights. "I'll call you back in a few days."

After I hung up the receiver, I stayed in my chair for some time, thinking over this new turn of events. With people like the Schaeffers working beside me, there was no telling what God could do.

My vision was reborn.

Franky Schaeffer and me at The Rutherford
Institute (May 1990)

Nine-month-old Joel with me (April 1982)

CHAPTER 12

The basic problem of the Christians in this country in the last eighty years or so, in regard to society and in regard to government, is that they have seen things in bits and pieces instead of totals.

—*Francis Schaeffer, A Christian Manifesto*

"How's your father doing?" I asked Franky the next time we talked. "I heard about the cancer."

"He's doing okay. My ole man is a strong bird. He's got a lot of life left in him. But what about you, John? Do you want to do the book?"

"Yes," I responded, "but I've got a better title. I want to call it *The Second American Revolution.*"

Franky liked the title and agreed on the spot to be my agent. I began researching and writing down ideas as soon as I got off the phone. It was early September, and I wanted to have a good draft by December.

When I agreed to let Franky be my agent, I had no idea how seriously he viewed that position. He called every day, sometimes two or three times, to see if I was working on the book.

Franky's energy level amazed me. I have never met anyone with his capacity for work and enthusiasm. His voice was animated and loud, and his monologues could go on for hours. I couldn't get a word in, and since I needed to get some work done, I learned to lay the receiver down on its side, tune out his voice, and keep on writing. An occasional "uh-huh" from me was enough to make Franky think I was listening to him. This kept him happy because he loved to talk, and it kept me happy because it allowed me to get some work done on the book. Franky's voice became a background sound track to my writing and actually helped me move forward.

For three and a half months, I got up around five o'clock every morning and began reading and writing, spending eight hours a day or more at my desk. My writing flowed, and ideas came quickly—until a dark day in December that changed music history forever.

End of an Era

On December 9, 1980, I woke up early—as usual—and started exercising—as I do every day—while listening to the radio. Every station I turned to was playing Beatles music. I love the Beatles, but I couldn't figure out why everybody was playing their music until a voice came on the air and said, "A great man died last night."

Immediately, I flipped on the television, which was all John Lennon. The night before, Lennon and his wife, Yoko Ono, had gone to a recording session. As they returned to their apartment, a psychotic fan named Mark David Chapman (who had once worshipped Lennon) shot him outside Lennon's residence, the Dakota apartment building in New York City. Lennon died on the way to the hospital. With John Lennon's death, the hopes of many who had fought for change in the sixties died as well.

Lennon had just come out with a new song, *Starting Over*, which had revived his career and was moving up the charts. Despite his famous statement about Christianity (that it would "vanish" and "shrink") and his imagining that "there's no heaven," Lennon remained one of my heroes. He was iconoclastic and outspoken. When the Beatles broke up, instead of retreating into a mansion, Lennon came to New York City and worked as an activist, fighting against the Vietnam War, inequality, and injustice. John Lennon was idealistic, and he paid the ultimate price for it.

I called Franky. "What do you think about Lennon getting shot?"

"Well, people die," he said. While it didn't seem to affect him, it made me more contemplative. Ringo's later comment, "I guess the Beatles can't get back together now," fell like a hollow thud in my heart. It was the death of an era, and I had been part of that amazing period.

It certainly forced me to stop and take a good look at my life.

Years later, when I was making my video series *Grasping for the Wind*, I shot some footage in front of the Dakota. The security guard showed me the place where Lennon fell that December night. It still brings a chill to my bones.

"You Say You Want a Revolution?"

With Lennon's lyric "You say you want a revolution?" ironically ringing in my ears, I was finally able, with Carol's assistance and typing of my manuscript, to complete *The Second American Revolution*.

The thesis of the book is that a revolution has taken place, changing the way we look at people and restructuring our basic institutions and laws. The state has become a sort of modern deity, with the Supreme Court now actively making laws. Since modern humanism denies even a tenuous connection to God's claim on this world by denying that there is any order to nature and insisting that man is totally autonomous, it invariably ends in the deification of man and the rejection of God. Humanism's dominance has paved the way for abortion, euthanasia, and the attack on religious liberty.

In response to the spread of humanism, I argued for a second revolution "in the reformative sense." "It should not be a revolution designed to kill people or tear down and physically destroy society," I wrote, "but a revolution in the minds and the souls of human beings—a revolution promulgated to be a total assault on the humanistic culture."

These are strong words, to be sure, but at the time I felt they were appropriate and much needed. Lennon and I may have disagreed about many things, but I felt a kinship with him in standing up for what I believed.

Falwell Follies

As I completed *The Second American Revolution,* I was invited to meet with Dr. Jerry Falwell and some of his advisers. Falwell was considering starting a legal group as part of his Moral Majority and asked if I would advise him.

I was eager to meet Dr. Falwell and found him to be genuinely likable, with an engaging sense of humor.

Since I had been working on my own and finances were the nadir of my mission, I thought that perhaps teaming with Falwell would provide the necessary resources to get something done. Dr. Falwell listened attentively to my ideas and was willing to let me explain how a legal group should be structured.

One of the more interesting people I met during my visit was Cal Thomas, who worked with Falwell. He later became a popular national columnist and served on The Rutherford Institute's board of directors for several years. Cal was very outspoken, very funny, and very direct—he'll tell you exactly what he thinks, without apology. He shares my irreverent spirit.

Cal left Falwell's employ in a disagreement over some of his boss's policies. A decade later, in 1999, Cal co-authored a book attacking Falwell and other evangelical leaders for falling into the politics power trap. Although Cal was heavily criticized for the book, I believe the debate it stirred was healthy.

After our meeting, a direct mail letter was sent out announcing that the Moral Majority was starting up a legal branch. To Falwell's disappointment, the response to the letter was extremely poor. I wasn't surprised, as it mirrored the response I had been receiving when I spoke in so many churches.

Falwell doesn't fool around, and when he realized that a legal group would not be financially self-sustaining, he dropped the idea.

Looking back, I guess I should have been forewarned! Jerry Falwell has been one of the most successful fund-raisers in this century. The fact that he couldn't raise sufficient resources to support a legal group should have told me how difficult the road would be for me. Even now, with The Rutherford Institute's numerous successes, we still find it extremely difficult to raise money for our cases, and financial droughts are a routine part of our calendar year.

Though we ended up never working together, I spent time with Falwell on several other occasions. Though people have accused him of being a right-wing nut bent on taking away people's freedom, I found him to be a sincere, genuine, and—despite his acclaim—easily accessible human being. I don't always agree with what he says and does, but I'll give him credit for taking a stand on issues and taking the heat for doing so.

Full-Scale Advance

I mailed my manuscript to Franky a week before Christmas. About ten days later, I received an enthusiastic phone call.

"My dad loved *The Second American Revolution,*" he said. "He actually cried. We need to meet soon and go over what to do now."

After almost leaving the "cause" to pursue a private legal practice, this was a tremendous boost. Having Francis Schaeffer's blessing was more than I could have imagined happening.

Just after New Year's Day in 1981, I was on a plane to Boston. For two days, Jim Buchfuehrer (Franky's business partner), Franky, and I mapped out a plan to market the ideas contained in *The Second American*

Revolution. We wanted to do far more than promote a successful book—these were vital ideas that we hoped would help arrest what was wrong in America and provide some solutions.

It was about this time that enemies started gathering around me. I've never consciously tried to make people dislike me, but adversaries have always seemed to be a part of my life. Once, when I heard someone say, "I don't have any enemies," I quickly broke in and pleaded, "Then please, take some of mine!" And later, especially when I took on the Paula Jones case, people I had never even heard of began attacking me.

In this particular instance, the antagonist came from the Christian Legal Society. Apparently still sore from our divergent goals over what Christian lawyers should be doing, this man actively lobbied against the publication of my book. With the Schaeffers' backing, however, I knew the book would find a home somewhere, which it did with David C. Cook Publishers.

Then another unexpected opportunity came my way. Near the end of my stay in Boston, Franky took me aside and asked, "Would you be interested in helping my dad write his next book?"

It was one thing having Francis Schaeffer's blessing; it was another thing altogether to actually work with the man on his next project. I was so honored to be asked that when Franky offered to pay me a flat fee, plus a small percentage of the royalties, I didn't even negotiate his terms. I accepted his first offer, without a single amendment—something you don't see a lawyer doing often.

Within days, I was busy researching and writing what would become the foundation of *A Christian Manifesto.*

Just as I wrapped up my work on *Manifesto,* one of Franky's daily phone calls provided another thrill. "Dad's speaking at the Christian Legal Society conference in South Bend, Indiana," he said. "It would be a good time for the two of you to meet."

I was elated at the opportunity and flew out to South Bend to hear Dr. Schaeffer give a strong call to Christian lawyers. He exhorted them to take a more active role in fighting for justice and religious rights. When Dr. Schaeffer said, "Christian lawyers need to get out on the front lines and fight, as John Whitehead has done in his case out in San Francisco," I was shocked. Instantly, I was a celebrity of sorts at the meeting—Francis Schaeffer had offered me as a role model!— and many of the lawyers started hanging around me, asking me about the San Francisco case.

It was somewhat ironic and a little fulfilling, in that previously I was viewed as little more than an irritant to CLS. In fact, for this conference, they had assigned me to conduct just one rinky-dink workshop. They had also tried to get my book buried before it was published because, at the time, they didn't want to become involved in the abortion issue. They also didn't want to take on controversial cases or litigate— and I was eager to do both.

So much had changed in the previous months. My "retreat" had become a full-scale advance. I was deeper into this movement than I had ever been!

After the meeting, Dr. Schaeffer sent a message asking me to meet him in his hotel room. His wife, Edith, opened the door and warmly greeted me. Franky was already there, and Dr. Schaeffer was sitting at a desk eating lamb with mint sauce (one of his favorite dishes). Always a humble man, he rose to greet me while Edith went back to her juicer. She was pouring as much fresh vegetable and fruit juice down her husband's throat as he could take in the hope of alleviating the cancer attacking his body.

"I really like your work," Dr. Schaeffer said. "You've written a great book. I'm going to endorse it heavily."

"Here, Fran," Edith said, placing yet another glass of juice in front of her husband. He already had several full glasses and seemed much more interested in the lamb than the juice. I followed his example and took a glass of the murky-looking liquid that Edith offered me.

"You know," I said, "I've been thinking of adapting some of the material that appears in my book and using it in *Manifesto*. Your book could be a precursor to *The Second American Revolution.*"

"Good idea," Dr. Schaeffer said.

I was shocked at how quickly the publisher got the book out—just two months after I delivered my first manuscript to Dr. Schaeffer, his book was in the stores. Even though *The Second American Revolution* was completed well before *A Christian Manifesto* was started, Schaeffer's stock was so high that publishers rushed through its publication, allowing *Manifesto* to come out months before my own book.

Manifesto became an instant best-seller, with some 400,000 copies selling the first year. Interestingly enough, because of blatant religious discrimination, it never appeared on the *New York Times* best-seller list. Franky recruited me as Dr. Schaeffer's attorney. I contacted the editors and tried to badger them into putting Dr. Schaeffer's book on their make-it-or-break-it list, pointing out that *A Christian Manifesto* was outselling some of their current titles ten to one. In fact, at the time of our negotiations, *Manifesto* was selling seventeen thousand copies *a week,* easily outpacing the number one book listed in the paper (a workout book by Jane Fonda).

The *New York Times* wouldn't budge.

"*A Christian Manifesto* is a specialty book," they insisted, "and we don't put such books on the best-seller list."

"Are you trying to tell me that Jane Fonda's workout book isn't a specialty book?" I retorted, but they weren't listening.

A Christian Manifesto was the launching pad for what was briefly known as the Christian activist movement. Previously closed doors literally flew open. Formerly apathetic audiences now responded with enthusiasm. Franky and I spoke at the Christian Booksellers Association annual meeting and all across the nation.

"We must do something to preserve freedom while we still have the time left!" I told audiences, and this time I was greeted with loud applause and amens.

Christians started picketing abortion clinics, and I saw how this new activism could be marshaled to include the fight for religious rights. Suddenly, a large segment of Christians weren't afraid to challenge our society. They *wanted* to be part of a second, peaceful "revolution."

Francis Schaeffer was the high point, the leader sounding the alarm bell. He has to be credited with igniting the pro-life movement and other important struggles for religious rights.

This was a real war, and it required *prepared* soldiers. An incident in Florida would convince me just how important being prepared is.

Home Fires

"Hi, John, this is Ed Rowe; I work with Anita Bryant."

It was the spring of 1981.

Ed continued, "We're getting a group of people together in Dade County, Florida, to fight an ordinance barring discrimination based on sexual orientation. We also want to get people organized to stand up for family and conservative issues."

Within days, I was on a flight to Miami. Anita Bryant was about as "hot" as you could get at the time. The gay movement had positioned its collective forces and was firing everything it had at this Hollywood celebrity, who was almost single-handedly taking them on.

Anita Bryant and her husband, Bob Green, lived in a mansion by a canal. In front lay a huge courtyard filled with exotic plants and birds. I admired the decorative tiling on the floor and the home's modern, Old-World style (it was made to look old, but was relatively new).

The beauty of the home was marred by internal strife, though. I hadn't been inside the house for more than a few minutes when I started feeling that something wasn't right. Since then, I have come to see that big houses, luxury cars, and expensive artwork are often a veneer for emptiness and pain. Nothing is a substitute for human love.

Anita and Bob sat apart, and the air between them was chilly. Their aides whispered that there was considerable tension in their relationship. I was dismayed, in part because I was well aware from my work with Pastor McIlhenny of how volatile and taxing it can be to stand against certain forces. If you want to go against the grain, you better be prepared to take a lot of heat because life isn't going to be easy.

After being in their home, I realized that Anita didn't need legal advice; she needed marital counseling. Within a short period of time, she and Bob were separated. Bob met with Carol and me when he came to the Washington, D.C., area.

"I still love her," he insisted, adding that he was virtually begging her to reconcile, but Anita wasn't interested.

Though Anita was initially successful, the sexual orientation ordinance that she so vigorously fought in 1981 surfaced again in the late nineties, ultimately becoming the law in 1998.

This encounter was a sobering lesson about the importance of a stable home life. There is enough stress fighting for religious rights without coming back to a home that is falling apart.

The ACLU

Joel Christofer Whitehead was born on July 4, 1981. We still couldn't afford health insurance, and Joel was born at home with the assistance of a midwife. Franky took Joel's famous birth date as "significant, an important sign," especially since my book *The Second American Revolution* was published within weeks.

In the fall, I received a phone call from attorney Wendell Bird, asking me to consult with him and the attorneys who were defending the state of Arkansas, which was being sued by the ACLU over a state law that mandated balanced treatment of "creation science" and "evolution science" in the public schools. Arkansas wanted to teach both creation science and evolution—the ACLU was arguing for an evolution-only curriculum.

Evolution, it must be remembered, is only a theory. I have

always argued that any theory with a scientific basis should be taught to students, and creationism certainly has a body of scientific opinion that supports the thesis of the intelligent design of the universe. Pure indoctrination is not democratic and definitely not the American way.

Although Wendell and I were not involved in the trial in Little Rock, it was riveting for me, in large part because I finally got to see firsthand how the ACLU operates. The state attorney general appointed two young lawyers to defend the state statute. Against this meager force, the ACLU marched a high-powered team of seven attorneys into the courthouse. They looked somber, professional, and were well dressed—a formidable team, to be sure.

With so much firepower, these seasoned professionals decimated the Arkansas attorneys. Their arguments were cogent and persuasive, and they had done all the research necessary to back up their case. They won overwhelmingly, and Arkansas was forced to pay the ACLU over a million dollars in attorneys' fees and expenses.

In spite of my experience with Falwell's unsuccessful efforts, I was still toying with the idea of founding my own organization, whose purpose would be to defend religious rights. I made a mental note that the team approach employed by the ACLU was definitely the way to go.

Fiasco in Greenville

My next stop was Greenville, South Carolina, where I was asked to speak at a conference on the First Amendment and religious freedom at Bob Jones University (BJU). As I was being driven onto the school grounds, I was struck by the encampmentlike feeling of the campus. Passing through the chain link fences and security guards, I felt like I was visiting a prison instead of an institution of higher learning.

At the time of my arrival, the university was fighting a losing battle over its tax-exempt status. The Internal Revenue Service had alleged that BJU violated public policy for, among other things, not allowing interracial dating. The case went all the way to the United States Supreme

Court, where the school lost.

Evangelist Lester Roloff, who had fought the state of Texas over obtaining a license for his home for delinquent boys, spoke before I did. A fiery speaker, Roloff kept the crowd sitting on the edge of their seats.

"After years of study," he shouted out, "I have finally discovered the reason why America is in trouble today!"

I tried to guess what he would say. Adultery, perhaps? Murder? Drugs?

Roloff paused, baiting the audience to get their full attention, and then exclaimed, "It was the Beatles!"

The crowd's cheers and amens deflated me.

"Now, John," some school officials warned me just before I went onstage, "you need to know that Bob Jones III is a little skittish about the question of civil disobedience."

That's just what I needed to hear, considering that civil disobedience was my topic! But I went ahead and delivered my lecture, based on *The Second American Revolution*.

"There are instances where religious people may need to break the law," I argued, "particularly when the government tries to force a Christian to violate his or her faith. Another instance would be to protect the life of another."

I backed up my arguments with both biblical and historical support. "In Acts 5:29 (RSV), the apostle Peter defies the authorities, saying 'We must obey God rather than men.' And Corrie ten Boom did the right thing when she violated German law by hiding Jewish people during Hitler's reign of terror."

These were the same words that were receiving such a warm welcome in the wake of Francis Schaeffer's wake-up call. But Schaeffer's influence apparently hadn't made its way onto the Bob Jones campus.

Bob Jones III got up as I sat down. I was still sitting on the stage when he announced, "I'd like to refute everything this man just said."

Hundreds of faces were riveted on me, seeing how I would respond. Of course, I was embarrassed, but I wasn't all that surprised. Jones's diatribe was a bit incoherent, but not original; I had heard it before in many churches.

I've never been back to Greenville, but I learned a valuable lesson there. Regardless of whether my fight for religious freedom is the fashion of the day, I can never expect it to find full acceptance in the wider Christian community. There will always be those who oppose what I am doing.

A Horse to Ride On

With the publication and film adaptation of *The Second American Revolution,* I knew I had a message to carry to the world. But I gradually became convinced that I needed more than a message—I needed a horse to ride on that would help me carry that message. The ACLU team approach convinced me that a "lone ranger" couldn't go very far. At every turn, I'd be buried by the firepower of a multimillion-dollar group.

Amid my family's Christmas celebration (quite raucous, since we now numbered six), my mind kept coming back to a point of reflection. And as we sang carols on Christmas Eve at the small Presbyterian church that we attended, I thought about the past twelve months. In many ways, it had been a "breakout" year. On the verge of quitting, I had been cast into the fray with more commitment than ever. I became consumed with the idea of starting an organization to carry the fight forward.

Although 1981 had been a pivotal year, 1982 would prove even more definitive in my life.

I'm holding Joshua while Carol and Joel relax
after Josh's home birth (October 6, 1983).

Joshua and I share a moment at the beach (April 1985).

CHAPTER 13

I was halfway across America, at the dividing line between the East of my youth and the West of my future, and maybe that's why it happened right there and then, that strange red afternoon.

—*Jack Kerouac*
On the Road

I don't know if Samuel Rutherford would be too pleased with me. After mulling over countless names, I chose his for my organization, which was established to defend religious rights. Rutherford, however, was primarily interested in protecting Christian rights. Protecting other religions or atheists, as I have done, would probably have horrified him.

Samuel Rutherford was a seventeenth-century educator who wrote *Lex, Rex*. What ultimately convinced me to use Rutherford's name was his idea that all men are subject to the law, and none are above it. It was this latter clause, in fact—which stated no one is above the law—that led me to take on the president of the United States many years later.

When I became serious about founding The Rutherford Institute

(TRI), I met with Franky and Dr. Schaeffer for their input. Both were enthusiastic and encouraging, while also realistic about the difficulty of funding such a group.

"You know, John," Dr. Schaeffer said finally, "I'm scheduled to be on *The 700 Club* soon; perhaps I could arrange a meeting between you and Pat Robertson. He has a great deal of money and might be interested in helping to fund The Rutherford Institute."

Through Dr. Schaeffer's introduction, Pat agreed to meet with me. In addition to Dr. Schaeffer, Franky, and myself, there was a plethora of Robertson advisers present. Pat came in last and took his place at the head of the table.

"I had a dream last night," he began, and I noticed a few of his advisers sigh. "In my dream, I stepped from my car and started walking toward my house when I saw a snake coiled on the ground. I saw another snake wrapped around a fence post, a third lying in the grass, and a fourth coiled around my doorknob!"

He spoke in his easygoing, sincere manner. "The moral of the dream, I believe, is this: The serpent is very subtle."

Dr. Schaeffer and I glanced quickly at one another, exchanging incredulous looks. Franky, ever the initiator, said, "Interesting," then jumped out of his chair and literally moved it to the opposite head of the table, essentially taking over! He nodded to his dad, who spoke with passion about the importance of the legal fights that lay ahead.

"John has defended a church that was sued for firing a gay organist, and he argued the first successful homeschooling case that used a First Amendment free exercise religious right. He's on the front lines, doing what a Christian lawyer should do."

Robertson and his assembled staff patiently listened, perhaps out of deference to the eminent Francis Schaeffer, a leading Christian voice.

"Well, thank you very much, gentlemen," Pat finally said. "We'll get back to you with a decision."

Several weeks later, I hurriedly picked up the phone when Carol told me that one of Robertson's assistants was on the line.

"Pat is interested in helping to fund TRI," the aide said, "but . . ."

I listened attentively as I was told that Pat would expect ultimate control if he donated the money.

"I'll get back with you," I said, and immediately called Franky.

"This isn't good, John," Franky said, and I agreed. TRI under the control of Pat Robertson—a man with political leanings and a strong agenda of his own—would not be the TRI we envisioned.

"To be a true revolutionary," Franky explained, "it's better to have a Volkswagen than a Mercedes-Benz." Our thinking was that if you run a "Volkswagen" organization, you'll be much more flexible—you can drop everything into the trunk and move when the right opportunity presents itself. If you try to create a Mercedes-Benz, you'll be nailed down by the expense and luxury of the organization you've created. A revolutionary has to travel light, so we didn't want to build a big, monolithic organization.

As time passed, I became more confident of our decision to remain independent. Months later, I received an impassioned call from Dr. Schaeffer.

"You won't believe what Robertson's people did to me!" Dr. Schaeffer bellowed into the phone.

"What?" I asked, somewhat surprised that Dr. Schaeffer had chosen to call me, of all people.

"They followed up my interview on *The 700 Club* with a Christian sword swallower!"

He was very angry, insisting that if he had known what was going to happen, he would never have agreed to appear on the show.

We decided to launch TRI even without Robertson's support. Its first board of directors consisted mainly of friends—including Franky Schaeffer, R. J. Rushdoony, and attorneys Tom Neuberger and Jim Knicely.

It was somewhat of a stretch to have Franky and Rush on the same board. Rushdoony had made clear to me his dislike for Francis Schaeffer; and Dr. Schaeffer, as well, indicated to me his nervousness about Rushdoony's theology. Though I no longer accepted the central tenets of reconstructionist thought, I appreciated Dr. Rushdoony's intellect and wanted him to be a part of TRI.

"Any relationship with Rushdoony is going to come back to haunt you," Franky warned. "You realize the baggage he brings with him, don't you?"

"Yes, I do," I admitted, "but Dr. Rushdoony has been very kind to me and my family, and I'm not going to disassociate from anyone simply because knowing him might hurt my reputation."

Unfortunately, Franky's fears were justified. I am still accused of being a Christian reconstructionist, which is absurd in light of what I have written and the civil liberties nature of my work.

Interestingly, Dr. Schaeffer has also been accused of being a reconstructionist. The two of us had many long conversations on the topic, and Dr. Schaeffer was consistent in publicly and privately disavowing reconstructionist theology. Rather than talking about a Christian takeover, Dr. Schaeffer believed that society was going into chaos and the only hope was Christian involvement in all areas of life—being the "salt," as Christ called it. This is a far cry from a Christian takeover, as evidenced by the fact that TRI has publicly fought for the rights of other religions to practice their faith freely, without government intervention.

Launching a Second Revolution

My publisher sent me on a month-long book tour to promote *The Second American Revolution*. For the first time, I experienced the entertainment nature of news programs, somewhat akin to Dr. Schaeffer's experience on *The 700 Club*. On one occasion, I discussed law and Christianity sandwiched between a stripper and two professional wrestlers!

Along with the book, we released a film adaptation using fictional characters to present the case for Judeo-Christian principles. Dr. Schaeffer was heavily involved in this project. He wrote a glowing blurb for my book: "This is certainly the most important book I have read in a long, long time . . . I recommend this book highly." Franky cowrote and directed the video adaptation.

Dr. Schaeffer arranged a premiere showing of the film version of *The Second American Revolution* at the National Archives in Washington, D.C., on November 15, 1982. The response was so overwhelming that two showings were required.

I sat next to Dr. Schaeffer during both sessions. As we watched the film roll, Dr. Schaeffer, with a father's sincere pride, said, "What a masterpiece!"

After each showing, Dr. Schaeffer and I conducted a question-and-answer session to standing-room-only audiences. After having my concerns virtually ignored in the recent past, it was intoxicating to see such a powerful response. Nationally renowned politicians such as Jack Kemp and Henry Hyde helped sponsor the event.

The major difference between then and two years prior was that I felt like a member of a team. Dr. Schaeffer, Franky, and I shared ideas, used them, refined one another's presentations, and worked together to present a united front. In spite of his acclaim, Dr. Schaeffer always treated me as an equal (while at the same time doting on everything his son did). He could easily have dominated the situation, but during the question-and-answer sessions he frequently deferred the questions to me.

It was thus with great concern that I watched Dr. Schaeffer's health decline. It literally hurt me physically to watch him have to stop to take breaths when he spoke to audiences. He and Edith moved to Rochester, Minnesota, to be close to the Mayo Clinic. However, in spite of receiving the world's best care, it was clear to Dr. Schaeffer's intimates that the cancer was winning.

Even with his ailing body, though, Dr. Schaeffer remained active.

I heard from him quite frequently, particularly when he needed legal advice.

"John," he said on one occasion, "I've organized a picket of a local abortion provider." There was a slight pause. "I'm a bit nervous about his response. Would you be willing to help me out if I get arrested?"

"Absolutely," I assured him.

Humble Beginnings

From the start, TRI had little money. Its first donation was from Carol and me: our entire savings account, which amounted to $200. We set up a small office downstairs in our home. TRI, which officially began on June 29, 1982, consisted of a desk, a telephone, a typewriter, and little else, as far as material support went. Since we didn't have enough money for bookcases, my books were stacked against the walls. The kids had to restack them when they routinely fell over.

Carol and I were the first and only staff. We put together an introductory letter, then sat in our rec room where we licked the envelopes and stamps, praying that our appeal to friends and business acquaintances would prove successful.

In early 1983, I received a letter from Becky Beane, a young woman in California who worked with Campus Crusade for Christ. She had read *The Second American Revolution* and wanted to work with TRI.

I knew we could use the help, but I was concerned about our financial situation. I telephoned Franky and asked him what he thought.

"Go ahead, hire her," Franky suggested. "If the sucker folds, it folds. We did our best."

Becky joined us that spring. With an assistant, we needed an office, and we found a small one in Dale City, Virginia, near our home. From there, Becky put together our first newsletter and dutifully mailed it to our fledgling mailing list. I still worked out of my small home office.

Several days later, Becky called me, obviously upset.

She had just received a call from a leader in the Christian Legal Society. "He rudely attacked me and accused me of stealing his mailing list because someone he knows received our newsletter!"

The enemy thing, again.

This was an absurd accusation; of course, it was inevitable that we would have some mutual acquaintances. But the missions of CLS and TRI were so different that we really couldn't be seen as competitors.

I decided to take quick action.

"Listen," I said when I got the culprit on the phone, "if you *ever* speak to my assistant like that again, I will personally come visit you and make you very sorry. Do you understand me?"

It was a threat, and I meant it as one. The old temper had flared up again.

He caved in immediately. "Please forgive me, brother. I promise not to do it again."

Circus Christianity

The historical situation was such that many of the early cases brought to TRI revolved around abortion, including the right to picket and protest. Pro-life work has always been a priority of TRI, in part because the right to life represents the most fundamental of our rights. If we are denied this first right, all other rights become meaningless.

Out of this work came the invitation from another Schaefferite, Lane Dennis of Crossway Books, to write a book that confronted the trend toward fascism in America—including abortion. The result was *The Stealing of America*.

When time came to promote the book, I was once again introduced to another side of Christian America when I accepted an offer to appear on Jim Bakker's show, *The PTL Club*.

Franky—and just about everybody I knew at that time—warned me not to do the interview. "Don't do it, John," he said. "You don't need to be associated with that program."

In spite of Franky's advice, I went on the show. My attitude toward the media is the same now as it was then—all media is good if you can get the message out. If you think you stand a reasonable chance of getting your point of view across, why not take advantage of it? That's why I don't shy away from granting interviews to *GQ* magazine or even *Playboy.* I felt my book's message was important, and the size of Bakker's audience was such that I was eager to get the word out.

I flew to North Carolina and was picked up in a limousine and driven to Heritage USA, which looked like a scaled-down theme park. I was led to the green room, where the various artists and entertainers congregated before the show. About ten minutes before we were scheduled to go on, Jim Bakker sauntered into the room. An aide caught Jim's elbow and introduced him to me.

"John Whitehead," Jim said, flashing a wide grin, "you are the one."

I was startled and confused by this enthusiastic greeting and cracked a lopsided grin. It seemed to lack sincerity—a virtue I soon discovered wasn't actively pursued on this program.

Once on the show, Bakker introduced me by saying that I had written one of the most important books he had ever read. The problem was that the book was not yet in print—and Bakker hadn't read it! My book company had managed to get Bakker a mock-up cover and then gathered various pages from my earlier books and slid them inside.

The interview was a bit wacky. Jim read the jumbled passages from my earlier books, wanting me to respond as if they were from *The Stealing of America.* I could feel the sweat start trickling down my back as I began to expound on various cases and the need to stop abortion, all the while trying to make sense out of a nonsensical conversation.

I was so relieved when that interview was over! I wanted nothing more than to grab the limousine driver and head back to the airport. Instead, I had to stay and watch the show's completion, which took the term *manipulation* to a new level.

The evangelists who appeared on the show that day congregated in front of the audience with Jim. One fellow stepped forward and said Jim Bakker needed their financial support because saving souls on television is expensive. Next came the defining moment. An evangelist grabbed the microphone and said, "The Lord has spoken to me that someone out there is going to donate $1,000 today."

After a short group prayer, a man raised his hand; he was ready to donate the money. With startling efficiency, a PTL usher was there to collect the check.

Then the Lord "spoke" to the evangelist again. "I believe someone is going to donate $5,000," he said. A young man, his wife, and three children came forward.

I felt sorry for them.

The Lord "spoke" several more times, raising the ante each time. All the while, I was watching the spectacle from behind the crowd of evangelists on the stage.

Finally, the Lord "spoke" and said someone was going to give $25,000 to Jim Bakker that day.

"Hallelujah! It's me!" came a voice from far back in the crowd.

Up jumped an elderly woman who came down the aisle and walked right up to *me! What do I have to do with this?* I thought.

"Brother," she said, "God has told me that I should sue the city of Little Rock, and you're to be my lawyer. We'll raise that $25,000 for Brother Bakker."

"What are you going to sue them for?" I asked.

"I fell on the state capitol steps a couple of months ago," she said.

Incredulous, I finally saw, with great relief, my limousine driver emerge. "What you really need, ma'am," I said, "is to speak with that gentleman over there." I pointed to a counselor and made a speedy exit.

I was literally jogging toward the door when I heard a man call out, "John, can I ride to the airport with you?"

It was a well-known Southern California charismatic evangelist with whom I had spoken briefly before the show. I beckoned him to follow, and he jumped into the back of the black limousine, looked me straight in the eye, and said, "Boy, you need the Holy Ghost to come upon you. You need to speak in tongues."

Memories of guitars playing in my ears and a woman trilling like a dove flashed before my eyes. As the limo lurched forward, the evangelist clutched my leg with what felt like a death grip and cited numerous Scripture verses, explaining why I couldn't be a good Christian unless I spoke in an "unknown tongue."

I know God is good because the airport soon appeared in the distance. "Forgive me, but I'm only a Presbyterian," I said. "And I've got to catch a plane."

The reverend looked perplexed at my response. I jumped from the car as he yelled out one more plea for me to seek the gifts he so enjoyed.

I barely made my plane that day. Easing into my seat, I noticed that I was sweating as if I had just played forty minutes of basketball. And as the plane finally touched down at Washington National Airport, I thanked God that I was on planet earth again.

Pressing Needs

Our fifth child, Joshua Benjamen, was born on October 6, 1983—at the same home with the same midwife who had delivered Joel. Our quiver may have been full, but our bank account most assuredly was not. We now had two children attending a small Christian school, a house payment, and the mounting daily expenses for seven people. My salary from TRI was minimal, and once again my ideals were being pitted against the reality of living in a world that includes bills and creditors.

It was at this time that I received a fortuitous phone call from Charles Kothe, dean of the O. W. Coburn School of Law, who asked if I would be interested in teaching during the 1984 spring semester.

"What made you think of me?" I asked.

"We announced that we would be offering a course on church-state law," Kothe explained, "and then asked the students who they wanted to teach it. You were their first choice."

Intrigued, I listened as the dean described my salary (nearly double our meager income from TRI!) and explained that they would pay our moving *and living* expenses while we were in Tulsa. It didn't take us long to decide. TRI was barely making it financially, and Becky Beane could run the office for the few months I'd be gone.

Franky was adamantly opposed to my taking this position, in large part because the law school was part of Oral Roberts University.

"He's as crazy as Jim Bakker," Franky said. "Imagine seeing a seven-hundred-foot Jesus!"

Well, whatever, I thought, *but we really need the money!* Besides that, teaching had been a lifelong dream of mine.

The day after Christmas, we packed our van and headed west toward Tulsa. The Whiteheads were on the road again, and this stop wouldn't be any less contentious than any that had preceded it.

My family in Tulsa (Easter 1984)

That's me playing Santa Claus back home in Manassas (Christmas 1985).

CHAPTER 14

"So which of these three do you think was neighbor to him who fell among the thieves?" And he said, "He who showed mercy on him." Then Jesus said to him, "Go and do likewise."

Luke 10:36–37

"Some day in the distant future," Franky predicted, "when the world has been destroyed by a nuclear holocaust, the people who survived will dig around Oral Roberts University and proclaim, 'My God! They worshipped hands!'"

Franky was referring to the giant praying hands that stand in front of the now-defunct medical center at Oral Roberts University.

Franky would have found even more to lampoon inside the university, particularly Oral Roberts's disdain for beards. Charles Kothe, the dean of the law school, warned me before I came out, "Beards aren't welcome here." So I dutifully shaved mine off. Just days after I arrived, I was walking through a hallway at the university. It was decorated with paintings of the disciples, all of whom were clean-shaven—except for Judas!

I have never understood the evangelical phobia over beards. In the early eighties, I spoke at the Moody Bible Institute and afterward joined a professor for lunch in the cafeteria. As we ate, I couldn't help but notice that students kept staring at me.

"What is it?" I asked.

The professor smiled. "It's your beard. They aren't allowed here."

Less than an hour later, I stood in front of a plaster cast face of Dwight Moody, the school's founder, and couldn't suppress my laughter. He had a full beard!

Shortly after I arrived at the law school, I was asked to give the chapel address, which all the ORU students were required to attend.

"I heard you're speaking at chapel," one professor said to me.

"That's right."

"Can I give you a piece of advice? Don't talk about abortion. That's one of Oral's taboo subjects."

This warning was repeated at least three or four times by several different individuals.

That pretty much convinced me to speak on abortion. When the day came, I walked to the podium before thousands of watching eyes. Oral Roberts sat behind me. For the next twenty minutes, I spoke on abortion and how important it is for Christians to get involved in protesting the killing of unborn children.

When I finished, the audience erupted in applause. I turned to find my seat, and when I looked out at the students, I saw that the applause had evolved into a standing ovation.

Then Oral Roberts stood up. I half expected a Bob Jones response—"I want to refute everything that man just said"—but instead Oral stepped to the podium and proclaimed, "I take that as being from the Lord."

One of the law professors at the O. W. Coburn School of Law was a young woman named Anita Hill. We had several conversations about being a Christian in the legal profession, and I found her to be a genuinely nice person. I don't know why Anita talked to me, other than the fact that perhaps she saw me as a kindred spirit.

Anita particularly won me over by the kind way she treated my children. Carol brought them to the law school frequently, and Anita would pick up the little ones and talk to them, asking about their toys, and treat them with genuine affection. Most of the professors simply ignored our kids, but Anita always stopped to talk to them.

When Anita Hill's name surfaced during the Clarence Thomas nomination hearings for the Supreme Court, I was surprised. It was difficult for me to believe that Anita made up the charges she leveled at Thomas, and I believed her testimony. However, I was let down and extremely disappointed when during the Paula Jones case Anita, along with Patricia Ireland of the National Organization for Women (NOW), distanced herself from the case.

Anita's argument (and that of many in the women's movement) was that since Clinton had been, in her opinion, good on the abortion and women's issues, his alleged conduct against Jones shouldn't be held against him. This was a political rather than a moral judgment, and in my view, politics should never take precedence over morality.

Death of a Mentor

I invited Franky Schaeffer to ORU to speak to the students. If my talk had been perceived as somewhat controversial, Franky's was off the charts. He gave an impassioned address, urging the students to actively protest abortion. It was one of the most radical talks I ever heard him give, with one of the most bizarre endings.

His time was running out, so I gave Franky the "cut" signal with my hand.

"Oops, Whitehead says I've gotta stop," he told the crowd in midsentence. Without saying another word or bringing his talk to a conclusion, Franky stepped off the stage and started walking away. The stunned students followed him with their eyes, not quite sure that he really was leaving. They became even more confused when Franky paused at the cookie table, picked up a treat, took a couple of bites, and then casually left the building.

Later that spring, Jim Buchfuehrer, Franky's assistant, called me with sobering news.

"Dr. Schaeffer just died," he said. "Franky wants you to be an alternate pallbearer."

The call didn't surprise me. Edith's juice notwithstanding, the cancer had been winning its battle with Dr. Schaeffer's body for some time. In a way, it was a merciful exit, as Dr. Schaeffer's last few months had been very hard on him and his family. While the cancer was eating away at his father, Franky had literally lived in Dr. Schaeffer's room, bathing and cleaning him. He never gave up the hope of recovery, but cancer is a cruel master with little concern for people's wishes.

The funeral was a solemn occasion and provided me with an opportunity for my own reflections. Dr. Schaeffer had carried enormous influence, which affected some people in strange ways. On one occasion, I had seen people reach out and touch Dr. Schaeffer's clothes as he walked by.

"What are they doing?" I asked Franky.

"They're trying to be healed."

"You've got to be kidding me!"

"I'm not."

I looked at their faces, and you could see the expectation. Francis Schaeffer never claimed a gift for healing; he never told anyone to do this, but his stature was such that people thought he carried enormous spiritual power.

Listening to the eulogies, I couldn't help but wonder where I would have been without Dr. Schaeffer. His life was a moving testimony to how profoundly one individual can affect another. Had it not been for Dr. Schaeffer and his son, I might well have given up and returned to a private law practice. That undoubtedly would have led to a more comfortable lifestyle financially, but a much poorer life spiritually.

Back in Virginia

After being asked to teach my course in the summer school session also, we returned to Virginia in July. It was time to refocus on TRI.

In the fall of 1984, I began research on what I consider to be one of the better books I've written, *The End of Man*. I was becoming alarmed over the development of science and technology outside of any moral system. Under the guise of scientific determinism, eugenics was being promoted under the name "biomedical ethics"; genocide was being called "population planning"; abortifacient drugs were being readied for widespread distribution; and artificial intelligence was threatening to overpower humankind, replacing human reasoning with electromechanical reactions.

I finished the book in the spring of 1985 and delivered the manuscript to my publisher, Crossway Books. The editors at Crossway were less than enthusiastic about receiving it. Not only did some of them question the book's message, they also questioned the format. It's a heavy book, with more than six hundred footnotes and a "select bibliography" that runs twenty-five pages!

"People just aren't going to read this," some editors argued. And they were right. The book sold few copies and essentially died soon after it went into print. I had written a noncommercial book, but I have yet to write anything with money as my aim. I simply thought *The End of Man* needed to be written. But evangelical audiences were not ready for—or interested in—the message.

Two years later, I was invited to speak at a crisis pregnancy center, out in the middle of nowhere. The board members took me to lunch, and one of the men present scowled at me every time I looked his way. After we ate, I saw him marching toward me and the thought went through my head, *This is it. If I'm ever going to be assassinated, now's the time.*

Instead, the man came up to me and said, "I want to thank you for writing *The End of Man*. That book led me to become a Christian."

When I got back home, I called Lane Dennis—the one editor at Crossway who had been positive about the book—and told him about this conversation. He couldn't believe it. "Not *The End of Man!*" he exclaimed. "I'd believe any of your books except *that one* could lead somebody to God!"

Who knows? Maybe the purpose of that book was just to encourage one man to reconsider his eternal destiny. It was one happy note for an otherwise frustrating experience. I thought I had written my best book yet, and no one cared.

Splinters

We came tantalizingly close to constructing a united front of concerned Christian lawyers in the fall of 1985. Watching that front crack and then fall apart was one of the most disheartening experiences I've ever known.

Over the previous three years, TRI had been steadily building. We had moved to a larger office and hired some additional staff, including two attorneys.

It began with great promise. I contacted the lawyers who had worked on cases for TRI and arranged a meeting at Chicago's O'Hare Airport. State chapters of TRI were just getting under way, and it seemed like a good time to bring everyone together.

The meeting presented historic promise. Finally, I began to believe that it was possible to build the equivalent of an ACLU-type organization. Everyone who came paid his own way. Attorneys from all fifty states were there because we believed that religious rights were important and together, we could accomplish something. Many excellent litigators—including Tom Neuberger, Don Campbell, Jim Knicely, Eric Johnston, Charles Bundren, and others—were ready to go to war to protect religious liberty.

There was a fresh exuberance with the promise of lawyers coming together to build a united front defending human life and religious liberty. Lawyers were willing to do free work—which is the only way TRI could afford to take cases—and hopes were high.

It worked well for several years. But the promise was deflated by something none of us foresaw—the rise of varied legal groups within evangelicalism, which slowly began, one by one, to pick off many of the former volunteers. Some of the top names in the Christian world discovered that, ironically enough, there was now money to be made from publicizing various court cases and legal issues. I knew there wasn't that much money to go around, as TRI had fought the funding battle for years. Before the evangelical world grew tired of court battles, though, there was a short season when Christians gave generously and often.

That opened the doors to new organizations. Ultimately, Pat Robertson would start the American Center for Law and Justice (ACLJ) and make a fundamental error with devastating consequences for the movement. Unlike TRI, which paid expenses of cases, ACLJ promised to pay at least some legal fees to some of the lawyers who argued their cases. Once lawyers started receiving money to fight for righteous causes, we were never able to get some of them to donate their time again. Thus, when funding levels inevitably dropped—as I knew they would—our momentum and volunteer base were decimated.

There are now almost twenty "Christian" legal organizations. While this might sound like good news, the downside of it is that there isn't one that handles the number of cases that TRI does—or has earned the reputation we have for being aggressive. Often, it only takes a phone call or letter from one of our attorneys to resolve a matter.

The rise of so many organizations also means that the good Samaritan principle, upon which I've based The Rutherford Institute, was being replaced by another axiom: "Money talks." (Or, as Bob Dylan said, "Money doesn't talk, it swears.")

Many lawyers no longer viewed these cases as a form of ministry; some hoped to carve fairly lucrative livings out of their "calling." One legal organization, which handles only a few cases a year, even managed to buy a private airplane!

The unity of the lawyers displayed in Chicago in the fall of 1985 quickly began to splinter as each group chased after the same headline-making cases, which would allow them to raise the necessary funds to keep their organization going. The final death knell of this united front occurred with the establishment of the Alliance Defense Fund (ADF) some years later. ADF enjoyed the support of numerous evangelical superstars. The idea was that these leaders would use their own donor base to raise money and give it to ADF to fund important court cases. My concern was that ADF was a giant middleman, threatening to suck up funds while providing little in the way of actual frontline help. I told the ADF leadership that there was no need for a group like ADF because TRI was already fighting important court cases.

I was surprised and dismayed at the reaction of the ministries when we talked to them about this. "Are you questioning our integrity?" was the general response.

I didn't understand the defensive posture of these groups and soon learned there is a steep price to pay for raising questions in the evangelical world. After the furor erupted over ADF, some people I've known well for ten or fifteen years no longer wanted to be associated with me and even stopped supporting TRI. And we ultimately learned that a large portion of ADF's funds go toward administrative costs and flying attorneys and staff members to long meetings, sometimes in exotic vacation spots, with all expenses paid.

Besides the rise of competing evangelical groups, political activism—ironically enough—also became an Achilles' heel in the fight for religious rights.

Playing Politics

The diversion of evangelicals into politics, beginning in the early eighties with the inauguration of the Reagan administration, sapped the Christian activist movement of its ideological strength. The nature of politics is such that success is achieved by compromise. The political process forces people to balance priorities and then lean heavily toward expediency. In the end, politics is won by getting the vote, not by winning the case or saving a baby's life.

How else can we explain the demise of Dr. C. Everett Koop, who coauthored *Whatever Happened to the Human Race?* with Dr. Francis Schaeffer. Once Koop became surgeon general, he suddenly became an antismoking zealot and completely buried his pro-life convictions—which was what earned him his nomination in the first place. He spent more time bringing back the surgeon general's uniform—and all the pomp and circumstance that go with the office—than he did taking on the abortion industry. Give me a street fighter any day over a politician.

Please understand, I'm *not* saying that Christians shouldn't run for government office. Running for office can be good and right. What bothers me is that people tend to grow weak in office, eschew their principles for the sake of maintaining power, and then fail to effect real change.

Watching "evangelical heroes" accept crumbs of success as long as they were welcomed at the White House was disheartening. Furthermore, the inconsistency and hypocrisy of some of the evangelical leaders I had worked with or come into contact with disturbed me. One well-known leader made a habit of using cases we were arguing to raise money for *his* ministry—and he never even mentioned us!

By 1986, I was reassessing where I should be and what I should be doing. I began to wonder, *Whatever happened to the real Christian message in the modern age?*

In his last book, literally written on his deathbed, Francis Schaeffer warned about *The Great Evangelical Disaster.* Now that he was gone, the disaster seemed to be overtaking the Christian church. I began to wonder, *Had evangelicals missed the real message of Christ somewhere along the line?* In their rules, their expensive church buildings, and their lust to build the next evangelical empire, had modern evangelicalism somehow missed the simple, but profound message of Christ?

I was about to be cast into a serious time of questioning.

PART FOUR

A TIME OF QUESTIONING

People do not like to think. If one thinks, one must reach conclusions.
Conclusions are not always pleasant.

—Helen Keller

Carol and me outside our home in Manassas,
Virginia (1986)

Here I am after receiving the Religious
Heritage Award (October 1990).

CHAPTER 15

Whosoever would be a man, must be a nonconformist.

—*Ralph Waldo Emerson*

By 1985, TRI was receiving enough financial support to move to a small office in Old Town Manassas, Virginia—appropriately located, we thought, on Battle Street. My staff now included several attorneys and administrative employees, and summers brought an influx of interns from law schools across the country. To reach our small base of operations, housed in an old building next to the train depot, you had to ascend a narrow, steep flight of twenty-five stairs. When the trains came through, the engineers would blow their whistles, making it impossible to continue a telephone conversation—which could be a bit embarrassing.

George Bush, along with Dan Quayle as vice president, was now in the White House. Pat Robertson had thrown his hat in the ring during the Republican presidential primaries. Many Christians backed Robertson with fervor. I watched the entire political parade, knowing that an election year always meant a dwindling of donations to TRI. People reduce their giving to charities as they funnel money to political candidates. This is a dangerous gamble with good money. And with a well-known evangelical in the race for a nomination, I knew the financial hit to my work would be even harder felt.

I began writing a book entitled *True Christianity*, in which I wrestled with many questions that were troubling me about the nature of our faith. What is the true essence of being a Christian? Is it an attempted takeover of society, as some evangelicals were saying? More fundamentally, is our mission as Christians to serve or to rule? Was the church or society—as an entity—more valuable than individuals? The more I read and reread the Gospels, the more I became convinced that some of my more strident beliefs may have been based on some popular evangelical interpretations rather than on Christ's true teachings.

I had by now rejected most of Christian reconstructionism and had come to see that people such as Mother Teresa were living out "true Christianity" in a far more profound way than many of my Protestant acquaintances—theological differences notwithstanding.

Mother Teresa saw Christ as One who came to serve. In her mind, caring for humans was more important than passing laws or electing the next popular candidate. How you take care of people is how you express your faith. Rather than trying to bring in a Christian order and preparing to rule, Mother Teresa prophetically called Christians to serve, which struck me as far more Christlike than any theology I had studied.

My dealings with Dr. Schaeffer had changed me as well. Though most people thought of him as a philosopher-writer-lecturer, in actuality, Dr. Schaeffer was very people-oriented and emotional. Many times I saw him with tears in his eyes, especially when he talked about the plight of the unborn. For Dr. Schaeffer, the pro-life movement wasn't about political power or winning or losing; it was about his passion for the unborn children who were being victimized unmercifully. He felt their plight deeply.

Also about this time, I received a call from one of Pat Robertson's advisers, inviting me to a meeting in Virginia Beach to discuss some important legal and constitutional issues. Of course, I hesitated. Remembering the previous meeting I had endured was sobering. Even so, TRI was always wondering where our next dollar would come from. Because I believed so strongly in what we were doing, I was willing to give just about anything a shot. I wasn't naïve or expecting great things, but I did harbor a little hope that perhaps something of substance would come from one of these meetings.

I should have known better. We assembled in a large, wood-paneled boardroom. By "we," I mean myself, about a dozen of Pat's assistants, and a couple of other lawyers. An empty chair waited patiently at the head of the table. I took the opportunity to look around the room, but I didn't know very many of the participants, which seemed odd considering I had been working in this field for some time. If these were key players, why hadn't I heard of them?

An interminable thirty minutes passed amid awkward gaps of silence and inane small talk before Pat walked in. Everyone rose to greet him.

The purpose of the meeting was to consider the perceived threat to Christians and their rights in society-at-large. This was a legitimate concern, which Pat asked me to address. I noted that much as the ACLU and other groups had done, we needed to mount a consistent attack in the courtroom and parallel that with educational programs for law students and the general public. This was part of TRI's agenda to protect constitutional freedoms, a strategy I had been working to employ almost from the moment I became a Christian.

Pat nodded approvingly, waited for me to finish, and then utterly deflated my hopes by saying, "God spoke to me yesterday."

Here we go again, I thought.

"I was praying about how we should address the concerns that our friend John Whitehead has just raised for us. God answered my prayer with two words."

Two words? I thought.

Pat went on, "God said, *Constitutional amendment.*"

I groaned inwardly, particularly as I heard Pat's staff "ooh" and "aaah" over this divine revelation. I had grown weary of this method of doing Christian business and was reminded of the time two men from Oral Roberts's ministry approached me. They literally carried what I called "the book of Oral." It's a collection of Oral's sayings, statements that he believes are from God. These are looked at with nearly the same reverence afforded Scripture.

The problem was that Oral wanted to move his ministry in a certain direction, and a previous "prophecy" seemed to argue against such a move. They asked me if I would look at the prophecy and advise them.

Ever the astute lawyer, I discovered an equivocal phrase. "You know," I said, tongue-in-cheek, "you could interpret this in another way."

Their faces lit up like a street lamp at dusk. They were so happy that I had found a loophole!

As Pat went on about his revelation, the meeting was really over for me. I knew that as constitutional amendments go, they are nearly impossible to ratify. An amendment protecting religious people would bring every strict separationist group out of the woodwork to fight it with a maniacal desperation. Even if by some miracle (and it would take a miracle) the amendment was ratified, it takes years upon years for an amendment to mean anything. The whole process would be a national debacle.

Besides, I saw the problem as one of immediacy. We needed to fight for the rights *now*, not tomorrow or next year. Listening to Pat speak, I felt as if my brain would explode.

I've got to get out of this place, I thought. The last thing I wanted to do was waste another day in another crazy meeting.

Over the following months and then years, I never heard anything else about the proposed amendment, or whether God had reconsidered His advice to Pat Robertson. Interestingly, five years later, in 1990, Robertson founded his American Center for Law and Justice (ACLJ). From the beginning, Robertson seemed to model his group after TRI, from its structure to the cases it took, even to the appearance of his promotional materials.

Imitation, it is said, is the sincerest form of flattery.

In Bed with the Government

I attended another Christian Booksellers Association (CBA) convention in the summer of 1985. My book *An American Dream* had been nominated for the Gold Medallion Award. This excursion provided another look into the somewhat quixotic soul of evangelicalism.

Shortly before the convention, the Iran-Contra scandal broke. American officials had diverted millions of dollars in profits from the secret and illegal sale of missiles to Iran to fund the contra rebels in Nicaragua. Evangelicalism's hero, President Ronald Reagan, was facing an impeachable offense if directly implicated in the scheme. The White House mounted a vigorous defense, claiming that Colonel Oliver North, National Security Council aide, had directed the operation on his own (a later congressional investigation found that many in the Reagan administration were involved).

In nationally televised hearings, North enthralled millions of Americans with patriotic rhetoric. By the time I reached CBA, North was the hottest celebrity on the planet. Evangelicals were sporting North buttons with slogans defending him. Without question, most of those present had naively bought into the rhetoric of the whole affair.

I stopped one well-known man and engaged him in what became a rather intense discussion.

"I see you're wearing an Oliver North pin," I pointed out.

"Absolutely. He's a modern-day American hero."

"Do you think there's any truth to the fact that he broke the law?"

"He's a Christian, Whitehead, and the liberals are out to get him and our president. What's your point?"

"I don't really have a point, except to ask, is Oliver North telling the truth?"

I was not trying to demean Oliver North. Obviously, he was patriotic and believed in his country.

But this last question—*Is he telling the truth?*—was an inquiry that many evangelicals seemed to consider irrelevant. "Our" president's legacy was on the line; if Oliver North had to break the law and then lie about it to defend Reagan, then so be it.

I became increasingly concerned about how closely Christians and Christian institutions should ally themselves with the government or governmental policies. History shows that many such alliances end up making Christians the tool of the state.

"I just think we need to be careful," I said. "We can never forget that Adolf Hitler co-opted the German church, which in the end remained silent as the Jews were led to the gas chambers."

"Are you trying to call Reagan *Hitler?*"

He wasn't getting the point. The conversation was over.

A New Home

By now, through our legal victories and educational endeavors, TRI had enough renown to be regularly called upon for its services. Our cases spanned the spectrum from defending pro-life protesters who were arrested for their picketing to public school students accosted in the hallways for handing out Christian tracts.

Unfortunately, it seemed that we had more people asking for our help than we had offering to support our efforts! The Jim Bakker scandal in 1987, coupled with the Oral Roberts fund-raising fiasco (telling people essentially that God would end his life if he didn't raise a certain amount of money), cast mistrust over virtually every evangelical ministry. I actually received letters from donors asking how I was different from Jim Bakker. Donations plummeted for several months.

But we continued to survive because I believe God does honor honesty and faith. Carol and I sold the first and only house we had ever bought, the one where TRI and two of our children had been born, and started looking for another place big enough to hold a family of seven. We were somewhat limited by my salary at TRI, though.

Scanning the real-estate magazines, Carol came across an ideal house in Culpeper, but her heart sank when she looked at the price, which was way out of our range. Later in the week, however, while looking in the same area for more affordable homes, she decided to check in on the dream home, just to see what it looked like.

To Carol's astonishment, the Realtor said the asking price had been lowered 30 percent, putting it at a level we could afford.

That June, we moved to a big house on ten acres of land out in the woods. It needed finishing work, but some friends donated a good bit of labor. The house sits on a hill surrounded by trees and streams. Foxes, cows, chipmunks, squirrels, wild turkeys, deer, and snakes share the property with us and our Jack Russell terriers. Our front yard quickly became a Wiffle ball, football, and soccer field. There's a basket-ball goal, and many weekends are still spent playing and arguing over calls on the ball field.

With so much tension and travel involved in my work, it is truly a blessing to have a peaceful place to call home.

Franky's Frustration

"I know I'm only speaking to half of you, because the other half are brain-dead."

Franky's comments, delivered at an evangelical function, were a deliberate repudiation of evangelicalism's worst elements. After Dr. Schaeffer died in 1983, Franky could easily have picked up the mantle to his father's legacy, but he made a conscious decision to be more radical and eventually committed the one, unforgivable sin: He started asking questions and critiquing evangelical culture.

Most of the evangelical powers-that-be view you as either for them or against them. There is no such thing, in their minds, as a "friendly" critique, no "iron sharpening iron." It is either accept what they say and do or be considered a rebel and an outcast.

During one CBA convention, Franky handed out flyers attacking several authors, publishing companies, and Christian magazines for equivocating on abortion. "If they were truly *Christian* publications, they'd be consistently pro-life," he told me.

At that point, it was over. The "head Pharisees" don't like to be questioned, and they don't like controversy. I could empathize with Franky, as I had faced similar reactions to some of my own questions.

"I want to break free from evangelicalism, Whitehead," Franky told me over the phone. "I just want to make a good film, and I don't care what the evangelicals have to say about it."

I thought he had the right idea. Christians should be involved in every phase of society, including Hollywood. This is part of Christ's call in Matthew 5:13 for believers to be a preservative and moral influence in society.

Franky was successful in raising enough money to make a low-budget film. Set in a futuristic world, *Wired to Kill* tells the story of two teenagers who seek justice for their parents' murders by building a remote-controlled robot programmed for revenge. Its violence and rough language ensured that it would be assailed by Christians. One large Christian radio station in southern California donated entire shows to attacking the film and Franky.

Initially, *Wired to Kill* was slated to open in more than eight hundred theaters, which virtually guaranteed it would be at least a minor success. Unfortunately, at the last minute Oliver Stone's movie *Platoon* was moved up and substituted for *Wired to Kill*, virtually obliterating *Wired*'s distribution. Franky's film opened in just a handful of theaters. Critics weren't particularly fond of the movie, and the evangelicals in general attacked it on a moral basis.

This debacle coincided with a number of other disappointments in Franky's life. The Hollywood business is a difficult one to break into. In *Sham Pearls for Real Swine*, Franky wrote, "Los Angeles is not a beautiful part of the world. But the physical ugliness of Beverly Hills, Hollywood, Burbank, and the Valley is easy to tolerate compared to the soullessness of many of the human life forms flitting through the Hades that is the movie industry, peopled by men and women with dead eyes."

Many promises were made and broken. United Artists asked Franky to write a script on speculation. At considerable expense to himself, Franky did so, but the man who had commissioned his work was fired soon after Franky completed his script—effectively killing the project. Then Franky wrote a very good screenplay called *Foreigners*. Zoetrope Studios, a production company owned by the acclaimed director Francis Ford Copolla, loved the script and wanted Franky to direct it. As Franky's lawyers negotiated his contract, Zoetrope declared bankruptcy.

There are limits to how many heartbreaks a man can survive, and I think Franky had more than his share. When Carol and I visited him in his Hollywood apartment, I was shocked at the sight of this demoralized man who had once amazed me with his adrenaline and vitality. His excitement was gone, his conversations short. The optimistic, confident magpie had gradually become sullen, sour, and serious. It was as if he had been gutted and left like a fish on the sand to die. Bitterness set in.

Franky used to be one of the most animated and entertaining men I've ever known, a classic joker, but the humor had largely died. The fearless man who had inspired me in the early eighties was now insisting, "I'll never speak to a Christian audience again."

That attitude eventually changed. I still believe Franky has much to share, though it seems he is at times inclined to purposefully offend pietistic sensibilities.

All of this may help to explain Franky's eventual foray into Eastern Orthodoxy. Evangelicalism and Franky just couldn't get along anymore.

True Christianity

Rather than taking Franky's approach of repudiating evangelicalism, I still hoped to help reform it. *True Christianity* is a small book that I hoped would state with simplicity Christ's teachings as I understood them, as well as give some of my views on how to put one's faith into practice.

I divided the book into three sections. First, I discussed the present moral malaise. Next, I critiqued what I saw as the main problems with modern evangelicalism: its infatuation with entertainment; various forms of Christian reconstructionism or "utopianism"; and the dangers of politics and compromise. Finally, I presented my case for a "true Christianity"—one that does not merely play off of emotion but is intellectually charged and controversial, one that actively seeks ways to help people while also fighting social evils. "Equipped with great spiritual and intellectual power," I wrote, "along with fervent devotion to Jesus Christ, Christians can change the world around them."

Operation Rescue

This desire to preserve what I saw as true Christianity filtered through my other writings. I wrote an article entitled "Activism: Has the Light Gone Out?" that presented what I intended to be a friendly, in-house critique of the pro-life movement. In the article, I argue that "any true activist movement must—as Christ did—originate and remain *outside* the establishment . . . For it is the tendency of the establishment to absorb all movements, honoring activists or radicals with their lips while denying them in principle."

I feared that this was exactly what was happening within the pro-life movement. The leaders had grown comfortable in funding their organizations and had fallen prey to the allure of political solutions. "Within Christianity," I wrote, "are counterfeit groups that prey off of the issues simply to raise funds for their 'nonprofit' organizations."

Later in the fall, I spoke at a pro-life rally in Washington, D.C. After my presentation, a coterie of people, including many pro-life leaders, cornered me. "What did you think you would accomplish with your article, Whitehead?" they asked me.

What bothered me was not their anger, but the focus of their anger.

They were upset because I dared to raise in-house questions. None of these detractors were even attempting to understand the critique; in their mind, to critique is to become an enemy.

"I wrote the article because I remain a pro-life activist," I tried to explain. "It wasn't to attack you, but to help us truly save the unborn. I just think we could go about this in a different way."

Their reactions only grew more heated. I expected them to take me away to be tarred and feathered at any moment, when a young man spoke up from the back of the crowd.

"Hey," he called out, drawing everybody's attention by his forceful voice. "Why are you criticizing John Whitehead? He's fighting for us!"

It was a warm day, and my defender was wearing a short-sleeve shirt. He had a distinctive, short, tight-curled haircut, and was a lean man a little more than six feet tall. He looked to be in his late twenties.

"My name is Randall Terry," he said. "I've been inspired by your books." He was carrying a copy of *An American Dream,* which he pointed to and said, "Your book helped me realize that revolution is occurring in modern-day America. We may need to support the overthrow of America if that occurs."

"That's not what I intended at all!" I protested, somewhat horrified at this serious misinterpretation.

"Anyway, I'm organizing a series of protests, and I'm calling my organization Operation Rescue (OR). Would you have any free time to meet and discuss it with me?"

Terry handed me a pamphlet about OR, which I read carefully the next day. It set forth a plan to disrupt the abortion business with nonviolent sit-ins, reminiscent of the civil rights movement. I saw great promise in his approach and called him immediately.

"Randy, I'd be happy to spend a day with you, discussing Operation Rescue and what this might mean, including what you can expect from the legal end."

Terry was encouraged by my response and traveled to the TRI

office in Manassas several weeks later. My first concern was whether he had carefully thought through the legal ramifications of Operation Rescue.

"Randy, I have to be honest with you. If you go through with this, abortion activists will target you, attack you personally and viciously, and try to take away everything you own through lawsuits. They will attempt to put you in jail and make an all-out effort to completely destroy you. Are you prepared for that?"

"Absolutely," Randy said, a little too quickly, I thought.

"This means you're going to have to be very well organized and the rescues well planned. These rescues can't be haphazard. You have to know what you're doing. Target several major cities at one time. If you're willing to put it all on the line, you must be effective. Above all, discourage *any* type of violence."

Randy seemed to be listening. He took notes and nodded his agreement while maintaining his enthusiasm and confidence.

As he left my office, I feared that my warnings hadn't succeeded in getting through to him just how aggressive his opponents could be.

Six months later, OR was making headlines around the world. People were getting arrested at every turn, and Randall Terry had become famous.

A typical rescue went something like this: Large groups of pro-lifers gathered early in the morning and sat down in front of an abortion clinic's doors. When police came and ordered them to move, the rescuers stayed put, whereupon the police started arresting them. To slow down the process and keep the abortion clinic doors shut a little longer, rescuers went limp, refusing all cooperation as police officers carted them away. After these officers had carried just a few rescuers, their arms started getting tired, and their methods grew more forceful. After cuffing a protester's hands behind his or her back, officers would slide their batons underneath the pro-lifers' wrists to lift them up. This resulted in numerous broken bones.

Soon, rescuers were facing a veritable orgy of lawsuits, which didn't surprise me in the least. In the first years of Operation Rescue, TRI spent more than $200,000 defending people arrested during sit-ins.

Virtually overnight, Randall Terry had become a household name. Though he was an unpretentious, forthright person whose goal was to protect life, he was widely caricatured in the media as a fanatical, hate-filled zealot who despised women and took malicious glee at denying them "reproductive services."

Randall Terry called me and asked if I would speak at an OR rally in Atlanta. I was pleased to do so and encouraged the large audience by telling them that TRI would help them if and when they got arrested.

"Thanks for your help, John," Randy said to me afterward. "How about sticking around for our strategy meeting?"

Everything I had predicted about the ruthlessness of Terry's opponents came true—and then some. Women's groups and the abortion industry fought OR with unadulterated hatred and venom. As a result, there was immense pressure and strain at the top of the OR leadership ladder.

Still believing that OR showed promise, I invited Terry to speak at a TRI state chapter meeting. Much to my dismay, Terry did little more than vent against Christian lawyers. "We're out there on the front lines," he charged, "but you all do *nothing* for us."

I was offended at this charge. The room was full of Christian lawyers who had donated their time on behalf of these people. In this instance, Randy wasn't just preaching to the choir—he was excoriating it!

A couple of years later, I wrote an editorial entitled "The Demise of Operation Rescue." Rescuers were being brutalized in courts across the country and punished with excessive fines and imprisonments. I wanted to offer a critique of what had gone wrong.

"There seems to be no coordinated and knowledgeable group of leaders acting behind the scenes in Operation Rescue to weigh the pros and cons of the specific acts taken. The various congresses during the revolutionary period and later during the civil rights and antiwar movements were critical to the success of those movements. Although these groups had flaws and did not always have unanimity on specific aspects of their respective movements, they acted in concert to use wisdom and common sense that gave an air of respectability to the movements.

"Operation Rescue, on the other hand, has no substantial brain trust to give strategic cohesion. For example, there seems to be no rhyme or reason why one city, geographical area, or clinic is targeted for protest activities. The entire approach of the Operation Rescue leadership appears to be *ad hoc*. On the other hand, opposition forces, that is, the various pro-abortion organizations and government agencies, are organized."

After this editorial came out, Randy wrote me a letter telling me that I had, in effect, "sinned" by criticizing OR. Earlier, he had attacked evangelist Charles Stanley, accusing him of sinning for failing to endorse Operation Rescue.

While I backed the idea of rescues, I think many made the mistake of throwing everything they had into it. In my editorial, I point out that "no movement can use only one approach and be successful; the opposition soon learns how to deal with such limited protests."

Within several years, laws had been passed and Supreme Court decisions rendered that made it very difficult to do effective protests and picket abortion clinics. I started getting regular distress calls from OR leaders. Some even came to my office, asking, "Am I really going to lose my house over this?"

After one such leader left, I told my staff, "OR is finished. If the key people are worried about losing their homes, the battle is over."

Self-interest is deadly to any movement.

Looking back, I now believe that if groups such as OR had never come along, the pro-life movement would be in better shape today, though I didn't see this at the start. OR didn't have ill motives, but they did have an "in-your-face" type of activism that tends to scare people.

A reporter writing a story on me for *Playboy* recently asked, "Why are you opposed to abortion?"

"Put abortion aside for a moment," I told him. "Let's talk about D and X abortions."

I then explained this barbaric procedure, in which the baby is turned in the mother's womb so the legs emerge first and then the body. When the baby's head reaches the vaginal opening, the abortionist inserts a blunt pair of scissors and then suctions out the brains. As the head is pulled out, it collapses, thus delivering the dead baby.

He was horrified. "But how many of those actually occur?" he asked.

"What if there's only one?" I responded.

It made him stop and reconsider his position on abortion.

Over the years, I've learned to use much less commentary and many more facts. Legitimate debate works in this country, but as soon as you are perceived as antagonistic, the debate is over. You've lost.

In the end, Randall Terry and those who followed him cannot really be blamed for the demise of the pro-life movement. Their goal was to save the lives of unborn children. The abortion fight was huge from the beginning, and OR just happened to play into the hands of the abortion industry. As a consequence, the abortionists got what they wanted—legal restrictions on abortion protests.

While tragic, this was probably inevitable.

Randall Terry has not disappeared from the scene, however. In February of 1999, I was in Nashville to attend the National Religious Broadcasters Convention, held at the Opryland Hotel. Walking through the hotel lobby, I was stopped by a familiar voice, "Don't pass by me without saying hello."

I turned and saw Randall Terry.

He had survived a very difficult time. Randy had run for Congress from the state of New York and lost. Numerous lawsuits had forced him to declare bankruptcy. And now that he was "broken," the media wanted nothing to do with him.

The positive side of this is that his humble, likable demeanor, it seemed, had returned, although it had come as a result of much pain.

Pigs and Goats

In 1990, TRI held a conference near Dulles Airport for the state leaders and other volunteer lawyers working with us. Even now, Carol still calls this weekend "one of the worst experiences of my life."

About a year before the conference, I received a call from one of our attorneys in California. I could barely understand him. It's never easy to listen to a grown man cry, and this one was having trouble controlling himself. I'm not sure why he called me, but through the weeping he managed to communicate that he had been on his knees in the shower for over an hour, water running over his naked body, while he cried about his broken relationship with his father.

I got off the phone, rather concerned. At the time, it didn't occur to me that his emotionalism would result in an attempted coup at Rutherford.

Just after people started arriving at the conference, a concerned lawyer pulled me aside and said, "John, you need to know that the California delegation is saying Rutherford needs to head in a new direction—with them leading the way, of course."

"You mean they want me out?"

"Afraid so."

Over the next hour or two, several others came up with essentially the same message. "I wouldn't worry too much," one of them chuckled. "They're obviously telling the wrong people!"

I scheduled five-minute reports, which gave each state delegation an opportunity to let the others know what was happening in their region. The California delegation extended its "five minutes" to more than an hour. It was an obvious campaign speech, delivered by the same man who had cried to me over the phone, talking about how important California is and how, essentially, California eventually defines our nation's culture.

I was tempted to cut him off, but a fellow lawyer urged me, "Let him talk. Everyone can see what's going on."

The coup never garnered enough support to make a serious challenge, but the attempt did succeed in effectively destroying the camaraderie we had worked so hard to build. Money and power certainly couldn't hold us together, as there wasn't enough of either to cement any bonds.

Driving back to my home in Culpeper, I knew that the solidarity of the attorneys would never be the same. Loyalty to one group and singularity of purpose were no longer possible. Power and ego, not to mention the seduction of money, meant that the state chapter system I had initially envisioned simply could not continue to work.

Loyalty, as I have always told my staff, may be the most important human attribute—as well as the most rare. Without loyalty, as Martin Luther once said, we are like pigs and goats.

But we live and learn. If you cannot adapt to circumstances, you cannot survive. I still had the fire in my belly. I wanted to try my best to follow what Christ called the greatest commandment—to serve God with all your might and to love your neighbor as yourself. For me, that would involve doing what I could to preserve people's rights and provide them with tools to help them better understand the world they live in.

Little did I know that this mission would soon take me to other parts of the world.

Receiving the Medal of Freedom from the president of Hungary,
The Honorable Arpad Gönz (November 1991)

At Focus on the Family in Colorado Springs with
Dr. James Dobson (April 1992)

CHAPTER 16

**Open your mouth for the speechless,
In the cause of all who are appointed to die.
Open your mouth, judge righteously,
And plead the cause of the poor and needy.**

—*Proverbs 31:8–9*

I know I should do it, I thought. *Yeah, there will be a lot of travel involved, and no, I don't speak their language. Of course, this will make it all the more difficult. But still, this is an opportunity I can't pass up.*

I held the invitation to speak in Hungary in my hand.

Definitely, I needed to go.

We had already established attorneys in Latin America, but this was the first time Carol and I would cross the Atlantic Ocean. She was no longer pregnant or nursing a baby, and the kids were old enough to leave with either my mother or Carol's. So we boarded a plane for Budapest in early October of 1990.

Before we left, we leafed through various travel brochures, all of which made Budapest look like paradise. Carol thought this might actually be somewhat of a vacation.

As soon as we touched down and started walking around, however, any thought of vacationing evaporated. There was a feeling of oppression in the atmosphere. The architecture, however, was undeniably beautiful, though cruelly marred by age and acid rain, which had carved grooves in the ancient stone.

"John," Carol pointed out, "nobody will look us in the eye."

She was right. The long years of Communist rule had left their mark. Suicide, the leading cause of death among teenagers, was at an all-time high. People walked with their heads lowered and their eyes darting, never allowing their glances to become fixed on an outsider. The Communists, through years of fear, torture, and inhumane treatment, had trained an entire society to believe they were not human. Though the Hungarian government had now been restored, the old philosophy still ruled many in their minds.

Further adding to the depression, the Hungarian economy was bad, and prices were very high. The average monthly wage for workers was a mere $200, but a pair of name-brand sneakers cost more here than in the United States.

Our hosts were Imré and Agnes Madaracz. Imré is a heroic attorney who resisted the Nazis, fought anti-Semitism, and then resisted the Communists. His wife, Agnes, a university professor, translated for us because Imré spoke little English and we spoke no Hungarian.

"Look here," his translator said for him.

I stopped in front of a building pockmarked with bullet holes that had chipped out the masonry.

"Most of these came from the Communist takeover in 1956, when the Soviet tanks rolled into Budapest and crushed the people's uprising," my host explained. "Thousands were massacred."

And the West essentially looked the other way, I thought to myself.

It took us several hours by bus to get to the conference, which consisted of speakers from countries throughout Europe. Listening to them talk, I saw that we could help Eastern Europeans in several ways: educational materials, advice (when requested), and money.

"John, what we really need," one representative told me, "are materials on legal and constitutional issues that will help us reclaim and rebuild our countries."

When the Communists took over in the fifties, they destroyed official records and titles of ownership, leaving the people no proof to reclaim their property. These nations needed structure, a place to begin again.

A colorful old pastor acted as master of ceremonies. He was tenacious about keeping us on time and was animated in his announcements.

"The bar will open at three o'clock," he said early in the day. Just an hour or two later, he said once again, "The bar will open at three o'clock."

The message was repeated once again—obviously, this was truly a highlight in their day.

At the appointed hour, the old pastor pulled a literal bar on wheels from a side room. The cart was lined with every kind of hard liquor you could imagine, and many that you couldn't! The pastor personally carried a bottle of a homemade brew he called "Transylvania Schnapps." He kept encouraging me to take a drink, but I took one look at that homemade liquid in a clear bottle and declined.

This ritual continued for a couple of more days, until I could no longer politely decline. I finally agreed to take a small glass. As soon as it hit my throat, I thought I was drinking acid! It burned like fire all the way down.

The final day of the conference, we listened to two Russian dissidents give harrowing testimonies about their lives in the Soviet Union. One of them, Alexander Ogorodnikov, had been locked up in solitary confinement in a cell that was three feet by three feet, with a hole dug for a toilet. He had no coat, even in the middle of winter. During the night, to keep from freezing to death, he would squat down and pull his shirt over his knees. He would jump up and down when he awoke, trying to bring some warmth and circulation against the intense cold. Even so, his hands often turned a deep blue.

Ogorodnikov's "crime" was organizing Christian seminars and

printing Christian material. Each time he was released from prison, he would set up another office, whereupon the authorities raided it and destroyed his machines. This went on until he was arrested and sent back to prison. Upon his release, the scenario was again repeated.

The Iron Curtain had not yet been lifted, and we asked the Russians why they didn't just keep on going after the conference. "And leave our Christian brothers and sisters behind? We could never do that," they replied.

Their dedication and willingness to suffer for their faith should put us all to shame. In fact, they told us they believed the West remained free only because of their prayers on our behalf.

Reforms were rushing ahead, but, coupled with a declining economy and the remnants of the old secret police, democracy was still a long way off. When I discovered that a large group of political prisoners had been punished in the winter by being taken outside in weather that was twenty degrees below zero and then sprayed with water, I immediately issued a press release telling the world about this inhumane treatment. As a rule, despots hate negative publicity. They want America's goodwill and usually respond quickly to exposed ills.

I also wrote to several key members of Congress. The only person who responded, interestingly enough, was Ted Kennedy.

In spite of what Westerners are told, decades will pass before there is any real freedom in the former Soviet Union, even without the Iron Curtain.

We reached an agreement with Imré and Agnes for them to act as TRI's representatives in Eastern Europe, which would continue the international work of TRI. They immediately went to work—protesting, marching, and arguing for the state to release government control of schools and churches. Since the Communists had destroyed the ownership records, it was—and still is—an uphill battle. Imré and Agnes wrote editorials and pamphlets in support of constitutional reform and translated some of my books and pamphlets into Hungarian and distributed them to the Hungarian Parliament.

TRI purchased simple equipment for their office—a telefax, typewriter, and a copy machine. Of course, they needed a telephone line to operate the fax. This is a major hurdle in Hungary. Telephone lines are extremely difficult to acquire, and it cost us more than $2,000 in American currency to obtain one.

For Carol and me, the biggest challenge in Hungary was the fatty food. After surviving one meal, I said to her, "They ought to just skip the food and serve cholesterol on a plate." We lost about ten pounds each during our stay there.

Since we had basically stopped eating—except for a couple of granola bars we had brought with us—we couldn't wait to touch down at London's Heathrow Airport. My first thought was food, and we literally ran to a small airport delicatessen, where I bought the first plastic-wrapped sandwich my hungry hands touched. I had never eaten a salmon sandwich before, but that day in October, it tasted great.

The next year (1991), mainly because of the work of Imré and Agnes, I received a letter from the president of Hungary, informing me that I was being given the Hungarian Medal of Freedom. With full bellies and a bag packed with crackers and granola bars, Carol and I returned to Budapest to meet the president, the Honorable Arpad Gönz. After walking down a red carpet, we shook hands, then he pinned the medal on me. We had a good conversation about the need to restructure Eastern Europe and its problematic economy. At one point, President Gönz led me to a window and pointed to a courtyard eight stories down.

"In 1956, the Soviets called a large rally to speak with the Hungarian people," he said. "They told them to meet in this courtyard. When the people arrived, the Soviets opened fire, murdering hundreds."

We were in Budapest for just three days, but by the time we reached the airport we were down to our last American candy bar, which Carol and I shared. The weather was foggy and raining and our flight was indefinitely delayed. The hunger pangs grew and the dampened weather darkened our own spirits.

"When we get back on American soil, I'm going to bend down and kiss the ground," I promised Carol.

We barely made it out of Budapest that day and then nearly missed our connecting flight in Frankfurt, where we were rerouted to Boston. Finally heading across the Atlantic, I let myself think about America. Although I have criticized it and have even fought its government in the courtroom, I wouldn't trade living in the United States for any country in the world.

When we landed in Boston, it was late on Thanksgiving Day. As promised, I stepped off the airplane, walked with Carol out of the airport, bent down on my hands and knees, and kissed the sweet American earth. A crowd of passengers standing nearby laughed and clapped for me.

It was great to be on home soil—even though I had many flights, and fights, ahead of me.

Art in the Headlines

In 1990, a big art controversy erupted when *The Perfect Moment,* a retrospective of photographs by Robert Mapplethorpe (who had died of AIDS in 1989), was hung in Cincinnati's Contemporary Art Center. Of the show's 175 photographs, five depicted homoerotic, sadomasochistic sex, and two others showed children's genitals. The museum's director was indicted on charges of obscenity, but a jury decided that Mapplethorpe's work had artistic value and voted to acquit.

I am a big fan of painting and art in general, but photographs of a man urinating in another man's mouth and one of a bullwhip pro-

truding from Mapplethorpe's anus undoubtedly stretched the definition of what art should be. These works are unfortunate since
Mapplethorpe was otherwise a very good photographer and artist.

Many evangelical leaders joined the conservative right, with Jesse
Helms leading the way, to fight the Cincinnati show. They lost.

A few months later, TRI entered the fray. Several people contacted
us, complaining that the National Endowment for the Arts was funding sacrilegious art with American taxpayers' money. Our case focused
on a picture by David Wojnarowicz that depicted Christ with a
syringe around His upper arm, mainlining heroin.

While I believe that Wojnarowicz has every right to create his art,
the real issue was whether taxpayers who are opposed to such art
should have to pay for it, and whether the government should fund
art that offends any particular religion.

We filed a lawsuit in the federal district court in Washington,
D.C., using the establishment clause—that government should
make no laws establishing a religion—in a "reverse" way.
Essentially, our contention was that the government was taking a
stand against religion by funding sacrilegious art, thereby actively
inhibiting religion.

While the court rejected our argument, the case resulted in a loud
and sustained public outcry, which helped change the NEA. Lawsuits,
therefore, often serve an educative function.

Dr. Dobson

I met Dr. James Dobson in March of 1991. Several years prior to
that, I toured the Focus on the Family facilities in California. Tom
Minnery, Dobson's assistant, told me, "Dr. Dobson is very embarrassed by all the oak paneling and expensive furnishings."

Naturally, ever distrustful of the establishment, I thought to
myself, *But not enough to require less grand surroundings*—which his
new headquarters in Colorado Springs would prove.

I'll never forget the sea of people in little cubicles (mostly women) who were answering Dobson's mail. It looked like some futuristic movie about worker bee people performing their tasks.

When I met Dobson, he was in a temporary facility awaiting the construction of the massive Focus structure that now occupies acres of land in Colorado Springs. That day, I was to appear on his radio show.

"He'll meet with you briefly, just before the show," an aide assured me.

I was deposited in a waiting area, where a young woman informed me that I would meet the doctor in thirty minutes. As I sat flipping through magazines, the young woman reappeared.

"You'll be taken to Dr. Dobson's office in fifteen minutes," she said.

Ten minutes later, she appeared for a third time and said, "I'll take you to meet Dr. Dobson in just a few minutes."

The staff's detailed movements reminded me of my Army days.

Finally, the young woman whisked me down a hallway and through a series of doors. Dr. Dobson rose to greet me.

At six feet, two inches, I'm fairly tall, but James Dobson is a large man and I felt like he towered over me. His hand swallowed up my fingers as we greeted each other. I felt right at home, given his easygoing mannerism and informal way of talking.

We had a brief, pleasant chat, mostly talking about the recent Rodney King debacle. Dr. Dobson was extremely gracious, saying he appreciated my work. After just a short while, he led me down to the studio to record the show. I shared the thirty minutes with a woman who wept several times while sharing her abortion story. Most of the show focused on her travails, though I was granted a brief moment to speak about The Rutherford Institute.

After the show, I accompanied Dr. Dobson and an aide through an exit door. We paused in a foyerlike room where an aide said, "I'm going to take a picture of you with Dr. Dobson now. Feel free to use the photograph in any way you see fit."

Dobson and I smiled for the camera, shook hands, and one of America's most beloved radio hosts soon disappeared around a corner.

The Rise of Bill Clinton

As I stated in Chapter 1, in May 1991, Arkansas Governor Bill Clinton and Paula Jones first met in a room at the Excelsior Hotel in Little Rock. Paula Corbin (later Jones) returned from that encounter flustered and told several friends that Clinton had sexually harassed her.

Six years later, I would be her attorney.

While those events were unknown to me at the time, Clinton's growing political base certainly didn't escape my notice. I was dumbfounded, to be honest. Remembering the unsuccessful congressional candidate's goofy grin, it was almost impossible for me to imagine him becoming president of the United States. But by 1992, our century's consummate politician had pulled it off.

One of Clinton's first acts coincided with the twentieth anniversary of the decision legalizing abortion, *Roe v. Wade*. As thousands of pro-life demonstrators marched in the streets of Washington, D.C., the newly elected Clinton paid back his pro-abortion supporters by *rescinding* five pieces of pro-life legislation:

1. The Foreign Assistance Act of 1961, which prohibited non-governmental organizations that receive federal funds (e.g., Planned Parenthood) from using those funds "to pay for the performance of abortions as a method of family planning."

2. The Department of Defense Code Section 1083, which prohibited the use of DOD funds to perform abortions except where the life of a woman would be endangered.

3. The exclusion of the importation of RU-486, the abortion pill.

4. The law prohibiting pro-abortion counseling and abortion referral services for family planning clinics for poor patients.

5. The temporary moratorium that had been imposed on federal funding of research involving transplantation of fetal tissue from induced abortions.

Announcing these moves on the anniversary of one of the most controversial Supreme Court decisions in American history was a clear signal of Clinton's agenda to promote abortion. But perhaps even more significantly—for events that would occur several years later during his impeachment trial—Clinton was making good on his *quid pro quo* for the women's vote. Clinton had promised feminist groups that he would protect the unrestricted right to abortion. The union between Clinton and the radical feminists—such as Patricia Ireland and Gloria Steinem—was sealed.

This union paid off handsomely for Clinton during the Jones lawsuit and all that followed. Although it cost the women's movement its credibility to defend Clinton, they remained his steadfast supporters. Anita Hill and Patricia Ireland, among others, essentially admitted that nothing was more important to them than unrestricted abortion—not even their integrity or intellectual honesty. Clinton had made good on his promise to protect abortion (Anita Hill called him a "known commodity"). In the end, that seemed to be all they cared about.

But before the Clinton scandal took up my time, a more immediate concern drew headlines—the Branch Davidian fiasco.

"You've Embarrassed Me!"

In early 1993, a religious group called the Branch Davidians, led by David Koresh, began a standoff against armed federal agents from the Federal Bureau of Investigation, the Bureau of Alcohol, Tobacco, and Firearms, and other armed government officials (state and local) in Waco, Texas.

A TRI affiliate attorney in Texas telephoned me.

"John," he said, "some of the citizens here overheard SWAT teams, dressed in black and carrying rifles, saying, 'Let's get those religious nuts.'"

I was troubled. This is highly inappropriate language for any government official to use. The government has no business having any religious motivation at all.

"Listen," I said in response, "if you can get through to some of Koresh's representatives, tell them that if we can show religious animus is involved, TRI will help them negotiate with the federal government and then defend them in court."

The media has ears and eyes all over this country, especially while blanketing a big story like this. Our attorney's inquiries didn't go unnoticed, and within minutes the media were reporting that TRI was offering to defend the Branch Davidians.

Angry phone calls pelted our office in Charlottesville. "John, you've really blown it on this one," a former supporter from Houston half yelled at me. "David Koresh is a religious nut; he's discrediting everything Christians stand for. How can you defend him?"

"I may not agree with his theology," I replied, "but he's someone in need. We're lawyers, we help people in trouble—and those people don't have to pass a theological test to qualify for our assistance.

"What about you?" I added. "What if we disagreed with your eschatology and decided not to defend you on that basis? Would that be right?"

"I'll never give money to you again," the caller insisted.

On April 19, before we could help the Davidians, federal agents charged what they were calling the "compound" with a vehicle equipped with a battering device. A fire erupted—whether the Branch Davidians or the federal agents started it has been hotly debated—and in the aftermath, eighty-five people died, including seventeen children.

I turned on the television just in time to see the building burning. It was totally destroyed in less than an hour.

"This is so unnecessary," I told my staff. "The government overreacted, and innocent people died as a result."

This principle played out tragically the following year, when on July 29, 1994, Paul Hill, an anti-abortion protester, shot and killed Dr. David Gunn outside a Pensacola, Florida, abortion clinic. At TRI, we already knew about Hill. He had written several papers on his extremist views and sent them to me for comment.

Our staff had responded to Hill with lengthy letters, pointing out the weak links in his philosophy and showing him that on a practical level, violence doesn't work. "Not only is violence outside Christian parameters," we wrote, "but it simply will not accomplish your supposed goal of reducing the number of unborn babies killed by abortionists."

Our pleas went unheeded. I believe Paul Hill's act of violence was a sign of frustration as much as anything else. The pro-life movement had come up against a brick wall comprised of police actions, court decisions, legislation, and the Clinton administration. When you impede free speech, as the government was doing through laws and court decisions, you create an explosive atmosphere. When somebody like Paul Hill introduces misguided theological teaching on violence, the result is certain to be incendiary. It's a very dangerous thing to deny any group its free speech rights.

While we didn't agree with Hill's reasoning, we knew he needed help. I didn't want to do to Paul Hill what other groups had done—initially help him but then abandon him. The ACLJ defended Paul against harassment charges before he shot the abortionist. As soon as the murder occurred, they dropped him. *Time* magazine reported:

> The ACLJ says it was representing Hill because the harassment charges [harassing abortion patients] infringe his First Amendment right to protest. But the ACLJ is not the ACLU, which routinely defends the rights of people it profoundly disagrees with . . . The very fact that the ACLJ dropped Hill when he became too hot to handle suggests that its previous defense of him was motivated by something other than abstract dedication to the First Amendment.

"Let's meet with him," I suggested to Rene Wright, one of our attorneys, the week after he was arrested, "and see what we can do."

I paused, adding, "I'm putting a condition on this. We won't accept his so-called 'necessity defense.' The necessity defense goes something like this: Because an abortionist is killing an unborn person, out of necessity to protect the unborn, there is a right to kill the abortionist. In this case I believe the argument was both wrongly argued and wrongly applied. We can use the argument that because of the bad teaching he received, Paul actually believed he had a right to kill the abortionist. Therefore, he shouldn't be put to death because he was essentially programmed to think this way." This was the nearest thing to an insanity plea.

There was no way Rene could slip into the prison unnoticed. Paul Hill's actions created worldwide headlines, and the media were all over it. Rene had to pass through a line of newspapers and cameras, and within minutes TRI's name was once again on the air—this time as the defenders of Paul Hill.

Rene visited Paul and discussed our offer with him, but he wouldn't budge. He insisted on the necessity defense.

"Then we can't help you," she told him. First, we didn't agree with what he had done. Second, his necessity defense would encourage more violence, which was wrong.

A physician called and complained, "John, you're embarrassing me! I've supported you for years, but never again." He hung up abruptly before I could explain.

Once again, our principled approach had hurt us. My goal has always been to help people who need our services. Paul Hill was one such person. I am an advocate of the approach taken by the ACLU, which is willing to defend people with whom they disagree. I am not Jewish, but I have defended Jews. I am not Buddhist, but I will defend the right of people to practice Buddhism.

In early October, Rene walked into my office and said, "I got a call from Paul Hill's wife. She wants to know if we can help save her husband from the death penalty."

Paul's guilt and conviction were foregone conclusions. Nobody believed he would be acquitted, but his wife was in tears, pleading for us to help him escape the death penalty. She ultimately realized there was nothing we could do.

Religious Apartheid

The Branch Davidian and Paul Hill controversies occurred while I was writing a book, *Religious Apartheid,* which addresses these very issues. The word *apartheid* means "apartness" or "separation." My book addresses how some groups are trying to separate religion from American public life.

For instance, a fourth-grade boy in St. Louis was removed from a public school lunchroom because he silently prayed over his lunch tray. Communities are regularly being sued for displaying long-standing Christmas decorations that include a cross or a crèche.

Another concern of mine was how our government was gradually creeping into private homes by constructing social programs that increasingly interfered with intact families. One example of this was Hillary Clinton's proposed health care plan, which in one stage proposed criminal sanctions for going to the wrong doctor! Religious beliefs were again under siege. However, much to my surprise, President Clinton eventually became somewhat proactive in defending religious rights, more than any recent president.

While Carol and I were on a promotional tour for the video version of *Religious Apartheid,* which Franky Schaeffer had directed, the country was consumed with the O. J. Simpson murder trial. The Heisman Trophy winner was embroiled in what reporters routinely referred to as "the trial of the century."

Several years later, however, an even bigger case came my way— one that implicated the president of the United States.

Carol and me on our first trip to
London in the early 1990s

My sons and me at the James Dean Gallery (July 1997)

CHAPTER 17

I have seen all the works that are done under the sun; and, indeed, all is vanity and grasping for the wind.

—Ecclesiastes 1:14

It was a warm day, especially for October (1993). Carol and I were in Great Britain, promoting the work of TRI. We made this pilgrimage annually for several years, and I even had the opportunity to speak at the House of Commons on our trip there in 1995. I thought we had been to all the London museums worth seeing, but the day before, we had seen a poster glued to a brick wall of a building, advertising an exhibit of "American Art in the 20th Century."

The next morning we were in a black London cab, eager to see what this exhibit had to offer.

I have dabbled in art all my life. While a kid, I was an inveterate doodler. In high school, I enrolled in an art correspondence class but lost interest when it seemed too much like school. About the same time, I enrolled in a drafting class, but had problems drawing in perspective (that is, drawing squares and rectangles three-dimensionally).

"You are hopeless, Whitehead," my teacher told me after reviewing my crooked lines and collapsed dimensions. Mentally, I phased out of the class and barely passed the course.

I tried my hand at painting in the Army but had no idea what I was doing and didn't spend enough time trying to develop a style.

By the early nineties, inspired by the paintings of Francis Bacon, my thirst for art became a new passion. The pain and human suffering Bacon expressed in his work moved me, and I began to haunt museums in whatever towns I happened to be in. I also started reading about various painters, growing particularly interested in Picasso, Duchamp, and Philip Guston.

When we returned from London, I bought some oil paints, a couple of canvases, and a few cheap brushes. Painting soon became one of my passions, an outlet for creative energy, plus a great way to relax and take my mind off work. I initially set up my "studio" in our bedroom, but Carol said my easel and I had to go when a few too many paint splatters ended up on the carpet. I tried to convince her that, in the style of Jackson Pollock, those pieces of carpet could be worth a lot of money someday. She didn't buy it. Next, I moved to a corner of the living room but, despite carefully laying a sheet over the carpet, was banished for the same reason. The only place left was the laundry room in our basement, with its cold concrete floor, where I have painted ever since.

I was surprised in 1995 when two of my paintings—including a portrait I had done of Carol—wound up in the finalist category of an art contest in Virginia.

When the Paula Jones case erupted, reporters frequently focused on my paintings. Ed Bradley of *60 Minutes* came to our office in Charlottesville to interview me for the program. After studying one of my oil paintings, he came to the conclusion that "maybe even John Whitehead doesn't know who he is." Actually, I think my paintings reflect me quite well. I don't paint people smiling. Instead, I try to capture the reality of the world as I see it, which includes a lot of pain and suffering.

My reason for painting is simple—I have an urge to create. I believe that I was put on the earth to create. This is when I'm truly at my best. Perhaps someday my art will recoup what I've paid for paints, brushes, and canvases. If not, I will still continue to paint and escape into a world where there are no rules, no reality.

Grasping for the Wind

As Carol and I walked through the London art exhibit, I was intrigued. This was by far one of the best collections of modern art I had ever seen in one place, with paintings and sculptures from Marcel Duchamp, Marsden Hartley, Man Ray, Arthur Dove, Georgia O'Keeffe, Charles Demuth, Joseph Stella, Edward Hopper, Alexander Calder, Arshile Gorky, Jackson Pollock, Andy Warhol, and on and on. I kept walking through it—a second time, a third time, even a fourth.

Knowing we had to leave for home the next day, I bought the museum's book of essays and illustrations. Studying it as we crossed the Atlantic Ocean, I began planning a project. I didn't know it at the time, but this art exhibit began a five-year intensive study of art, literature, film, politics, philosophy, music, and general culture that culminated in my book and video series, *Grasping for the Wind.*

I began buying more books on art, film, and related subjects, adding to my library (which presently contains more than five thousand books). The more I studied, the more convinced I became of a pattern. None of the disciplines—art, film, science, or politics—is isolated. They all seem to work together, sometimes almost in unison, giving birth to a new worldview and thus bringing about change. And it was clear that these disciplines had moved away from a Judeo-Christian worldview, even ridiculing it.

Judeo-Christian theism helped establish the philosophical foundations of Western culture and democracy. Indeed, without Judeo-Christian presuppositions and principles, it is unlikely that the modern concept of life and freedom would ever have developed. But one finds scant Christian influence in the modern world.

The barrage from Darwin, Freud, Marx, Nietzsche, and others against the Christian worldview has been devastating. Their diatribe, however, would not have been successful had it not been for abuses practiced by the church and the false pietism that dominated the Western world in the nineteenth century. Moreover, as Christians vacated the system, they lost their influence. Thus, when the barrage was unleashed, there was little resistance.

In looking at the great works of modern art and taking into account recent scientific and political developments, I asked myself, *Are we better off for these changes?*

In some ways, yes. The great strides, for example, in minority and women's rights are important. But overall, life appears more chaotic, and people are desperately searching for meaning in drugs, new sexual experiences, entertainment, and the extraterrestrial. Overall, we do not seem to be better off.

While researching and writing, I was reminded of a verse in Ecclesiastes that verbally paints humanity's strivings apart from a real understanding and knowledge of God as merely "grasping for the wind."

I had my title, and the book-video project, *Grasping for the Wind,* was born.

Protracted Project

Wherever I went for the next twenty-four months, I carried a book with me. While my kids played Little League baseball, I sat on the bleachers reading, stopping only when my child came up to bat.

When I started writing, I couldn't stop. The manuscript ballooned to more than 1,300 pages, with some 2,000 footnotes—all written out by hand on yellow legal pads. Although I can type using the two-finger method, I write all my books out in longhand, as I've found this to be the only way my thoughts flow freely. Since my handwriting often resembles a foreign language and Carol types all my books, these are rather stressful times for us.

From the book manuscript, I eventually wrote seven thirty-minute screenplays. After I completed an outline in the summer of 1994, I showed it to Franky Schaeffer.

"It's a great idea, John," he said. "This time, you've outdone yourself."

I asked Franky if he would be interested in working on the project. My idea was to develop a video series that would examine all the changes in Western society. I would be the on-screen narrator, much like Rod Serling in his classic television series *The Twilight Zone*, and Franky would be the director.

Franky quickly signed on. We were back together again, working on a video series—only this time, it would not go quite so smoothly.

I originally conceived a ten-part series with location shoots planned in Europe. I wanted to film at Freud's house outside London, the Vatican, and in Paris museums, but financial constraints made this impossible. I had to scale down the project to a seven-part series, with all of it shot in the eastern United States.

As Franky and I discussed the scripts, I told him I didn't want him to use the MTV-type jumpy shots that he had used when filming *Religious Apartheid*. It didn't work and often confused audiences.

"I want a straight video presentation," I said. The *Grasping for the Wind* series was a major, two-million-dollar undertaking, with as many as sixteen crew people at a time employed for in-studio shooting, and I wanted to do it right.

I had no idea what I was in for. Though shooting began in May of 1995, we didn't complete the series until two years later, in the summer of 1997. We began in Albany, New York, and the incredibly cold, blustery day presaged the ordeal that lay ahead of me.

If you've never worked on a video, there's no way you could begin to imagine all that can go wrong. There are far more variables than whether you remember your lines. There are cameras and lights all around you; if the wind picks up and one lightbulb goes out, you have to reshoot the entire scene. Waiting soon becomes interminable as a crew member works to get the right angle for the lights while another constantly adjusts the sound, and yet another warns of problems in the background.

Albany was so cold, and I just wanted to get it over with. We completed one take that I thought was perfect until the soundman explained that an airplane had flown overhead. We had to shoot the entire scene again.

We did a lot of shooting in Times Square during the spring of 1996. I stood on an island in the middle of traffic, about a hundred feet away from the cameraman. I wanted cars to move past me in the foreground, so every take had to be timed perfectly to coincide with the traffic lights.

In situations like these, it sometimes took us half a day to shoot thirty seconds' worth of video.

Alexis Crow, who worked with me at TRI, was the project coordinator for the series. Carol, who traveled with me throughout the shooting, helped me learn my lines, took hundreds of pictures, and endured the erratic mood shifts I went through as the project wore on. She and Alexis kept me sane through the increasingly difficult confrontations with Franky.

My goal for the series was to present our message through a professional product that we could all be proud of. One of the problems I address in the videos is the level of excellence frequently achieved by those who don't hold to Judeo-Christian views, compared to the mediocre ventures that are so often characteristic of many modern "Christian" productions.

Unfortunately—at least on this project—Franky didn't seem to share my views. When he was on location or in the studio directing camera angles, things went fine. But when it came to the hard work of creating a truly excellent project, Franky's interest waned. As a result, entire video episodes required serious adjustments.

Alexis had major concerns with Franky's work on the project. Thus, the relationship between Alexis, who was responsible for making sure that we ended up with an excellent set of videos, and Franky degenerated badly. Fortunately, because of our experience with *Religious Apartheid,* we had written this contract to give us ultimate control.

Some of the problems consisted of rather small details—music transitions poorly done, glitches in video production. Others, however, required major revisions. But for whatever reason, Franky wasn't willing to sit through this tedious chore.

Some of our phone calls devolved into screaming matches. "It's fine, John," he would say. "There's nothing wrong with it! What's your problem?"

I knew we needed to make a change, but out of my sense of loyalty and remembrance of our early days and his father, I found it very hard to do what I knew needed to be done. So I kept Franky on, while Carol and Alexis kept warning me that he was damaging the project.

Finally, though, we could no longer work together. I sent him a check for what remained on his contract, although I wasn't obligated to, and told him we no longer needed his services.

The videos were now in limbo. Since we had paid Franky the full amount we had budgeted for a director, hiring someone else was not an option. I finally decided that the most economical route was for me to finish the series as director. I had worked on several videos, and while I lacked the technical knowledge, I thought I could take a crash course in video production—which is exactly what I did.

When the shooting was finally completed, Carol and I spent many weeks sitting in video production suites, making transitions, editing the sound, and taking out the annoying little bugs that get into any production. But finally, in the summer of 1997—more than four years from the time I began working on the book—the seven-part video series was completed.

Grasping for the Wind was released in early 1999—right in the middle of the Clinton scandal. It explores humanity's search for meaning over the last two centuries through the works of Western philosophers, writers, artists, filmmakers, politicians, and musicians.

It is a work that I'm proud to have been a part of.

But not everybody in the Christian community appreciates what I've done, as I was about to find out.

Gadfly

One morning in the fall of 1996, just before getting out of bed, I imagined a fly on my pillow. First I saw its large netted eye and then, as I pulled my head back, the rest of the fly's body was revealed. This imagery became the logo for Gadfly Productions, a subsidiary of TRI. Webster's dictionary defines *gadfly* as an "intentionally annoying person who stimulates or provokes others, especially by persistent, irritating criticism." That sounded like me!

I wanted to force people to think, even if it meant irritating them—and little did I know just how well I would succeed.

Part of this new effort included *Gadfly* magazine, which was a natural outgrowth of my *Grasping for the Wind* video series. My goal was to produce a general audience publication that would examine culture objectively and honestly. It was not to be an evangelical publication; we wouldn't force Christianity into the magazine's content, nor would we edit the honest use of language (including what many consider objectionable language).

My oldest son, Jayson, was now a law school graduate. He accepted a position as associate editor of the magazine, and then moved to editor. We assembled a group of writers and produced our first magazine in January 1997. *Gadfly* has received excellent acclaim from some surprising sources. It was nominated by *Utne Reader* for "Best Cultural Magazine of the Year," and the *Washington Post* described it this way: "*Gadfly's* approach is . . . refreshing . . . it's a cultural magazine that fits no identifiable ideology. It's odd, eccentric, and eclectic."

That is exactly what we were shooting for.

The reception of the evangelical community, however, has been in stark contrast, as I discovered at the 1999 National Religious Broadcasters (NRB) convention. TRI's Becky Templeman, who was working our booth, started stocking our rented periodical bin on the first Friday of the convention (the NRB convention typically rents out fifty or more of these each year). Much to her delight, she could barely keep the bin full. *Gadfly* was, in her words, "going like hotcakes."

This happened all throughout Saturday as well. Carol and I flew in late Saturday night. The next morning—Sunday—while I was getting ready in my room, Becky was down on the floor, ready to restock the periodical bin for the afternoon session. An older man with an NRB badge stopped her.

"What are you doing?" he asked.

"I'm refilling my bin," Becky answered.

"I'm sorry. There's a problem. You can't display your magazine anymore."

"Why not?"

"You'll need to speak to the convention administrator."

Becky walked into the administrator's office, who had a copy of *Gadfly* open on his desk. Apparently, someone had taken a red pen and circled every objectionable word he could find.

"I'm sorry, Rebecca," the administrator said. "Some patrons to the convention find the information in your magazine offensive. There are objectionable words throughout. We've read your publication thoroughly and cannot find one redeeming article in the whole issue."

Becky explained the purpose behind the magazine. "We're not trying to specifically reach Christians," she said. "We're trying to open dialogue with artists and people of pop culture."

"I understand that," the administrator replied, "but this magazine has no place at NRB."

The first I heard of this was when my phone rang that morning.

"Hi, Mr. Whitehead. This is Becky."

"How's it going?" I asked cheerfully.

"We've suffered our first frontal attack. We've been censored. They won't let us display *Gadfly*."

My heart sank. This type of thinking is what Francis Schaeffer called "the great evangelical disaster." Evangelicals are fearful of anything that appears intellectual. The tragedy in all this is that we won't reach the kid who listens to Marilyn Manson by using a sanitized approach. There is biblical warrant for this: Jesus spoke Greek because that was the language the people of His day understood. Today, most evangelical Christians speak a language that sounds foreign to modern culture. The NRB board was playing right into this.

Our lawyers believed we could have fought the NRB and won, but I decided not to pursue it. Frankly, I didn't want to waste my time.

Becky dutifully stashed the remaining copies behind a black curtain, but word soon leaked out about a renegade banned magazine. Within hours, numerous people were regularly stepping behind the drapes, leaving with copies in hand. Becky stayed true to our directions—she didn't hand out a single copy. But she didn't stop anyone from sneaking their own copies, either!

Any pioneering work that challenges the evangelical community to think will inevitably be attacked—but that is by no means a badge of shame. Christ's teaching was so thoroughly cutting-edge that the religious authorities of His day had Him put to death.

The Calm Before the Storm

After finishing my work on the video series back in 1997, I was ready for a break. My four boys and I climbed into our Chevy Blazer and drove out to Fairmount, Indiana, where James Dean grew up and is buried. All my boys have seen his movies. Although Dean was born about ten miles away in Marion, Fairmount has become a mecca for people of all sorts, from Bob Dylan to actor Dennis Hopper.

It was good to get away for a couple of weeks, and I felt refreshed when we got back. "It's been an unusually quiet summer, don't you think?" I asked Carol late in August.

"It certainly has," she said. "I wonder how long it will last."

The usual controversies that followed my work at TRI just hadn't erupted.

However, within thirty days I would be sucked into a political, legal, and media wind tunnel, the likes of which I had never experienced before and probably never will again.

(Courtesy of Glass Onion Productions, Inc.)

(Courtesy of Glass Onion Productions, Inc.)

In a Boston studio filming *Grasping for the Wind*
(June 1996)

CHAPTER 18

There is something in corruption which, like a jaundiced eye, transfers the color of itself to the object it looks upon, and sees everything stained and impure.

—*Thomas Paine*

Carol and I went out to dinner in late November to celebrate a profile of me that appeared in *Time* magazine.

"This is great," Carol said, reaching across the table and taking both of my hands into hers.

Carol had walked with me through many years of "just getting by," speaking in small, out-of-the-way churches and being sent home with barely enough money to buy gas. Our work had been underfunded and underappreciated by evangelicals for many years. Throughout it all, the greatest nemesis we faced was apathy.

In this day and age, if you don't get the attention of the media, your work goes virtually unnoticed. It's interesting that while Hillary Clinton was debating whether to run for the Senate, a major factor affecting her decision, according to her associates, was which position would garner the most media attention. An article in the March 15, 1999 issue of *USA Today* said,

[Aides] say [Hillary] has little interest in the options once thought to be her future: heading a college or foundation or accepting lucrative appointments to corporate boards. She is said to believe such positions would thrust her straight into obscurity.

Nor does she want to travel the world speaking out on issues such as women's rights. Although she has relished those opportunities over the past six years, they have brought her limited attention from the news media. As a former first lady, friends say, she fears she'd get none.

Aides say she has come to believe that only as a senator could she command the national spotlight.

I had been working on behalf of religious rights for two decades, but it wasn't until the Paula Jones case that the major media started paying attention. The article in *Time* (November 24, 1997) did an excellent job of putting our struggle into context.

Time writer Jay Branegan wrote, "The Institute pioneered the tactic of using constitutional free-speech guarantees as a legal weapon for people, claiming they were denied the right to religious expression— a frequently successful court strategy now imitated by other religious-rights advocacy groups."

Most of the article focused on me and my views. "Whitehead has a reputation for following his own path. By standards of the religious right, he qualifies as a bit of a cultural maverick."

It might have taken decades for the media to take notice of the work I was doing, if they ever did. Once the coverage started, though, from early in the morning until late at night, I was swamped with media requests. It never let up. Practically every news agency, from the BBC to Greek television, wanted an interview. A French news program actually offered TRI a considerable sum of money for the phone on which Ron Rissler received the calls from the anonymous "X" concerning Monica Lewinsky!

Though many evangelicals have been suspicious and even hostile toward the media (one well-known Christian ministry frequently demands "quote approval" before it will grant an interview with its founder), I came to have great respect for what is often called "the fourth estate." *Time*'s Jay Branegan, the *New York Times*'s Neil Lewis, CBS's Phil Jones, the *Washington Post*'s Peter Baker, and National Public Radio's Chitra Ragavan, among others, distinguished themselves with insightful, accurate reports.

It was by no means all pleasant, however. In fact, when Bob Bennett, President Clinton's attorney, went on the *Larry King Live* show on January 9, 1998, he unleashed a barrage of criticism that marked the White House's early spin or strategy of trying to discredit me in the public eye. This is what he said:

KING: Who is this Rutherford group?

BENNETT: Well, that's interesting, Larry. I'm trying to find out the few dimensions of that, to tell you the truth. They are, in my view, a reasonably extreme organization who are financing Paula Jones's lawsuit. The critical point which I don't think anyone really appreciates is, the American taxpayer is financing Paula Jones's lawsuit and that is because The Rutherford Institute is paying her legal expenses.

KING: And they can deduct that as a . . .

BENNETT: That's tax deductible dollars. I'll be accused now, of having said that in answer to your question, of causing them problems. That's not my point. I believe they are a conduit of funds that want to hurt the President. Why would an organization whose fundamental mission deals with the Constitution and religious liberties be financing this lawsuit? Larry, I pulled in preparation for tonight their filing in the state of Washington with the Secretary of State.

KING: For tax purposes?

BENNETT: Yes, and their tax-exempt status, and here is what they say. They say The Rutherford Institute's purpose for existence is to assist in securing legal services in helping people for the violation of their constitutional rights as religious people. They say they want to preserve free speech in the public arena, protect the right of churches, defend parental rights and family autonomy, support the sanctity of life, and assist individuals who are oppressed for their beliefs in proletarian countries. I don't know where Paula Jones . . .

KING: This statement could have been issued by Billy Graham.

BENNETT: I'm not sure. It could have.

KING: The separation of church and state.

BENNETT: No, no, I think Billy Graham could have issued that statement, but I'm sure Billy Graham would not issue that statement and then finance Paula's lawsuit.

KING: You make this as just "We hate Clinton, we are out to get him."

BENNETT: Oh, I don't have any, I don't have any question about it.

BENNETT: [on a settlement] Now, the second reason I don't think it will settle is 'cause I don't think Paula Jones herself is political, is that organizations like The Rutherford Institute, which is probably, and I am trying to find out but they're resisting giving me the information, is probably a conduit of other extremist money and they are not paying hundreds of thousands of dollars for there to be a quiet settlement.

As my staff and I read various reports and listened to administration friends and officials talk on radio and television, it became readily apparent to us that the White House has a group of people whose job is to spin and attack and ultimately destroy whoever is perceived as the current political opponent. Believe it or not, this is what some of our tax dollars are spent on.

Bennett was the first one who tried to demonize me, but many more would follow. James Carville and other Clinton supporters even implied that I was a Nazi supporter. At a social gathering, I was finally able to talk to Dee Dee Myers, who had once been Clinton's chief spokesperson.

"What's with James Carville?" I asked her. "What motivates him to say these things? Is it money? Power?"

"No, it's simply good strategy," Myers responded.

"It's good strategy to demonize people and even lie about them?"

"Hey, it works," she said with a shrug.

That's when I realized that for the White House, morality held little sway. They didn't care whether what James Carville and other spin meisters were saying was either moral or even true. For them, it was simply a matter of good strategy. If discrediting an honest man works, then do it. Search and destroy someone's reputation, if necessary.

Shortly after I became involved in representing Paula Jones, some of the reporters who regularly travel with Clinton warned me, "Watch out, when you get Clinton on the ropes, he's one of the best political counterpunchers who has ever lived. The more he's under attack, the better he is."

It was about this time—December of 1997—that I came across the government vehicle on my property, which was parked conspicuously and deliberately as a warning, if not a threat. Although the van never reappeared, our private investigator, who has worked with the FBI, said it was clearly an attempt at intimidation.

I soon realized there was little the president's administration wouldn't do to win this case and prepared myself for a rough road ahead. I wasn't about to be passive. I was prepared to fight back.

Open House

The president's team turned up the heat by serving me with a notice of deposition and demanded access to TRI's donor list. This was a brazen act of intimidation. It is very rare for lawyers to depose lawyers, and in this case the tactic was clearly designed to hurt TRI and me. If donors found out that the government knew exactly who had given to us and how much, many would be less inclined to continue giving. (In fact, during the Jones case, several potential donors told me they didn't want to donate to TRI for fear of an IRS audit.)

The argument concocted by the White House was that TRI was a group funded by wealthy right-wing people who wanted to bring President Clinton down (which certainly was not the case). Our response was that this request was clearly unconstitutional. The Supreme Court has long recognized that revelations about donors and membership in advocacy groups is a violation of the First Amendment right of association.

However, I still wanted to demonstrate to the White House, Bob Bennett, and the media that we did not have anything to hide. Our resistance to the subpoena was based on principle, not fear. With the help of Nisha Mohammed, TRI's media coordinator, we prepared a rather dramatic way of doing this.

In mid-January, we held an open house for the media. As our press release stated, "The Rutherford Institute has nothing to hide. We invite all interested members of the media to come have lunch with us and talk about whatever interests them." I made sure that Bob Bennett got a special copy of this release. In essence, I was telling him that we were willing to let everybody see our records except him and the president!

All the major television networks and print media showed up. I explained why I was resisting the White House attempt to depose me and obtain our records. We served lunch and gave the media a tour of our offices, including our financial department, so they could see how TRI operates.

The event was a total success, leading to some very positive relationships with the media that remain intact to this day. And we owe it all to Bob Bennett!

Realizing, however, that we had a legal nuclear warhead aimed directly at us, I believed it was essential to solicit help from other legal groups. I wrote Nadine Strossen, who heads the ACLU, and explained what the president's lawyers were trying to do to us—the same thing they could subsequently do to the ACLU.

"If successful, the current attempt by the attorneys for the president will set a disastrous precedent for the activities not only of The Rutherford Institute, but also of the ACLU and other similar organizations," I wrote. "Under such a precedent, the next controversial case the ACLU files against a powerful individual or group could also be met by an attempt to examine the ACLU's eligibility for tax exemption or other governmental benefits."

Shortly thereafter, the ACLU filed a brief on our behalf, arguing that by trying to gain access to our records, the White House was violating TRI's First Amendment rights. I had always respected the ACLU, although our views differ on various issues, but gained even more respect for them because they helped us when we needed it. No evangelical groups even offered to help us. In fact, one leading evangelical legal group told us it couldn't help us for fear of an IRS audit.

With the ACLU backing us, Bob Bennett saw that we had dug in for a fight. He offered a settlement that we found acceptable. On January 14, 1998, we handed over all TRI publications that referred to Bill Clinton and a few other items that were already in the public record. They didn't get the giving records of a single donor.

We had won.

In the end, however, Bob Bennett got his revenge. My old classmate, Susan Webber Wright, who was the presiding judge in the Paula Jones case, was not impressed with my refusal of Bennett's subpoena. This made her predisposed to grant Bennett's motion to have me excluded from the president's deposition on January 17, 1998.

At first, I was incensed and determined to fight this. Don Campbell, however, thought otherwise.

"John, I think we might be able to win this thing, and I'm asking you not to fight it. We don't need a hostile judge."

"Okay," I responded. "I won't fight it."

I truly did want to give Paula Jones the best chance of prevailing in her lawsuit.

Ironically, though much of the nation was tuned in on January 17 to the fact of the president's deposition, Carol and I scarcely had time to give it any thought at all. We were in New Orleans, attending a conference put on by the National Association of Television Program Executives, to promote my video series, *Grasping for the Wind.*

It wasn't until the next week, when I got back to the office, that I was able to read the deposition for myself. Many of the president's answers were an embarrassment for an intelligent man: He "may have seen Monica" or "maybe he popped his head around the corner when she was present," for example. What struck me was that the man whose memory I knew as particularly strong suddenly couldn't recall things that had taken place only months earlier. Amazingly, more than 260 times during his deposition, the president said his memory failed him.

In hindsight, we now know why. The truth was too dangerous to admit. Clinton knew that if anything surfaced, he would be faced with a terrible choice—perjure himself, or risk political annihilation. A very real fear of Clinton during this time was Ken Starr's pursuit of him. In fact, Starr's work in getting Monica Lewinsky to go on record challenging many of the president's assertions and making many of them appear to be deliberate lies eventually caused Clinton great political embarrassment. One thing is clear, however. It is inconceivable, with what we know now, that Clinton could never remember whether he was alone with Monica in the Oval Office.

As I look back, I believe that the impeachment proceedings could have been avoided if Clinton had told the truth during this deposition or settled with Paula Jones earlier on. Our team made it clear that, prior to this deposition, we were willing to settle. Dick Morris, one of the president's former advisers, has said that Hillary was adamantly opposed to such a settlement. Rejecting this option proved to be a costly mistake and a curious one, as we now know that Bill Clinton knew exactly what was hanging in the balance, just waiting to be exposed. His decision to go to trial was by all accounts a reckless one.

Friendly Foes

At the very beginning of the media onslaught, I had to make an important decision. Would I fear the media? Was I going to hide from reporters?

I quickly decided that I would look reporters straight in the eye and be honest and as forthcoming as legal constraints would allow. I also decided to treat every newspaper, and every reporter, the same. I would give quotes to the *New York Times* and *Wall Street Journal* as well as to my own hometown newspaper, the *Culpeper Star-Exponent*. This attitude—that I would speak the truth, whatever the cost— proved to be far more costly than I originally thought, though the consequences were from the camps we least expected.

While in New Orleans, I was awakened by a telephone call from my son Jayson.

"Dad, you won't believe it," he said. "The *Washington Post* has a long feature on you with several large photographs. It's amazing coverage."

Megan Rosenfeld, a seasoned reporter for the *Post*, had covered the Watergate hearings and profiled some of the bigger names in Washington, D.C. A few weeks earlier, she had sat in front of me with her notepad and tape recorder. As I've already said, I was determined to answer each question candidly.

"What do you think about homosexuals?" she asked me. "Especially how Christians are responding to them?"

"I believe a great majority of evangelicals are out to lunch on the subject," I said. "Christ would not have been that way . . . Homophobia is wrong."

Being an astute reporter, Megan knew exactly where I was coming from and framed my words correctly. Her article said, "[Noting that] he still thinks homosexuality is wrong, [he believes] one must have compassion for people with AIDS, just as Jesus Christ reached out to lepers."

Several days later, Robert Knight of the Family Research Council called me, saying he was appalled at my comments in the *Post*. "How could you attack the brethren?" he said.

"It's easy," I replied. "When I think anyone is wrong and I'm asked, I'll say so."

"You're helping the homosexual agenda," he retorted.

"If reaching out to homosexuals in compassion helps their agenda—whatever it may be—I guess I'm doing it. That's what Jesus did. He wasn't afraid to eat with people the Pharisees called sinners. He touched lepers when everyone else said they were unclean. Frankly, sir, I think you're wrong, and your attitude will never win a soul to Christ."

At this, Knight became irate and the conversation ended.

Thereafter, the *Washington Post* article was circulated to conservative Christians throughout the country. Soon, I was under a constant barrage of criticism from evangelical groups over my position on homosexuals. Quotes were taken out of context, often leading me to be attacked for something I didn't even believe. Of course, all one had to do was read what I actually said to see that these statements were not true. But it was clear that I had accurately diagnosed a serious problem in evangelicalism—homophobia (a fear of homosexuals) had replaced the compassion of Christ.

This type of attitude has had disastrous consequences on our nation. Though our country was founded in part on Judeo-Christian principles, there is virtually no semblance of Christianity in today's major social institutions and popular culture. After all the crusades and pleas by televangelists over the airwaves, Christianity has less impact now than at any time in our nation's history, for one simple reason: We have stopped practicing true Christianity. With all the modern communications at our disposal, the message of Christ has become buried in the medium, leaving much of evangelicalism with an inauthentic faith that bears little resemblance to the servant-based, hope-giving, grace-filled gospel of Jesus Christ. Christ reached out to those in need; those who call themselves Christians must be willing to do the same.

I felt squeezed in the middle. Those on the right were saying, "He's a traitor. He's Judas, betraying all of us!" Those on the left were equally vehement: "He's a right-wing nut! He's insane!"

And then Hillary Rodham Clinton stepped into the fray.

Shooting the Messenger

Of all the tragedies that came out of the Clinton-Jones-Lewinsky scandal, perhaps the saddest was the drama played out behind the scenes, in the First Family. When the Lewinsky story first broke, Clinton (according to an article in *Vanity Fair*) pulled Chelsea out of college during finals week to provide a positive photo opportunity for the press, framing the president as a "family man."

Most openly aggrieved, of course, was Hillary, who "stood by her man" through numerous allegations. Hillary even went on the *Today* show and vocally attacked TRI, labeling us part of the "vast right-wing conspiracy" that was out to destroy her husband.

Ironically, few evangelicals were willing to defend me at this point. My most vociferous advocate was a leftist, Nat Hentoff, who writes for the *Village Voice*. Nat is a self-proclaimed atheist, but has more integrity and honesty about him than any evangelical I know. In response to Hillary's charges, Nat wrote:

A target of . . . Mrs. Clinton has been The Rutherford Institute in Charlottesville, Virginia, headed by John Whitehead. On his invitation, I have lectured before some of his lawyers and have written in the *Post* on a number of Rutherford's court cases . . . And much of the time, the Rutherford forces legitimately prevent the state from suppressing individual religious expressions.

But although Whitehead has become rather notorious for financially supporting the Paula Jones case, neither the print press nor television has bothered to look into the actual work of The Rutherford Institute . . . Accordingly, the Institute's name has conspiratorial overtones to many. And once the White House gets around to expanding Mrs. Clinton's conspiracy membership, there I am with connections to John Whitehead.

Nat's defense shocked many people on the left, but it showed his integrity—a trait sorely lacking in many of those on the right who should have been coming to our defense.

Another angry critic was Geraldo Rivera. Though he had never met me, Geraldo initially made me sound like evil personified.

Rivera Lively

Geraldo Rivera was an avid supporter of the president and seemed blinded—at least early on—by his partisanship. At TRI, we received several calls alleging that Geraldo had bought into the White House political spin that TRI was a right-wing group out to get Clinton. Consequently, Rivera attacked us unmercifully.

"They're using taxpayer funds to get at the president!" he railed. (By this, he was referring to our status as a nonprofit, tax-exempt public advocacy group. We did not actually receive any tax money to support our work, but people who contribute to us are able to claim a tax deduction for doing so.)

Once again, I was determined not to be "afraid" of the media. Instead of crying "foul" and using Geraldo's attacks to raise money, we decided to call his producer and ask for an opportunity to respond to Rivera's comments.

I appeared on his program on Monday, January 19, 1998, fully prepared to do battle. Geraldo is a tough interviewer, and I knew he didn't like me. In fact, he lit into me right away, saying he was angry that TRI was a tax-deductible group. But I was ready:

WHITEHEAD: You know what, it shouldn't make you angry. It doesn't make me angry that the ACLU is a tax-exempt organization . . . The ACLU has defended Nazis and the Ku Klux Klan. I think that's great. This is America. This is freedom, and it's tax exempt. Without groups like The Rutherford Institute, the NAACP, the American Civil Liberties Union, the American Jewish Committee and all these groups that we work with. . . The ACLU just filed a brief on our behalf. We work with the ACLU. They know how important what we do is.

RIVERA: I don't care what your motive is. All I care is that for every dollar deducted, thirty-five cents is lost to the federal Treasury. That means, despite my feeling on your lawsuit, my mother, Jimmy who is directing us, Barney who sits alongside me, anyone else, if they are all contributing to your lawsuit, many think it's brought by partisans, for partisan reasons which may or may not be true. I get angry that I have to participate in your action.

WHITEHEAD: Well, you can be angry about it. And that's great you are angry because we're in America, you have freedom to be angry and we protect that.

RIVERA: You'll represent my rights if need be?

WHITEHEAD: Exactly. Can I say one thing? Anytime that you want, you can bring your cameras into my office. We had open day for the press two weeks ago because people were saying, "Well, what do you do?" So we bothered to show them the room where the money comes in. We are a group that has a $3.7 million a year budget. We have 248 cases in the courts on all different kinds of issues. We spend our money on these people protecting their rights. Now I got people telling me, "I'm angry because you happen to be on a case where the president is involved." But I'm more concerned about the principle here.

RIVERA: John, the only beef I have is that you give people a tax deduction, and you are probably right. My beef should be with the IRS. Tell me why you have taken this lawsuit.

WHITEHEAD: Now, why we took the lawsuit was the same as it was in any of our cases. Again, we have 248 going on right now.

RIVERA: Would you stop there right now? On your honor, what percentage of your activities are going to the other 248 as opposed to or compared to this one?

WHITEHEAD: I couldn't tell you in percentages, but I would say . . .

RIVERA: Is it not fair to assume that the vast majority of your attention is now focused on the Paula Jones case?

WHITEHEAD: Not the vast majority. No. In fact . . .

RIVERA: The simple majority?

WHITEHEAD: Well, whatever majority you want to say, but there is no majority here. Most of my time is spent on programs like this explaining why or wondering why people are attacking President Clinton.

RIVERA: I think when you bring a lawsuit on behalf of football players who only want to say a prayer after the game, I'm with you. I'm with you. That is righteous, and it should be tax deductible. But when it gets above in this world of politics, that's where I think people should pay the damn tax.

WHITEHEAD: Can I say one thing? We didn't get involved with this for politics. It's a legal case to us, and do not damn The Rutherford Institute because of one case out of 248.

After that show, I appeared on *Rivera Live* regularly. And within a month, Geraldo was introducing me as "my friend." One time, he even introduced me by saying, "I really respect The Rutherford Institute because they believe in what they do." On another occasion, after Geraldo and I had a particularly hot debate, he closed the show by saying, "I think you're a pit bull. I hope you take that as a compliment."

I learned a valuable lesson. Square up, be honest, don't compromise, and media personalities, even those like Geraldo Rivera who start out hating you, will eventually respect you. In turn, I also learned to respect Geraldo.

Larry King Live

On January 30, 1998, I was asked to appear on *Larry King Live*, the very show on which Bob Bennett unleashed the demonizing strategy against me. I found Larry to be a genuinely fair, decent human being, both on and off the air. After asking about some of the particulars surrounding the case, King began to delve into my personal views:

KING: Your reaction to the fact that this president has now exceeded Ronald Reagan's popularity rating, with a 68 today. It was 58 a week ago.

WHITEHEAD: Well, I said before, I wear two hats in this case. I wear the hat of a citizen. As a citizen, I find the whole situation as tragic. I'd be in that 68 percent if I was polled and said the president is doing a good job. There is no doubt about that. As a lawyer, I must pursue my case. And as most people don't know, I knew Bill Clinton when he was at the University of Arkansas . . .

KING: You are not a right-wing radical now, are you?

WHITEHEAD: No, I am not a right-wing radical. I fall down on both sides, left and right.

KING: Do you think the right-wing radicals have hurt their own cause by knocking Clinton so much?

WHITEHEAD: Yeah, I think that the broadside attacks on Bill Clinton are a mistake. I think strategically they're bad mistakes because obviously most people are satisfied with the man's job so it's hard to knock it. To be really honest, if you look at the man right in the face, the job he is doing, it's hard to knock him.

KING: When someone, therefore, is popular and his plans are popular and the people are happy with him, doesn't it make it tough for a jury? You are going to have to pick a jury. Let's say Paula Jones goes to trial. You have to pick a jury that probably is all working and pretty happy.

WHITEHEAD: Well, that's been obvious. A lot of commentators have commented on that. How do you get a fair trial when you have a president involved in a case?

KING: A popular president.

WHITEHEAD: A popular president. If he is popular at that time. We don't know this. The evidence is still out. You know the public can go up and down. It is very, very difficult. This case—I believe we've got a good case based on the evidence, but when you get in a courtroom, it may be a different thing.

I had the opportunity to appear on Larry King's show several times and always found his questions to be fair and honest. And respect for TRI in the media continued to grow.

Johnny-Come-Lately?

In concert with initial media reactions were attacks that struck me as entirely misdirected. After having voiced my support of Anita Hill and her claims of sexual harassment against Clarence Thomas when he was a Supreme Court nominee, Anita and other feminists refused to follow suit and support us when "one of their own" was threatened. Instead of attacking the man accused of blatant discriminatory behavior against a female subordinate, the women's groups attacked me!

Patricia Ireland, president of the National Organization for Women, essentially called us "Johnny-come-latelys." In an open letter to Ireland, which was disseminated to the national press, I wrote:

> The truth, then, is that [The Rutherford] Institute has been actively involved in women's issues for more than sixteen years, and it is the abortion issue that motivates NOW to so vehemently attack the Institute. NOW sacrificed Paula Jones to its abortion agenda, and it is difficult for NOW to live with the fact that the Institute filled the void NOW itself created. Had NOW done its job free of politics and come to Jones's assistance, the Institute would not have had to do so. NOW has demeaned and humiliated a woman seeking her day in court because it was unwilling even to foster an appearance that NOW would in any manner be in opposition to Bill Clinton's own political agenda. In this sense, NOW has become the pawn of White House politics. NOW is thus desperate to find a plausible cover for its actions.
>
> In the process, NOW has trampled on the right to a jury, the right to have one's day in court, and the right to sexual integrity regardless of the identity of the predator or the victim. NOW has now taken the lead in politicizing one woman's fight for sexual integrity in the workplace. That this should happen to even one woman is unacceptable. It is unfortunate that NOW has abandoned the

moral high ground in favor of politics. The Rutherford Institute will not follow suit.

Patricia Ireland did not respond to me. Shortly after my open letter, the producers of Larry King's show wanted to stage a debate between Ireland and myself.

"I'll go on anytime, anywhere," I promised, but the producers said they were "unable to find a time when both of you could be on together." The blatant hypocrisy of the women's groups and the absolute disintegration of their integrity in the wake of these charges was one of the more frustrating aspects of working on this case. Essentially, the liberal women's groups made a decision to abandon sexual harassment in favor of abortion rights.

Juggling the demands of the media, the attacks of the president's supporters, and the underhanded barbs thrown by liberal groups and conservative evangelicals alike was one thing, but we also had to learn how to handle Paula's spokeswoman, Susan Carpenter-McMillan, which became one of the most difficult struggles of all.

The "Protector"

"She said what?" I asked.

Nisha, my media coordinator, shook her head in disbelief. "According to this reporter, Susan Carpenter-McMillan told the media that she and Paula looked for the lawyers with the best legs."

"That cannot be true," I moaned. "You cannot talk that way to the media when you're trying to win a sexual harassment case!"

Susan Carpenter-McMillan, Paula Jones's self-appointed spokeswoman, is a petite woman who took Paula "under her wing," so to speak, teaching her how to dress, apply makeup, and, ostensibly, handle the media.

The thing is that I believe Paula, with the proper support person, could have handled the media better on her own. Certainly, Carpenter-

McMillan's attempts to address Paula's appearance proved helpful—the big hair and heavy makeup needed to go in this media-savvy age—but this transformation came at a price. Susan took a lot of the "small-town girl" out of Paula, a personality that, in the long run, would have been much more appealing to most people than a savvy, street-smart woman who knew how to dress for the camera and always had a sound bite ready for the press.

Nisha soon discovered that Susan's relationships with men differed dramatically from her dealings with women. To men, in Nisha's words, Susan could be "sweet, simpering, and vulnerable." With women, an entirely different character emerged.

After the flare-up about Susan's statement regarding how the lawyers were chosen, Nisha and I knew we needed to control the media from our office. We simply could not afford to be sideswiped with statements that hurt or undermined our case.

Nisha drafted a letter to Susan, with a copy to me. "We need to be aware of what is being said," Nisha wrote. "We certainly don't want to make sexually suggestive remarks in a sexual harassment case."

A few days later, a somewhat flustered Nisha entered my office.

"Well," she said, "Carpenter-McMillan responded."

"And?"

"She blew her top. She ranted, she raved, and she accused me of treating her like a child."

Initially, this was surprising to me, as I had seen no indication of hostility in my previous dealings with Carpenter-McMillan.

The situation was exacerbated by the fact that the public relations onslaught of this case was an entirely new ball game for us. Some days, I spent between eighteen and twenty hours trying to satisfy the media's requests. I got to know some reporters so well that they even tipped us off on late-breaking developments. In fact, many developments happened so quickly that we sometimes learned of them only when we were asked to comment on them.

We were determined to project a consistent message: "This is not about politics. This is about sexual harassment. This is about one woman's right to be free to work without having to endure unwanted advances."

Both Susan and Nisha fought it out over media relations. Susan thought that the media were her specialty, but I felt that her wise-cracking method was making things worse. Ultimately, it was about who won the case, and I didn't want any comments that would jeopardize Paula Jones's day in court.

Eventually, Susan refused to talk to Nisha. When Nisha called her, Susan forcefully responded, "I won't talk to you. I'll only talk to John."

"Susan," I said, "we're not going to go down that road. Nisha is coordinating our media, and she needs to be involved in any phone calls that address this."

It was just one more hurdle to overcome in a case that was getting more bizarre by the minute.

About-Face

In late January of 1998, I got a call from someone close to the Clinton administration. "You're driving them crazy at the White House," she said. "They can't get a handle on you."

She thought it was hilarious watching the Clintonites "work over-time" to discredit me but not be successful in their efforts to tag me as a right-wing extremist—especially after the *Washington Post* article appeared, which accurately profiled me and the Institute's work.

In February 1998, the White House strategy suddenly changed. Lanny Davis, Special Counsel to the president (*USA Today* once described him as the president's "scandal spokesman"), had opposed me in a particularly nasty way for weeks. He claimed I was a demon in the flesh, a zealot out to get the president, a maniac determined to "overthrow two elections."

Then, virtually overnight, Davis started calling me a "really fine lawyer."

After a joint interview with Davis, Lanny even asked me, "Hey John, need a ride back to your hotel?"

Lanny was driving a Jaguar.

"No, thanks," I said. The attacks had been so vicious, there was no way I was going to get into an unknown vehicle! I needed to see more than changed rhetoric before I'd trust my life to that group.

When I talked about this surprise turnaround with a few knowledgeable people, their explanation made perfect sense: "The spin didn't work, so the White House had to change its strategy," they explained. "The way this administration does that is to pretend the original strategy never happened."

I survived the media assault, in part because I knew it would be temporary. I knew the media attention would eventually go away. For a while, I was recognized everywhere I went and was often stopped on the street or in airports and given verbal expressions of support. I could have been on radio or television practically twenty-four hours a day. There was hardly a newspaper in the country that didn't have my name in it several times a week, if not daily.

"It'll end," I kept telling Carol. "It can't go on forever."

I didn't want to fall into the media trap. TRI and I were pursuing other cases and concerns, as well as doing promotional work for *Grasping for the Wind*. The Paula Jones lawsuit did not, and would not, define us.

But it certainly would bring many additional battles in the days ahead.

In my office at The Rutherford Institute with Clinton mask
and assorted toys my kids have given me

Surrounded by reporters, including CNN's Bob Franken, outside
the D.C. Federal Courthouse (January 27, 1998)

CHAPTER 19

And what rough beast, its hour come round at last,
Slouches toward Bethlehem to be born?
—*William Butler Yeats*
The Second Coming

It was January 22, 1998, 6:00 A.M.—much too early for the telephone to be ringing. Carol and I had put in a long stretch the previous day in New Orleans, standing on the floor of one of the world's biggest television and video conventions (NATPE) talking to people about *Grasping for the Wind*.

"John, are you awake?" the gruff voice said.

I always thought that was a silly question. If I wasn't awake, how could I have answered the phone?

"Yeah, who's this?"

"It's Campbell, John. I'm calling from Dallas. We have a chance to take Monica Lewinsky's deposition tomorrow. We can do it in Washington. I want you to help."

Don Campbell never called me for small talk. In our sixteen-year friendship, this wiry Texan had never once engaged in anything but legal conversations or good-natured joking. He wouldn't ask me to be there unless he thought it was important, and I wanted to do everything in my power to assist him.

"We'll have to check on flights, but we should be in our D.C. office by this afternoon," I told him. The deposition was scheduled to begin the next day at 9:00 A.M.

Don told me what hotel he would be staying at, and we planned to rendezvous early that evening. Carol quickly called the airline, and within a few hours we were on a plane headed to Washington, D.C.

Don and I wanted to know the answers to a lot of questions about Monica's meetings at the White House, gifts she had received from the president, and meetings Lewinsky had with presidential adviser Vernon Jordan, among other things. Her answers were important to our case. We were trying to show that there was a pattern of conduct by the president with women that would corroborate Paula Jones's allegations that Bill Clinton had sexually harassed her.

The pattern was definitely there. Among other things, both Paula and Monica were in their early twenties when a sexual relationship was proposed; both had been government workers; both were asked to perform oral sex. But where Paula declined, Monica would say that she had initiated the contact, later engaging in oral sex with the president on numerous occasions. And where Monica received favors for sex, Paula complained that she was treated differently at work after she refused Clinton during the hotel incident.

The cold Washington, D.C., wind slapped us in the face as we got in the taxi at the airport and headed to TRI's D.C. office. Numerous reporters and television cameras were already set up outside our building on Fifteenth Street. In the hallway, more were waiting and would wait overnight, expecting Monica Lewinsky to walk through our office door. Don arrived around five o'clock that afternoon, and we met in his hotel room. As we reviewed our notes for several hours in preparation for the next day's deposition of Monica Lewinsky, Don received a call from one of the attorneys in his firm. I listened in on the extension. "You're not going to like this. I just got off the telephone with Judge Wright and the president's lawyers. Judge Wright just ruled that we cannot depose Monica Lewinsky."

We were both stunned. Ken Starr, the independent prosecutor who had been dogging the Clintons for years, had filed a motion in our case to stay all proceedings with Monica Lewinsky. We never thought for a moment that Judge Wright would agree or that she would take the further step of excluding all Lewinsky-related evidence completely. Taking a key witness away would greatly hamper our case.

The next morning, Don and I climbed over reporters to get in the door of our small D.C. office. We knew we would have to make a statement. Virtually every television channel was covering the event live. As I stepped in front of a CNN camera to talk to veteran reporter Bob Franken, I got the feeling that we had turned some kind of corner in this case. What concerned me was that I didn't know if what was waiting around that corner was good or bad.

Events soon unraveled at astonishing speed.

Starr Witness

No sooner had I returned to my hotel room that night than I got another call.

"Chief, I've got some interesting news for you," Steve Aden, a TRI attorney working with us on the Paula Jones case, said. "I don't know how you're going to take this. But Ken Starr's office has subpoenaed The Rutherford Institute."

"What do they want? Does Starr want me to testify? Does he want records? What?" I asked. I was ready to believe anything at this point.

"Starr doesn't want you to testify," Steve said. "But he does want every record related to Paula Jones and President Clinton to be delivered to the grand jury. That's a big load."

"We have a tough decision to make, Steve. I don't like all this meddling in our case. But at the same time, I don't want to defy a federal prosecutor empowered by the courts and Janet Reno. I need time to think. I'll call you later."

What to do? It was a big decision. My initial response was to fight the subpoena. But did I really want to risk being held in contempt over records that Starr was undoubtedly going to get his hands on anyway? After consulting with other attorneys who advised me to comply, I decided to go ahead and deliver the documents.

I was scheduled to appear at the Federal District Courthouse in Washington, D.C., on January 27 to deliver the documents. From a half-block away, Carol and I could see the antennas on the television trucks. When our taxi pulled up in front of the courthouse, a throng of reporters converged on me. By now, my face was easily recognized by the media.

"John, is that the president's deposition in your briefcase?" one reporter yelled.

"Are you appearing before the grand jury?" another asked.

"I can answer questions when I come out," I said over my shoulder as microphones banged me in the head and video cameramen walked backwards, shooting my entrance into the courthouse.

Once inside, Carol and I breathed a sigh of relief as we went through the metal detector and up the elevator to where the United States Grand Jury meets.

I was met by two FBI agents who looked, well, like FBI agents—short haircuts, nondescript blue suits, and black shoes. They flashed their identification badges and led me to a federal marshal, to whom I delivered the documents under my control.

As I walked toward the elevator, reporters who had somehow gotten into the building tried to interview me. I was polite but firm. "Wait until I get outside, please."

Stepping into the cold January morning, I was soon engulfed by a throng of microphones, cameras, and aggressive reporters. I briefly read a statement, making it clear that I was delivering documents in compliance with the law. "That's why I'm here. Any questions?"

A reporter bellowed out, "How do you respond to Hillary Clinton's charge that you're part of a right-wing conspiracy to overthrow her husband?"

I smiled. "If Mrs. Clinton will give me a time, place, and date when the right-wing conspiracy meets, I'd be glad to help expose it so I can get on with my work without further questions about it."

The president had threatened action against Saddam Hussein several days before. So, of course, I was asked, "Do you think the president would start a war to divert attention from his legal problems?"

"Well," I said, "I've seen *Wag the Dog.*"

It wasn't long until the bombs started falling.

Allegations

While war began in Iraq, the legal battle continued at home. Our office began receiving numerous phone calls, mostly anonymous, providing tips about alleged Clinton activities. One anonymous caller claimed that Clinton, while governor, had a sexual encounter with a young woman he had met while jogging. There were several other tips, some of which seemed credible, though it was difficult to verify any of these stories to the extent that would be necessary if we wanted to make them part of our case. I'm convinced that two we followed up were true, though we ended up dropping our investigation, for reasons I'll explain in a moment. The first tip came in February 1998.

"I'm a close friend of an Air Force pilot who was attached to *Air Force One.*"

"And?" our attorney asked.

"The pilot told me that stewardesses on *Air Force One* were constantly being sexually harassed by President Clinton during 1993 and 1994."

The reason this was relevant and appropriate to our case is that all stewardesses on the president's plane are U.S. Air Force personnel, either enlisted or officers. Thus, all of them are technically under the commander-in-chief, making their ordeal very relevant to a lawsuit concerning on-the-job sexual harassment.

"My friend first told me about this in 1994," the caller explained. "He was outraged by Clinton's behavior."

The caller gave our attorney the name of the pilot, whom we immediately located and called. Unfortunately, the pilot refused to return our calls.

In desperation, we set up a meeting with a retired Air Force pilot who had flown *Air Force One* for several past presidents.

"You'll never get what you want," he told us. "The pilots of *Air Force One* are similar to Secret Service personnel. You'll never get them to speak about incidents aboard the president's plane unless you get a subpoena."

"Is there nothing else we can do?" our attorney asked. We didn't believe we had enough information to get a subpoena. Besides, by this time TRI was rather strapped for funds, and we felt it highly unlikely that after great expense and effort we'd get the pilot to talk anyway.

The retired officer sighed. "There are two men who might be able to help you. Both of them are Air Force officers, and one of them was a pilot for President Reagan."

As soon as he got back to the office, our attorney placed a call to the former pilot for President Reagan. His wife answered the phone.

"I'm one of the attorneys representing Paula Jones," he explained, "and we're following up a tip we received in this case informing us that President Clinton may have sexually harassed female personnel attached to *Air Force One*. We'd like to speak to your husband about it."

"The colonel is not available," she said firmly. After a short pause, she added, "Can I be candid with you?"

"Yes, of course."

"My husband has never, and will never, share with me or anyone else anything about what happens on *Air Force One*. He will take that information to his grave. Do I make myself clear?"

"Yes, ma'am, you do."

The wife said, "Fine," then hung up.

We waited two days and called the second pilot, whose name the retired officer had given us. It was evident, when we spoke to the wife of this pilot, that she had been previously warned about our inquiries. We were told that her husband was not available, although this was questionable.

Because of the negative responses, we determined to drop further inquiries.

The second tip that we believed credible came to us in August of 1998. A caller told us about an incident involving President Clinton at a country club in Maryland that had supposedly occurred earlier in the year. Keep in mind, in the spring and summer of 1998, Clinton was still involved in the Jones case and Independent Counsel Ken Starr was preparing his report to Congress. The scandal was still very much on people's minds, in spite of the president's denials.

Nevertheless, according to the caller, the president was still unable to rein in his libido. Approximately six to eight weeks prior to the telephone call, Clinton, we were told, after playing golf, had become "attracted" to a waitress in the clubhouse. Clinton allegedly contacted Vernon Jordan to see if Jordan could arrange a meeting.

When Jordan started asking questions at the golf club, the young woman realized that he was inquiring about her. She was both frightened and angry and spoke with an influential club member, who intervened on her behalf by addressing this with the owner of the club. Jordan was contacted and told to cease his inquiries or else risk termination of his club privileges. Furthermore, the owner warned, if this type of behavior continued, Clinton would no longer be allowed to use the golf course.

The last thing Clinton needed was another fresh, salacious story, so the inquiries were dropped.

After some investigation, we identified the scene of these events: the Maple Run Golf Course in Thurmont, Maryland. Upon further inquiry, we discovered that Clinton used the course eight to ten times in 1998, the last time in July 1998. Vernon Jordan also played the course. The last time Jordan and Clinton played the course together was in May 1998.

We determined not to pursue the head of the golf course, more out of concern for the young woman than for the president. We figured we would end up in the same situation as in the *Air Force One* debacle. We had good information, but probably not enough for a subpoena. Also, we weren't sure that uncovering this would build our case to any substantial degree.

There were so many similar accusations that we felt certain some of them had to be true. Financial resources and time constraints prohibited us from following up on every lead.

Personally, I was amazed that our president was leaving himself so vulnerable and acting so recklessly, even while the national spotlight was already focused on his Oval Office door. In the Starr Report, Lewinsky noted how Clinton tends to deny reality. He never expected to be held accountable—and, in a way, he wasn't. He got off again.

It was a bruising fight, but in the midst of it, I got the thrill of a lifetime—an opportunity to take a recess from the lies, allegations, and daily motions and attend a movie lover's ultimate dream: the 1998 Academy Awards.

Real People

There was a phone call from a friend who has worked in the movie industry. "I just got my application in the mail for lottery tickets for the Academy Awards," he told Carol. "Would you and John be interested in attending?"

"Absolutely!" Carol responded.

"It's not a certainty," our friend warned us. "Whether I get tickets—and where those tickets are—all depends on a lottery."

My friend was careful about raising false expectations, and I pretty much put the thought of attending out of my mind until he called back and said, "Good news! I got 'em! And they're great seats."

For a man who was raised on films, this was truly a dream come true. I rented a cheap tux, Carol bought an evening gown, and we bought our tickets for Los Angeles.

We arrived at the Shrine Auditorium early, just to make sure we didn't miss anything. There's a reception beforehand, with many of the industry people milling around. Waiters go around with food—in this instance, little pizzas—and wine so you can snack before the program begins.

Karl Malden was standing in a small group just a few feet away. I wanted to say something to him but was hesitant, not really sure about the proper etiquette. Clearly, many ambitious people were "working" the room. You could see the aspiration in their eyes as the lesser-knowns flattered the well-connected producers, executives, directors, and stars. There was a lot of hustling, cell phones, unnatural hugging—the type of phoniness I find very distasteful.

"Who are you?" a gentleman asked me. I didn't recognize him and he didn't recognize me, and I was caught off guard by his blatant introduction. Clearly he was thinking, "Is this someone I should know? Someone who could help advance my career?"

"I'm John Whitehead, a lawyer."

"John Whitehead, that sounds familiar," he began. I could see his mind working hard to place me. "You're not that Jones guy, are you?"

"Actually, I am," I said.

The man walked off without saying another word.

When we walked into the auditorium to take our seats, we found, much to our delight, that our host hadn't overestimated our seating arrangements. They were fantastic, about halfway back on the main level. In fact, we were just two seats down from Billy Zane, who played the "evil, rich" fiancé of Kate Winslet in *Titanic*. Zane sat next to Frances Fisher, who played Winslet's mother.

Attending in the flesh is a much different experience from watching the Academy Awards on television. During commercial breaks, the audience relaxes and the stars stand up and mill around. Then the host counts down as the television cameras are poised to rejoin the millions of viewers, and the doors are locked to prevent any distractions. It was amusing to see Jack Nicholson running for his seat and reaching it just before Billy Crystal welcomed the television audience back to the broadcast. And Sean Connery walked right by us.

As we talked with our friend and his wife a couple of weeks before the event, he said, "You know what's even better than being inside the awards ceremony? The *Vanity Fair* party. That's where you really get to see the stars up close."

Because of my connection to the Paula Jones case, Carol and I had actually been invited to this fete. Held in a small club, the *Vanity Fair* party is considered the hottest event in town.

Carol and I walked up to the party's very small room—about forty by one hundred feet—which was packed full of Hollywood's hottest stars. Fans lined the entrance, screaming out as their favorite stars walked by. I still couldn't believe we were going to be allowed in until the man at the door checked for our names on the list and motioned us forward.

The cream of Hollywood and the entertainment world was present. In one corner, Brad Pitt held court. People filed up to him, shaking his hand, making small talk. Madonna stood in the center of the room, talking with Ellen Degeneres and Anne Heche. Arnold Schwarzenegger was there with his wife, Maria Shriver. Billy Crystal and Robert Duvall were having a lively discussion, but Duvall's tall, young date looked bored.

In person, many of Hollywood's leading men are surprisingly small in stature, yet a number of them (especially the executives and directors) had far younger and taller dates—inevitably blonde-haired with obviously manufactured bodies. I don't know why, but you kind of expect the stars to be larger than life. When they turn out to be smaller than you, it's a shock! An almost completely bald, older man—probably at least eighty years old—who was no taller than five feet, five inches (in heels), walked by with a twentyish, six-foot-tall, statuesque blonde woman clinging to his arm.

"Only in Hollywood!" Carol and I said to each other.

There were a lot of hors d'oeuvres, champagne, and every imaginable kind of liquor, all free, but most of us had to eat standing up. There were only a few seats.

It was fascinating watching famous people in their natural habitat, many of them, such as Kim Basinger, fused to their newly won Oscar statuettes. Kate Winslet walked through in her *Titanic* gown. Later in the evening, Carol saw her in the ladies' room, and listened in as she talked about that famous dress.

Robin Williams entertained reporters as he made his way inside. The old sixties rebel, Tom Hayden, walked right by me. I wanted to go over and introduce myself to Oliver Stone and tell him how much I enjoyed his recent release *U Turn*, but thought better of it. Stone had his hands full with several women, and appeared to be quite intoxicated or high on something.

As I walked into the men's room, I saw Eric Idle of *Monty Python* fame doing a little jig in front of the urinal; he's a naturally funny guy, apparently all the time.

Back inside the room, Dee Dee Myers and her husband walked up to us and introduced themselves. We talked about the Jones case and the president's mounting troubles.

"Despite all his problems," Dee Dee said, "I'm still a true believer."

As we stood talking, a man moved toward me. I had never seen him before, but he walked right up to me, as if to fight, poked me in the chest with his fist, and said, "John Whitehead, you should be ashamed of yourself."

He then turned and departed as quickly as he had arrived.

I was stunned and looked at Dee Dee in disbelief.

"Don't worry about him," she laughed. "He's just acting up. He's harmless."

We stayed at the *Vanity Fair* party for more than four hours and left exhilarated by the night's magic. As I lay in bed that night, my mind kept returning to the same thought. Seeing the stars in their natural environment, without the press harassing them, they were simply normal people. Billy Zane wore a full head of hair in the blockbuster movie *Titanic*, but in person his head was shaved. Rod Steiger could barely descend a flight of stairs on his own. The celebrities certainly have more money than most of us and their faces are recognized worldwide, but inside they are just as small and fearful as the rest of us. And in the end, they will have to stand naked before the Maker, just as we will.

It was a night to remember, probably a once-in-a-lifetime experience, and a welcomed respite in the midst of a stormy case. As I finally drifted off to sleep, I had no idea of the legal bombshell that was about to drop from the office of my old classmate, Susan Webber Wright.

Ed Bradley and me after the *60 Minutes* interview, standing in front of my "Self-portrait with Balloon"

(© Harry Benson 1998)

In my basement studio where I paint (Spring 1998)

CHAPTER 20

**The Spirit of the Lord is upon Me,
Because He has anointed Me
To preach the gospel to the poor;
He has sent Me to heal the brokenhearted,
To proclaim liberty to the captives
And recovery of sight to the blind,
To set at liberty those who are oppressed.**
—*Jesus Christ, Luke 4:18*

On April 1, 1998, Susan Webber Wright granted the Motion for Summary Judgment by the president's lawyers, thus dismissing the Paula Jones case. No one expected Wright to grant this motion. In fact, Clinton was in Africa and, upon hearing the news, asked if it was an April Fool's joke.

It certainly was no joke for us or Paula Jones.

Camera crews began gathering at the TRI office in Charlottesville by midmorning. Nisha and I discussed options, and I finally said, "Well, I better go down and make a strong statement." My desire was to "rally the troops." I knew the lawyers in Dallas and Paula and Steve Jones were getting tired. It would be tempting to just drop the matter at this point.

There were several boom trucks in front of our office. I walked up to the microphones and cameras and made a forceful statement, saying I believed we should appeal the judge's decision. I certainly didn't think it was time to throw in the towel.

Susan Carpenter-McMillan went on the air that same day and proclaimed, "John Whitehead doesn't speak for Paula Jones."

"What's that all about?" Nisha asked.

"It means Paula is having second thoughts about continuing," I said.

Later that evening, Carpenter-McMillan and I both appeared on *Larry King Live*, though we weren't in the same location. Susan was overly gracious, thanking me on the air for all I had done.

Well, maybe Paula is going to fight this thing, I thought.

It took Paula a few weeks to decide what she wanted to do. The ordeal for her was almost eight years old. She had to think through whether she wanted to continue a battle that could easily drag on for several more years.

A little more than a week later, I got a call from Don Campbell. "Paula wants to appeal," he said.

"That's good news," I responded. "I think that's the right thing to do. Let's discuss options."

We decided to make the announcement in Dallas on live television on April 16.

Going Forward

"Hi, John."

"Hi, Paula."

"Hello, Susan," I said to Carpenter-McMillan, the ever-clinging, ominous force hovering around Paula Jones.

"Good to finally meet you in person, John Whitehead," Susan replied.

"Hey, Steve," I said, noticing Steve Jones coming up the hallway. We were all assembling at the law offices of Rader, Campbell, Fisher & Pyke in Dallas.

"Hello, John," Steve said coldly. As I note previously, Steve had been irritated with me and TRI for some months concerning what he perceived as positive remarks I had made about Bill Clinton. Also, I had let him know that his independent fund-raising efforts through the Paula Jones Legal Defense Fund—which had no connection whatsoever to TRI's work on Paula's behalf and which never sent a dime to TRI for the case—had hurt TRI's ability to raise funds to pay the ever-increasing legal expenses of his wife's case against the president. Steve's arrogance and haughty manner had alienated almost everyone who was defending his wife. I think it's difficult for any man to have his wife become famous while he remains unknown, and Steve was no exception.

Don Campbell and I had just finished drafting a statement for Paula to read that afternoon at a press conference announcing that she had decided to appeal Judge Susan Webber Wright's decision dismissing her case. The media representatives were everywhere.

This was a big day. We were ready to continue the fight.

Paula was understandably nervous as we descended in the elevators, preparing for the drive to the Fairmont Hotel in downtown Dallas. When we arrived, we were met by guards who took us in a back way to avoid the media. We congregated in a side room to the main ballroom where the press conference was scheduled to be held.

Paula sat reading over her statement, anxiously puffing on the cigarette that looked as if it were glued to her fingers. Taking deep draws and swallowing the smoke, she silently moved her lips as she read the words that would soon be broadcast around the world.

Susan paced nervously around the room, taking short, staccato tokes from her cigarette, talking incessantly to anyone who would listen. Steve sat patiently, apparently content to watch things unfold around him.

It was almost 2:00 P.M.—time for the press conference. The Rader, Campbell, Fisher & Pyke attorneys and Paula, Steve, Susan, and I lined up for the procession to the stage where the podium awaited. Carol and Nisha followed us and sat with the reporters.

As the door opened, Paula snuffed out her cigarette in an ashtray. I was standing beside her.

"Aren't you nervous, John? I am," she said.

"No, and you shouldn't be, either. Just read your statement slowly, smile, and sit down. Everything will be okay," I said, looking at her. She seemed to relax as we spoke.

We walked out and took our seats. Then Don Campbell introduced Paula, who began reading her statement. She said she had decided to appeal the judge's decision. She thanked her attorneys and TRI and then, as the toll of four years of turmoil and courtroom drama caught up with her, she began to cry. This petite, young woman was carrying a heavy emotional and spiritual weight.

Though she stumbled, Paula kept enough composure to finish her statement.

Sitting there beside the podium listening to her speak, I thought, *How has she survived? How did this little woman from Arkansas ever get to where she actually threatened an American presidency?*

I looked over and caught a glimpse of Paula's husband, who had endured a lot as well. In fact, a week after the press conference, Steve lost his job with Northwest Airlines, where he had worked for seventeen years. Though he had great influence over Paula, when we got together for meetings, Steve no doubt felt like the odd man out. And, of course, there was the humiliation factor as well. Steve wanted to be an actor. He was now a household name, but the entire reason for his fame was that the president of the United States had exposed his genitals to Steve's wife. That's not exactly self-esteem-building material.

Neither Steve nor Paula has the appearance of someone who would change history, but their litigation shows how great moral issues do not arise in neat packages. If we care about human rights, we must be able to see the real issues and be willing to fight for them, even if the people involved are less than perfect. Social change does not come from ideal situations.

Any student of history knows this. Norma McCorvey, the "Jane Roe" in the landmark *Roe v. Wade* abortion decision, was a humble young woman with a ninth-grade education who was facing her third problem pregnancy. The schoolchildren in the history-making civil rights case *Brown v. Board of Education* were just regular, poorer-than-average schoolchildren who were undoubtedly unaware of the historical change they were initiating.

Few individuals in great cases are especially significant *per se*. They were just living their lives and became important because of the role history gave them to play. Lawyers, clients, and judges often fall into our nation's heritage rather than strategize their way there.

So it was with Paula Jones. The reason I was so adamant about pursuing this case went back to why I undertook Paula's representation in the first place. I care about human rights issues and believe that Paula's right to sexual integrity in the workplace had been grossly infringed. I've been involved in human rights issues for almost thirty years, and the Jones case had the potential for important progress in the area of sexual harassment. Since most of my staff (about 80 percent) are women, I have a growing interest in this area of human rights, especially the way women are treated.

Unfortunately, several of the Dallas lawyers did not share my opinion. Instead of seeing the larger issue of women's rights and fighting for that, they wanted to win this battle on technical points of law. This is endemic among lawyers today. Jurisprudence—the history and theory behind law—has been buried among technical minutiae in many law schools, robbing young lawyers of the context for their labor. Without understanding the history of law, they fail to understand their responsibility to handle it in the future.

David Pyke, one of the Dallas lawyers on Paula's team, went so far as to question my aims on national television. "This women's rights stuff was Whitehead's idea," he scoffed, making it clear that he did not agree with me. Like a typical conservative, Pyke wanted to fight this case within the law as it existed, without any passion for the human rights issues involved.

The irony is that Paula Jones herself does not know that much about women's rights. Her original inspirations for her lawsuit may never be clear—and perhaps they are not clear even to her. Apart from her desire to clear her name, we may never know just why this young woman from Arkansas was willing to endure such travail to make her case against the president.

But for the purpose of history, none of this is really important. The words I helped pen for Jones in our April 16 press conference state my belief clearly. As Paula read: "I have also considered the fact that the court's ruling affects many women other than myself. Despite the continuing personal strain on my family and me, in the end, I have not come this far to see the law let men who have done such things dodge their responsibility. They should not be able to abuse their positions of power at the expense of female employees. And I do not believe, when this suit is over, that my case will merely show that people in power can get away."

The amazing—and most frustrating—thing was working with all the egos involved in the case. Everybody positioned themselves to be on television. It was still difficult trying to build a cohesive message for the world when so many different versions were being told to the press.

Fighting for Life

This season was by no means "all Paula Jones, all the time." The irony is that although I was the one who felt most strongly about appealing Judge Wright's decision, dropping her appeal would have been by far the most convenient thing for TRI to do. We had several other major cases on our docket, and I was well aware that pursuing

Paula's case would cost us hundreds of thousands of dollars more, funds that could have been applied to other concerns.

Even so, I clearly believed that going forward was the best thing for Paula. If you surrender, there's no hope of receiving a settlement. Paula had put in so much time and effort that I wanted to see her at least get something for her pain and suffering.

One major case in which I became involved during this time concerned Karla Faye Tucker, a Texas woman who was facing execution. Tucker had been convicted of several grisly murders, but had become a Christian while in prison. For a brief period of time, her plight renewed attention on capital punishment.

Larry King and I talked privately about Tucker, and we both believed that she should not be executed. I even wrote to Archbishop John Cardinal O'Connor on behalf of Tucker, asking him to contact the pope. Shortly thereafter, the pope attempted to intervene in the Tucker case.

At one time I believed, with reservations, that the death penalty was a way to protect people. But when I studied the question more thoroughly, I discovered the statistics did not bear this out. In fact, the murder rate has actually increased in some states with the death penalty.

Like my stand against homophobia, this belief was destined to create havoc for me with conservative, politically active evangelicals, the vast majority of whom are staunch defenders of capital punishment. But I'm more concerned with helping people, and one conversation in particular challenged my previous support for the death penalty.

One day while discussing the abortion issue, an abortion advocate challenged me by saying, "Yeah, you people save them as babies and then execute them twenty years later."

Is that really what they think of us? I asked myself. *Even more important, is this how they would have thought of Christ?*

The more I studied the New Testament, the more I came to see that the death penalty doesn't square with the teachings of Christ. In fact, I believe that being against the death penalty completes the pro-life cycle from birth to death. All punishment in Christian terms must be not only for the sake of society but also for the criminal—this is the radical nature of the Gospels.

Christ was people-oriented. As such, punishment in the Christian sense must be dominated by love. Christian love means the undefeatable desire for the other person's good. Clearly, love will sometimes invoke punishment, for a love that exercises no discipline is not love at all. But punishment must be administered in such a way as to make the wrongdoer emerge a better person.

Obviously, you do not cure a man or a woman by killing him or her. You do not seek a person's highest good by sending her to the electric chair or by forcing that person to submit to lethal injection. Execution declares the human being hopeless and states that neither human skill nor the grace of God can do anything for him. Capital punishment is the ultimate denial of remedial punishment.

In addition to writing to Cardinal O'Connor, I wrote to Texas Governor George W. Bush, asking him to commute Karla Faye's death sentence. "The fact that minority convicts have been put to death at proportionately higher rates than nonminorities only underscores the truth that governments should not be in the business of killing their citizens," I wrote. "As a nonprofit civil liberties legal and educational organization, The Rutherford Institute has learned from years of experience that minorities—religious, racial, ideological—are consistently at great risk of having their constitutional rights trampled upon. When the right at issue is the right to live, the risk of inequity is always too great."

Bush wrote back saying, "When I was sworn in as the governor of Texas, I took an oath of office to uphold the laws of our state, including the death penalty."

On February 3, 1998, Karla Faye Tucker was executed.

"Pervert"

"Which one is the biggest pervert?"

That was the question posed by the Westboro Baptist Church (WBC) in Topeka, Kansas, which placed a photo of my face next to a caricature of Bill Clinton wearing sadomasochistic garb.

Citing my "sympathetic view toward gays" and the fact that a Christian radio network had dropped our program, *Freedom Under Fire*, the pastor of WBC wrote, "It's a close question as to who is the biggest pervert—Clinton or Whitehead. To educate and warn true, God-fearing Christians, WBC will picket this disgraceful Judas at Rutherford headquarters in Charlottesville, Virginia."

Without realizing it, Pastor Fred Phelps and the WBC had made my day. I've never feared being picketed, so I instructed my staff to make sure we had plenty of doughnuts ready to serve the picketers.

I thought, however, that it was only fair to warn Pastor Phelps what he was up against, so we faxed him a letter that stated,

> Because we lease office space located at 1445 East Rio Road in Charlottesville, Virginia, we cannot grant you permission to picket on private property without the threat of being removed by the owner of the property.
>
> The Rutherford Institute will, however, protect your right to picket on the public sidewalk adjacent to the property. If you determine to picket our national office, and county officials would attempt to interfere with your right to do so on public property, we would be willing to legally assist in protecting your constitutional right of free speech.
>
> I hope your trip to this area is a safe one.

It probably would have made headlines for us to defend the very people who picketed us, but much to our disappointment, Pastor Phelps and WBC never showed up.

The radio station that Phelps alluded to was the Moody Broadcasting Network. We were informed by letter that Moody was ceasing its broadcast of TRI's daily radio program, *Freedom Under Fire*. "The Rutherford Institute has taken the Paula Jones case in her action against President Clinton," the manager of Network Development wrote. "Without casting judgment on that decision, we feel it would be wise to temporarily suspend the program in light of the current publicity surrounding the case. We continue to have great respect for Rutherford and the excellent service they provide. However, our mission is to present Christ with as few distractions as possible. It is our desire to reinstate the program after the current media hype dies down. This may take a few months."

Though some of Moody's independent stations continued broadcasting *Freedom Under Fire*, we were sad to see Moody take this action. And when the Paula Jones case was over, Moody did not reinstate the program.

Who Are You?

In March, *Gentlemen's Quarterly* magazine *(GQ)* sent a writer to do a story on me. The editors at *GQ* were surprised that I agreed to this because they had bought into the White House spin that I was a right-wing conspirator intent on bringing the president down. Steve Kotler followed me around for a week at my home and office, questioning everyone he came in contact with. Published in the September 1998 issue, the article is one of the best that has ever been done on me and presents an entirely different view of me than most people have.

One of the best things about the *GQ* profile was the photographer who took pictures. Harry Benson had traveled extensively with the Beatles, photographing them on their first trip to America in 1964 and many times thereafter. Harry had been told that I was a Beatles fan and brought a copy of his book on them for me. While he was autographing it, I went down to the office and brought up my own copy of the book. We talked for several hours as he took photos and shared intimate stories relating to his travels with the Beatles. As an indication of his stature as a photographer, he had recently taken photos of Ronald and Nancy Reagan for *Vanity Fair,* the only ones allowed since Reagan's illness, after having been personally selected by Nancy Reagan for this honor. I considered myself in good company.

Ironically, while the evangelical world showed less interest, the media kept calling. In April, May, and June, the producers of *60 Minutes* came to our offices for preinterviews for a program they ultimately aired in October. The camera crew spent time at my home and at the TRI office. Ed Bradley then flew into Charlottesville to do the main interview.

For two hours, with only a few small breaks, Ed relentlessly pursued me with questions that generally focused on whether I was a right-wing fanatic out to destroy Bill Clinton. His researchers dug up information that was so old I didn't even remember it. Bradley asked about my relationship with Rushdoony and even quoted from some fund-raising letters I had written ten or fifteen years ago. He showed clips from videos Franky Schaeffer had directed, and it was hard not to cringe a little when Franky's style of directing was touted as my own.

I wasn't caught off guard, though. One of the producers had told Nisha before the interview that they wanted to give me a chance "to address issues that people are wondering about."

Ed Bradley was the one who looked downright miserable. Because of CBS's sensitive audio equipment, we couldn't turn the air-conditioning on, and hot lights relentlessly sprayed their heat on us as we talked. At one point, Ed opened his shirt and inserted his handkerchief to absorb the perspiration.

As the interview came to its finale, Ed Bradley asked me to explain one of my oil paintings that hangs behind my desk.

"That's a self-portrait," I said.

"It looks kind of morbid," he said.

"You think so? I think it looks happy. Some of my paintings might seem morose, but this is one of the happier ones."

"You call this happy?" Ed asked.

"There's a balloon by my head, and balloons are happy."

At this, Ed looked into the screen and said, "Who is John Whitehead? Maybe Whitehead doesn't even know himself."

The interview was over.

In spite of the grilling, when the show aired in early October, both Carol and I were pleased. Ed opened the broadcast by asking, "Is Whitehead the right-wing zealot the White House says he is, or is he, as he says, simply a product of the sixties with no particular agenda other than to do the right thing?"

Though many more quotes were edited out than were included, several salient points were preserved. I was quoted as saying, "Ninety percent of our cases now are always against the government, some government official who is out of control, and that government official needs to be brought under the rule of law." This helped frame our representation of Paula Jones in its proper light.

Thirty million people watched as Ed Bradley talked about my Christian experience (among other things). Carol told Ed how much I had changed after becoming a believer. *Sixty Minutes* helped us accomplish our goal of telling our story to people who normally wouldn't have heard it.

After the program aired, there were a few people who criticized me for not explaining myself more. These viewers apparently don't understand the nature of editing. After two hours of being taped, my answers were boiled down to a few minutes on-screen.

Overall, however, I received numerous calls and E-mails congratulating Carol and me. One newspaper reporter greeted me on the phone with, "Congratulations, you survived *60 Minutes*."

Chuck Colson wrote me a note that said, "I watched you and your wife on *60 Minutes* this week, rejoicing the entire time. You handled yourself magnificently and got a powerful Christian witness in . . . You were superb, a real pro. And I was proud of you." Coming from someone whom I respect, this note made my day.

In Times Square in New York, filming
Grasping for the Wind (May 1996)

Reporters strain to hear me outside the St. Paul, Minnesota, Federal
Building, where a three-judge panel heard arguments to reinstate
Paula Jones's lawsuit against President Clinton (October 20, 1998).

CHAPTER 21

'Tis too starved an argument for my sword.
—William Shakespeare

Shortly after our April press conference, we began drafting our appeal briefs in preparation to argue Paula Jones's case before the Eighth Circuit Court of Appeals in St. Paul, Minnesota.

Though our position was the same, our client had dramatically changed. Back in July, Paula had traveled to New York City, where she underwent plastic surgery on her nose. The taunts and jokes about this prominent feature had finally cut too deep. When someone offered to pay for the procedure, Paula quickly agreed to alter her appearance.

Of course, this elicited even more jokes for a few days. The double standards being waged were truly disconcerting. A woman was sexually harassed by a paunchy politician—and people mercilessly ridiculed the victim for having a larger-than-average nose.

I certainly don't blame Paula for changing her looks. It is difficult to live in the public eye and be the butt of continual attacks and jokes about your appearance.

As we made final preparations, I received a phone call from an attorney who represented Abe Hirschfeld, a New York real estate tycoon.

"Hirschfeld is offering to give Paula one million dollars to settle the case," he explained.

I was adamantly opposed to any contact with Hirschfeld. This type of offer was unprecedented and betrayed the principles for which the case was brought in the first place. This wasn't about Paula getting rich or the president getting in trouble. It was about the principles of how women are treated in the workplace. Giving Paula a million dollars to "just go away" wouldn't solve anything.

Though Paula and some of the Dallas attorneys (against my advice) participated in a press conference with Hirschfeld, Abe's offer subsequently fell through. I wasn't surprised.

On the day of our oral argument (October 20, 1998), the media literally swamped St. Paul, hoping for a Paula sighting, though she never showed up. Walking into the courthouse required threading our way through a gauntlet of microphones, cameras, and crowding reporters.

Jim Fisher, one of Campbell's partners, argued the case on appeal before a packed courtroom. An additional room had been added to accommodate media personnel who couldn't fit in the courtroom. These reporters heard the arguments over a loudspeaker.

It was hard not to chuckle when the presiding judge opened the proceedings by welcoming everybody to St. Paul.

"Welcome to our beautiful city," he said. "I hope you enjoy your stay." He waxed on about St. Paul's attractiveness. If I hadn't been in a courtroom, I would have thought I was listening to a travelogue commercial. I guess everyone is moved by the presence of the media.

Much to my satisfaction, the judges were prepared and asked thoughtful questions. It was clear they had read the briefs, which made me believe we had a chance to win the appeal.

Chief Judge Pasco Bowman and Judge C. Arlen Beam, two Ronald Reagan appointees who had ruled for Jones previously, saying that her case could proceed against Clinton, asked skeptical questions of Clinton's lawyer. Both were already thinking ahead to the next step in trying to determine how to handle the Lewinsky evidence (which had been excluded from our case) "if we send it back."

After the short hearing, one of the press people who has covered this court for years told me, "Bennett better get ready for a Supreme Court appeal or a trial, whichever way he wants to go."

Apparently, the media thought we were going to win, too.

While the case looked promising, things were not going as well in the background. A nearly explosive tension was building at TRI with the Joneses and the Dallas attorneys, particularly over the Paula Jones Legal Fund (PJLF).

The PJLF represented one of the more bizarre and disappointing elements of my involvement in the Jones case. Bruce W. Eberle and Associates, a Virginia direct mail organization, signed an agreement with Steve and Paula Jones in July 1997 to raise money through a direct mail campaign. As reported in the press, Eberle's agreement with Steve and Paula guaranteed them $300,000 in profit and called for an up-front advance to the Joneses of $100,000. Eberle must have been anticipating a great response to his campaign to guarantee this kind of money.

TRI entered the case in October of 1997, offering to provide legal services for free, as we do in all the cases we handle. Nevertheless, Eberle sent out a letter, signed by Paula, in November 1997 requesting donations so that Jones's attorneys could "keep fighting." The letter from Paula specifically stated that "this money is not for me. It's all going to help my legal case." This was simply not true. Neither TRI nor the attorneys handling the case received a penny from the PJLF.

Not surprisingly, the letters unleashed a barrage of confusion. People wrote to us, wanting to know if TRI was part of the PJLF and whether PJLF money was coming to us.

"When I send money to you, am I paying to board Paula's dog?" one supporter asked me.

"No, that's the PJLF, not us," I would write back in my explanation.

Essentially, two entities were raising money for the same cause, but only one entity—TRI—was actually using the money to advance the legal argument. We asked the PJLF to make it clear in their direct mail that neither the lawsuit nor TRI would receive any money from donations to the PJLF, but they refused to do so.

It was only a matter of time until the press uncovered the ruse and chastised all parties involved. Bob Bennett, the president's attorney, played the PJLF for all it was worth, even filing a motion before Judge Wright arguing that "the fund exists not so much to pay legal fees, but to pay for such items as plaintiff's clothing, haircuts, a personal computer, care and boarding for a pet, the towing of her car, and first and foremost, her large public relations operation."

It was a public relations fiasco. The name of the escrow agent that Eberle used to advance postage money to Steve and Paula was the "Washington Intelligence Bureau." A reporter discovered that the address given for the "bureau" turned out to be a warehouse in northern Virginia. The name of the list broker was "Omega List Company." I joked to my staff, "These names alone will suffice to get Hillary really excited about her 'vast right-wing conspiracy.'"

In spite of our pleas for either compensation from the PJLF or at least full disclosure as to what the funds were being used for, Steve and Paula wouldn't back down. It is one of the few times I have seen greed overcome the lust for power, but it certainly wasn't the first time I have seen greed overcome common sense and integrity.

Another troubling concern was our increasingly raucous relationship with Susan Carpenter-McMillan. As Paula's spokesperson, Carpenter-McMillan was ever present and, even worse, prone to media gaffes (such as her comment about how Paula's lawyers were chosen). When she appeared on talk shows—especially when she was paired with acid-tongued James Carville—the programs routinely devolved into a circuslike atmosphere.

It was embarrassing on both sides.

"Susan," we insisted early on, "you are not qualified to speak to the press on legal matters. It is important that a lawyer who understands the legal issues involved comment on them."

Susan agreed to stop talking, but then did pretty much what she wanted to do. I honestly believe Paula would have been better off without Carpenter-McMillan. One of the reasons Paula never won over the hearts of the public is that the public was rarely given a chance to hear from her. Carpenter-McMillan always spoke for Paula, depriving her of the opportunity to appear more "real" before the world.

Further exacerbating the situation was Steve Jones, who was an extremely difficult person for the Dallas attorneys to work with. Steve is high-strung and has a controlling personality. Though most of the time he apparently had no clue what to do, he frequently acted as if he could run the lawsuit on his own. He acted as if he were an amateur lawyer—something a lot of clients tend to do.

More than anything, most of us were put off by his patent ungratefulness. Several days after Paula's case was dismissed, Steve lost his job with Northwest Airlines, where he had worked for seventeen years. I knew Steve and Paula had little money, and I wanted to help. Even though our relationship was already rocky (the PJLF had by no means been resolved), I offered to help Steve by putting TRI's legal team to work on his behalf. We found Steve an attorney and offered to pay his legal expenses to fight for his job. When Paula's case moved toward settlement, Steve wrote the attorney we had hired for him and said he no longer wanted to work with TRI.

I was informed of this by Steve's attorney. "Steve said he no longer wants to be connected with Rutherford."

"Well, fine," I said. "You can keep working with him, though."

I, along with at least twenty TRI affiliate attorneys, had put in a number of long days in an effort to rehabilitate Paula's image, frame the case in its best light, and work for a judgment on Paula's behalf. TRI paid more than $400,000 in legal expenses alone. This did not include any attorney fees, which we estimated to be in the millions of dollars. Yet, it was only when I demanded from Paula something in writing for our files that I received a short, handwritten note with a thank-you.

The Dallas attorneys had also had enough.

"I don't think there's anything more we can do, John," Don Campbell told me.

I agreed, and the Dallas team drafted a letter notifying Paula that we would not continue the case beyond the appeals court level, which was as far as we had contracted to fight the case. Once the judges reached a decision—either to drop the case or continue it—Paula would need to proceed with different representation.

Shortly thereafter, Paula called me.

"I don't know what to do!" she said. "What if I need another lawyer?"

"You can get a lawyer, if you need one," I assured her. "After all this publicity, they'll be lined up waiting."

I refused to recommend any particular lawyer, though I did give Paula some other advice. "I think you deserve much more out of this than you'll get from any possible settlement," I said. "Now is the time to make money, Paula. Otherwise, there won't be any. With the media, you can be white-hot on Monday and not get any calls on Wednesday. You deserve something after all you've gone through. A lot of people are making a career off you; it's time you thought about that yourself."

"Well, thanks," she said.

"God bless and take care."

"Thank you, John."

That was the last time I spoke with Paula Jones.

Settlement

When the Court of Appeals asked for additional information in late October of 1998, we believed it was a sign that the judges were preparing to reverse Judge Wright and reinstate the case. My media friend's hunches seemed to be right. While this was good news for Paula, we knew that we would not take the case to the next level, but rather pass it on to another team of lawyers.

Apparently, we weren't the only ones who believed Wright was about to be reversed. Within days, the president's lawyers called Don.

"Can we discuss a settlement?" they asked.

When Don told me the news, I had mixed emotions. My gut feeling was to fight this thing out to the end. We had already spent most of the money that would need to be spent. A new team of lawyers could continue the case "on the cheap" and still press on to victory.

Knowing what Don was going through, however, I didn't voice my thoughts. The Dallas firm had expended at least a million and a half dollars in attorneys' fees, passing up other lucrative cases to represent Paula for free.

"Maybe settling is best," I agreed.

Attorney-client privilege prevents me from going into too much detail, but I can say that shortly before Thanksgiving, a settlement was reached. The media reported that the agreed-upon sum was $850,000, which would be split between Paula, the Dallas law firm, Paula's former lawyers, and TRI.

We all knew that the president would never apologize, so that demand was pretty much bartered away. Clinton will do only what he is forced to do. It's similar to his public admission of an "improper" relationship with Monica Lewinsky. If it hadn't been for the semen-stained blue dress, in all likelihood, the White House never would have abandoned its characterization of Monica as a stalker and the president as an innocent victim. To this day, I don't think Monica realizes how closely she came to being savagely portrayed by people within the administration. Though Monica probably would not admit it, Linda Tripp's advice that she not clean the blue dress ultimately saved her.

As a result of the settlement, the Court of Appeals dismissed the case. The Jones legal saga against Bill Clinton had finally ended.

"Would You Do It Again?"

By year's end, I was involved in other cases and issues, occasionally hearing about Paula on the news. When I saw her dancing with Abe Hirschfeld in New York City, I just shook my head in dismay. Within a month, Hirschfeld was arrested for alleged criminal activity. He posted a one-million-dollar bond—the same amount he had talked about giving to Paula.

Later, it was announced that Paula and Steve had separated and Paula, with their two sons, had moved back to Arkansas and bought a house there. Steve then filed for divorce. Next, reports surfaced that Paula was considering cutting a country music album and was associated with a psychic hot line.

Without question, one of the most common inquiries I receive now is, "Knowing what you now know, would you represent Paula again?"

"Absolutely," I respond.

The issues of the rule of law and the decent and equal treatment of women are important enough that they demand TRI's involvement and support. If I conditioned when and how I help people based on their personalities, spouses, and spokespersons, I would take very few cases.

One unfortunate but probably inevitable result of taking this case was the strain it placed on Don Campbell's firm, eventually causing a division among the lawyers. Fortunately, Don and I are still good friends and continue to work together.

And in spite of the strain, spent resources, and media attacks, I have no regrets about my involvement. I gave my final explanation at a speech delivered to the Thomas Jefferson Center for the Protection of Free Expression in Charlottesville in May of 1999.

"Political considerations ran roughshod over legal rights in the Paula Jones sexual harassment case against President Clinton," I stated. "Though the Jones case had the potential to strongly stigmatize sexual harassment in the workplace, instead it allowed a president's wife and feminist leaders to excuse boorish and harmful behavior and became a lesson in how politicians and the media can redefine problems.

"Here was the ultimate confrontation between the rule of law and the rule of power. I fought for law, but power won."

I told the crowd that "I did not see this case as a political issue. For me, this was a much bigger issue than Bill Clinton or political parties. Here was a case that could show for all time that there is no king in America. The law would be shown to be king.

"In the end, sexual harassment law and human rights were not advanced. Jones was robbed from the right, forsaken by the left, and cut short in the courts. I came to realize that the president may, indeed, be subject to the rule of law but that the rule of law is subject to politics."

In my speech, I also voiced my displeasure with Kenneth Starr, who took from Paula Jones a key component in her case (with all the Monica Lewinsky related evidence) as he sought to build his failed attempt at impeachment. Also unfortunate was a U.S. Congress that "subordinated its integrity to the public opinion polls."

Unfortunately, I continued, "Clinton was protected by a media consumed by political implications. And feminists abandoned a sister to protect the unfettered right to abortion. They made it clear that Paula Jones would have been one of their own, but for the identity of the defendant, who happened to be a pro-abortion president of the United States. It seemed clear to the feminist leadership that, in choosing between the two issues, the unrestricted right to abortion is more important than stopping predatory sexual conduct in the workplace."

As for "lessons learned," I suggested that "individual behavior should matter in these cases." I added that "nothing can get changed in America without serious media attention to its merits, not just its details. The media fanned the flames of confusion by focusing on the details of the case and endlessly speculating about the political ramifications.

"I actually believe that Americans were better informed about the broader issues of policy and politics when newspapers were dominant, before the age of television."

What did I see as the most important lesson? "We must return to the notion that it is the individual who is important—that each and every human being inherently has great worth and dignity and thus deserves respect."

New Beginnings

After the Jones settlement, my life shifted in other directions. By Christmas 1998, I was notified that my video series, *Grasping for the Wind*, had been selected as a finalist in the prestigious New York Film Festival. Carol and I attended the banquet on January 22, 1999, in New York City's Times Square, where we had filmed portions of the videos.

As I stood there on the stage holding the Silver World Medal and watching all the clapping hands, for a brief moment I heard no sound, just silence. In that short span, I heard a small voice say, *This is just the beginning.*

Do I really look like that? A political cartoon portraying me,
Susan Carpenter-McMillan, Paula Jones, and Don Campbell.

One of our favorite family pictures (Fall 1987)
Front row: Elisabeth, Joshua, and Joel.
Back row: Jayson, Carol, me, and Jonathan.

CHAPTER 22

The world expects of Christians that they will raise their voices so loudly and clearly and so formulate their protest that not even the simplest man can have the slightest doubt about what they are saying. Further, the world expects of Christians that they will eschew all fuzzy abstractions and plant themselves squarely in front of the bloody face of history. We stand in need of folk who have determined to speak directly and unmistakably and come what may, to stand by what they have said.

—*Albert Camus*

"Get a load of this, John," one of my staff said.

"What?"

"Tom Harkin, the senator from Iowa, said on the Senate floor that TRI is 'funded by conservative sources in the United States' and is the 'mastermind' behind the Jones case."

"So in other words, we're the tool the vast right-wing conspiracy is using to bring down the president?"

"I guess so."

I suppose these attacks were inevitable. The Senate trial of President Clinton was an amalgam of evasion, blame-shifting, and name-calling. Though the Jones case was settled, the political impeachment battle was far from over, and TRI took its share of hits.

The day before the president was acquitted, New York Senator Charles Schumer took to the floor of the Senate and unleashed a diatribe:

> It is the small group of lawyers and zealots in organizations like The Rutherford Institute who decided that they would invest time and money to exploit a personal weakness that people knew the president had, find a case to air it publicly, investigate the president's private life to the point of obsessiveness, and use it to bring him down.

It is shameful how these senators shifted the blame for the impeachment debacle from the president's actions to those who investigated him. The only reason we were forced to investigate "the president's private life" is because he lied about it in his deposition in the Jones case.

When I was discussing this with a friend from the media, he pointed out something that didn't surprise me. "You know, John, Hillary Clinton campaigned pretty hard for Schumer's election. I don't think it's an accident that he has taken the lead in defending her husband."

Schumer's and Harkin's words reeked of White House political spin. Both were irresponsible statements by professionals who should know better. I wrote to both of them, demanding a retraction, but neither one responded.

Certainly, TRI did play a part in a case that undoubtedly harmed the president, but there was no conspiracy or intent on my part to force Clinton out of office. My desire was exclusively to make Paula Jones's case. Admittedly, our work helped unearth Monica Lewinsky and led to the damaging and almost politically fatal January 17, 1998, deposition of the president. However, the sad truth is that Clinton's proclivity for sexual trysts was the true origin of his problems.

In all honesty, I have at times felt sorry for Clinton. Though he out-politicianed the entire Congress throughout the arduous impeachment ordeal (he may well be the best politician of our era), always remaining one step ahead of his political enemies, his personal life has to be a mess.

I took no delight in being the harbinger of these sordid facts, but I did take umbrage at being blamed for their existence. In many expressed views, I was labeled responsible for Clinton's problems.

February 1999 brought another bombshell. Judge Wright issued an order finding Bill Clinton in contempt of court. The false statements made by the president in his Jones deposition and later public statements denying any sexual relationship with Monica Lewinsky were irrefutably exposed by the infamous blue dress and Clinton's own confession.

Once again I was in the papers. We had taken the deposition and now had to submit the costs of Clinton's prevarications. In July, Judge Wright levied $90,000 in damages against the president. A portion of this amount was awarded to TRI for expenses and attorneys' fees.

I was beginning to feel that my life, to a certain degree, was being typecast as Paula Jones's attorney, a position I held for just a little more than a year. Although I am not ashamed of my role in her defense, I would never want all my other work, not to mention the many victories TRI has won in and out of the courtroom, to be relegated to an asterisk after the century's most famous sexual harassment case.

The best way to prevent being typecast, of course, was to throw myself even more into the cases we already had, as well as into the worthy cases that would follow. That's why I was very attentive when I got a call from another woman who felt she had been victimized by sexual harassment.

"How did you hear about us?" I asked her.

"I saw you on television and heard about your work with Paula Jones. I thought you'd be the best one to represent me."

This woman claimed to have been raped by a partner in a large Los Angeles law firm. To make matters worse, after her allegations, the firm subsequently treated her very unfairly, attacking her instead of the offending partner. It was Paula Jones all over again—the man in power riding roughshod over a subordinate female employee.

TRI took her case, and now there are many others. Though so many have said we were in this only to "get Clinton," our work will prove them wrong.

Of course, some of these new cases have created their own controversy, particularly my defense of Walter Decyk in the spring of 1999. Tom Neuberger, who had helped me with Chuck McIlhenny's case in San Francisco, called me with "one of the most pitiful situations" he had ever seen.

"What happened?" I asked.

"Walter was viciously beaten one night after leaving a restaurant. He's gay, and that's why he was beaten up. They left him with a fractured leg, back injuries, and a host of other ailments. To make matters worse, when Walter went back to his job as a tollbooth operator, his employer found out why Walter had been beaten up and started subjecting him to verbal slurs and threats of termination!"

"Had he ever been threatened with losing his job before?" I asked.

"No. By all accounts, he is an exemplary employee. This is all gay-related. His supervisor now calls him 'Ms. Decyk' or 'ma'am.' Further exacerbating the situation, when Decyk was finally let go, the Bay Authority denied his request to continue his medical benefits, which he needs to seek treatment for his injuries."

"Let's take his case," I said.

The reason I wanted to represent Walter was that it was simply the right thing to do. And I thought it was what Christ would have done.

Tom Neuberger and TRI eventually negotiated a settlement between Walter Decyk and his employer, the terms of which are confidential. Interestingly enough, though, Walter is one of the few clients we've represented who has actually written back to us and thanked us. Homosexual advocates have called our settlement a "miraculous win," and Walter wrote to me, saying, "The issue that stands out in my mind the most is your view that no one person, group, or political organization is above the law or has the right to deprive another American citizen of their constitutional rights."

Not surprisingly, various evangelicals and conservatives immediately accused me of advancing the gay rights agenda, but I've never been one to turn down someone in need—nor do I believe Christ would ignore the human suffering of anyone, including a gay man. Jesus, after all, spoke highly of the despised Samaritan who put to shame his religious persecutors by demonstrating true compassion, teaching us that we should help all people, whether they are Christian or non-Christian. To fail to do so is not only inhumane, it is clearly non-Christian.

Recently, the British were asked to name the greatest people of the twentieth century. Many were surprised when Mother Teresa was chosen number one. Why Mother Teresa? Because she selflessly gave her life to help people. Mother Teresa didn't preach from a huge, expensive church. She didn't wear a Rolex watch. She didn't own a Mercedes. She didn't go on retreats at expensive resorts. She simply knelt and washed the sores of the afflicted. This is true Christianity.

Slaying My Dragons

My life has not been an easy one. And, to spare the feelings of people I care about, much has been left out of this book. I don't believe that my life would be the same today if I hadn't gone through what I've suffered. I wouldn't be the same person, either, if my circumstances had been different—or easier. I do believe I have changed for the better because of the tough times. But in order for me to change, I had to slay many personal dragons. And I needed help. I believe that's why Carol came into my life, to help me fight my battles. In the process, I learned many valuable lessons.

I've learned to not take myself too seriously or to hold grudges. I also firmly believe that you cannot do anything worthwhile by playing it safe. It hurts, but taking chances works. When David slew Goliath, he knew it wasn't going to be easy. That's why he picked up a few extra stones—in case he missed the first time.

I've always told my children, "Stick up for the downtrodden, the little guy. If you see a child getting picked on at school, help him. Don't laugh, and especially don't join in. Helping the helpless is why we are here on this planet."

Also, I don't believe in giving up. Most of the people I worked with in the early days are gone. They grew cynical or depressed, became soul-deadened with affluence, and gave up fighting for what is right. If our cause is just, I believe we must stick it out to the end.

What bothers me is that I look at churches and find no distinguishable difference in the divorce rate. And many evangelical leaders are filled with the same greed and ambition as the most cutthroat corporate moguls.

Truth isn't finding its way into our churches, which are swamped with weight-loss programs, softball teams, raffles, and retreats. In many ways, churches have become antifamily, taking parents and children away from the home to build the illusion of a successful "ministry" in which programs are held virtually every night.

Sometimes I feel like Balaam's donkey in the Bible story. If God can speak through me, He can speak through anyone. That's why I see hope in every person, no matter who they are or what kind of situation they're in. God allowed me to do a few good things. And He sent

a few good people my way to help me along. I believe that the endur-
ing message of my life is not about human rights, religious freedom,
or the law. It's that there is a God who cares about people.

I hope you understand that though I have mentioned names in
this book, this memoir is not about "payback" or trashing anyone. I'm
no different from others—I'd prefer that people like me rather than
hate me. I'm not out to create enemies. But I believe in my message
more than I believe in being popular.

It's interesting how God has used me. I grew up hating authority,
and I now spend my efforts helping people who have been abused by
authority. God has taken a twisted, alienated person and through trials and tribulations, reshaped me.

But I still have a long way to go. There is still much work to be
done and many dragons to slay.

INDEX